Property and Trust Law in Nigeria

Property and Trust Law in Nigeria

Imran Oluwole Smith

This book was originally published as a monograph in the International Encyclopaedia of Laws/Property and Trust Law.

Founding Editor: Roger Blanpain
General Editor: Frank Hendrickx
Volume Editors: Alain Verbeke & Vincent Sagaert

Wolters Kluwer

Published by:
Kluwer Law International B.V.
PO Box 316
2400 AH Alphen aan den Rijn
The Netherlands
E-mail: lrs-sales@wolterskluwer.com
Website: www.wolterskluwer.com/en/solutions/kluwerlawinternational

Sold and distributed by:
Wolters Kluwer Legal & Regulatory U.S.
7201 McKinney Circle
Frederick, MD 21704
United States of America
E-mail: customer.service@wolterskluwer.com

ISBN 978-94-035-4724-4

e-Book: ISBN 978-94-035-4734-3
web-PDF: ISBN 978-94-035-4744-2

This title is available on www.kluwerlawonline.com

The Author

Prof. Imran Oluwole Smith, PhD, SAN, FCI Arb (UK), FCTI is a Professor of Private and Property Law at the University of Lagos-Nigeria; a Senior Advocate of Nigeria (equivalent of the Queen's Counsel in the UK); a solicitor of the Supreme Court of England and Wales; and a Professorial Research Associate at the School of Oriental and African Studies (SOAS), University of London, UK. He has taught and undertaken research in different aspects of law such as Land Law, Equity and Trusts, Environmental Law, Planning Law, and the Law of Credit and Security. He was the co-convenor of the Course: 'Law and Development in Africa' between 2010 and 2012 at the School of Law, SOAS, University of London, UK.

He has rendered consultancy services to law firms and government establishments on different aspects of Nigerian law within and outside Nigeria, and served as an expert in the areas of Private and Property Law before the High Court of Justice in England. He is an Arbitrator and a Mediator of international repute and a Tax Law expert. Professor Smith is the Head of Chambers, 'Wole Smith & Co.'– a firm of Legal Practitioners in Lagos-Nigeria, and the Head, Smith & Co.– a firm of legal consultants in the United Kingdom.

Professor Smith has published widely in his areas of teaching and research. He is the author of the following books: *Practical Approach to Law of Real Property in Nigeria*; *Nigerian Law of Secured Credit*; *The Constitution of the Federal Republic of Nigeria, Annotated*; *Landlord and Tenant Law in Nigeria*; and *Law of Adverse Possession: An Anglo Nigerian Perspective*. He contributed to, and edited many books including the following: 'Law and Development in Nigeria'; 'The Land Use Act: Twenty Five Years After'; 'Secured Credit in a Global Economy'; 'Law and Land Rights in Nigeria'; 'Essays on the Lagos State Urban and Regional Planning and Development Law'; 'Essays on the Lagos State Mortgage and Property Law'; and 'Essays on the Lagos State Land Registration Law'. He is currently, the editor in chief of the Journal of Private and Property Law and Chairman, Editorial Board of the Nigerian Banking Law Reports (a publication of the Nigeria Deposit Insurance Corporation). He has numerous articles in learned local and foreign journals to his credit.

Among other positions, he was, at different times, the Head, Department of Private and Property Law, and Dean of Law at the Lagos State University and the University of Lagos, Nigeria, respectively; Director of the Law Centre, Lagos State University, Nigeria; Director, LLM and MLS part time postgraduate programmes at the Lagos State University, Nigeria; Member, School of Postgraduate Studies Board, University of Lagos, Nigeria; Member, Council of Legal Education, Nigeria; Member of Council, Lagos State College of Education (now, Adeniran Ogunsanya College of Education); member of the Governing Board, National Universities Commission (NUC) in Nigeria; and member, Technical Committee of the Tertiary Education Trust Fund (TETFUND). He has also served as a member of the Judicial Panel of Enquiry into Ajah land disputes in Lagos State.

Professor Smith is a Fellow, Chartered Institute of Arbitrators (UK); Fellow, Chartered Taxation Institute of Nigeria; and a Notary Public for Nigeria.

Table of Contents

Table of Contents

List of Abbreviations

Law Reports

AC	Appeal Cases
All ER	All England Reports
All FWLR	All Federation Weekly Law Reports
All NLR	All Nigeria Law Reports
ALR Comm	African Law Reports Commercial
CCHCJ	Selected Judgments of the High Court of Justice
Ch.D	Chancery Division (Law Report)
CLR	Commonwealth Law Reports
CPD	Common Pleas Division
DLR	Dominion Law Reports
EALR	East African Law Reports
ECSLR	East Central State Law Reports
ENLR	Eastern Nigeria Law Reports
ER	English Reports
Exch	Exchequer Division (Law Report)
FNLR	Federation of Nigeria Law Reports
FSC	Federal Supreme Court (Law Report)
FWLR	Federation Weekly Law Reports
HCNLR	High Court of Nigeria Law Reports
HL	House of Lords Cases
IR	Irish Reports
KB	Kings Bench (Law Report)
LEPLR	Legalpaedia Law Report
L.J. Ch	Law Journal Chancery
L.J.QB	Law Journal Queens Bench
LLR	Lagos Law Reports
LR.CP	Law Report Common Pleas
LR.QB	Law Report Queens Bench

LT	Law Times (Reports)
MJSC	Monthly Judgments of the Supreme Court
NCLR	Nigerian Commercial Law Reports
NSCC	Nigerian Supreme Court Cases
NSWLR	North South Wales Law Reports
NWLR	Nigerian Weekly Law Reports
OGSLR	Ogun State Law Reports
OYSHC	Oyo State High Court (Law Reports)
PC	Privy Council (Law Reports)
QB	Queens Bench
QLRN	Queens Law Reports of Nigeria
SC	Supreme Court (Law Reports)
SCNJ	Supreme Court of Nigeria Judgments
Term Rep	Term Reporter
UILR	University of Ife Law Reports
WACA	West African Court of Appeal (Law Reports)
WLR	Weekly Law Reports
WNLR	Western Nigeria Law Reports
WSCA	Western State Court of Appeal (Law Reports)
ZLR	Zambian Law Reports

Journals

AJICL	African Journal of International and Comparative Law 26.1 (2018): 64–83
ALJ	African Law Journal
BLI	British Law Institute
Conv	Conveyancer
CLQ	Comparative Law Quarterly
JAL	Journal of African Law
JPPL	Journal of Private and Property Law
JUS	Justice: Journal of Contemporary Legal Problems
LASU LJ	Lagos State University Law Journal
LQR	Law Quarterly Review
NBJ	Nigerian Bar Journal
NJCL	Nigerian Journal of Contemporary Law

Legislations

CA	Conveyancing Act
CAMA	Companies and Allied Matters Act
L.E.N	Laws of Eastern Nigeria
LFN	Laws of the Federation of Nigeria
L.N.N	Laws of Northern Nigeria
L.W.N	Laws of Western Nigeria
MPL	Mortgage and Property Law
NURPA	Nigerian Urban and Regional Planning Act
PCL	Property and Conveyancing Law

List of Abbreviations

General Introduction

§1. General Background of Nigeria

I. Geography

1. The Federal Republic of Nigeria is a country with a population of more than 213 million.[1] The country is located on the West coast of Africa occupying approximately 923,768 square kilometres of land bordering Benin in the West, Cameroon in the East, with Chad and Niger in the North.[2] The lower course of the Niger River flows south through the eastern part of the country into the Gulf of Guinea. Southern low lands are created by swamps and mangrove forests on the Southern coast. These low lands are mountainous in the south-east and plains in the north, with hardwood forest in the inland territory.[3]

2. The country is made up of 36 States, a Federal Capital Territory located in Abuja,[4] and a total of 768 local government areas.[5] Abuja became the new Federal Capital in 1991; Lagos having been relieved of that status for political, social, and strategic reasons[6] although it remains the economic hub of the country. The new Federal Capital has a population of 3,464,000 going by the world population

1. *See* Nigeria population (2021) available online at www.worlddometers.info/worldpopulation/nigeria-population/ last assessed on 20 December 2021.
2. Phillips, D.A., *Nigeria* 10 (Chelsea House Publisher 2004). Also *see* Achebe, C., *Home and Exile* (Oxford University Press 2000).
3. *Demographics of Nigeria,* Wikipedia available at: http://en.wikipedia.org/Wiki/Demographics_of_Nigeria. Assessed on 23 Apr. 2015.
4. Constitution of the Federal Republic of Nigeria 1999, ss 2(2) and 3(1). The Federal Capital Territory (FCT), Abuja is not a State as it is not one of the thirty six States listed in the first column of Part I to the First Schedule to the Constitution, but defined separately in Part II of the First Schedule thereto. It however has the basic paraphernalia of a State having a defined territory and having been vested with the three essential organs of the State with necessary modifications and adaptations: *See* the Constitution of the Federal Republic of Nigeria 1999 as amended, s. 299 paras (a)–(d). Consequently, all the legislative, executive, and judicial powers vested in the State House of Assembly, the Governor of a State, and the State courts are vested in the National Assembly, in the President of the Federal Republic of Nigeria, and in the courts of the FCT respectively.
5. *Ibid.,* s. 3(6).
6. The former Federal Capital Territory of Lagos was seen as a politically aligned territory (especially following the creation of Lagos State in 1967 with Lagos as the capital), densely populated with limited land mass and strategically porous and prone to encroachment by external aggressors. The Akinola Aguda Committee which was set up in August 1975 found in its report that the location of the

review,[7] and 6 Area Councils.[8] There are 6 geo-political zones in the country namely, north-east, north-central, north-west, south-east, south-west, and south-south. There are approximately 500 ethnic/linguistic groups in the country with three, namely Hausa-Fulani, Yoruba, and Igbo as the largest tribes. Half of the population of Nigeria are Muslims, 40% are Christians, while 10% follow the traditional indigenous religion or no religion. The predominant form of Islam is the Sunni and, among the Christians, Protestants are 26%, African Christians, 18.25% and Roman Catholics, 13.45%.

3. The diversity of climate observed in Nigeria is aridity in the north, tropical at the centre, and equatorial in the south. These variations are governed by the interaction of south-west monsoon and dry north-west winds. The maximum temperatures are 34–36 degrees Celsius in the north, and 30–32 degree Celsius in the south. Annual rainfall is more in the Southern part. In the Niger Delta, the annual rainfall is more than 3,500 millimetres.

II. Political and Historical Profile

4. The geographical entity known as Nigeria today is traceable to the emergence of various autonomous ethic groups with different areas of influence in the form of Kingdoms and communities long before the fifteenth century. They were known for primitive farming, hunting, trading in ivory, hide and skin, and other artefacts from which they irked a living. Trade by barter and later, the use of cowries as a medium of exchange was popular, while the institution of pledge and pawn became important methods of raising capital. Territorial expansion and protection of territorial integrity led to outbreak of intertribal wars and the proliferation of slave trade within Nigeria.

5. In the fifteenth century, the Portuguese initiated the transatlantic slave trade, but by the end of the sixteenth century, the Dutch challenged the Portuguese influence in the region, and the French and British competition later undermined the Dutch position.

6. In the first decade of the nineteenth century, two developments brought about a change in virtually all of the area now known as Nigeria. The first was the Usman dan fodio jihad between 1804 and 1808 which established the Sokoto Caliphate in the north-western Nigeria culminating in the evolvement of thirty emirates – all directly under Sokoto Caliphate; and the second, the declaration of transatlantic

former Federal Capital Territory of Lagos was inappropriate to forge unity among Nigerians of different ethno-cultural background and create a sense of belonging among them. A neutral environment located in a fairly central position like Abuja was considered a prerequisite for effective administration of every part of the country. *See* Aguda, A., *Flash Back* 89–102 (Spectrum Books Ltd 1989).

7. See World Population Review available online at https://worldpopulationreview.com. Accessed on 20 Dec. 2021.
8. Constitution of the Federal Republic of Nigeria, 1999, s. 303.

trade as illegal by Britain in 1807 and the development of alternative but legitimate trade along the coast, with the Royal Niger Company taking the lead.

7. Following the Berlin conference of 1885 and consequently the adoption of the dual mandate by the Super Powers, Britain established effective occupation by creating two protectorates in the Northern and Southern Nigeria with Lagos as the administrative capital territory. Lord Lugard was the High Commissioner of the Protectorates from 1900 to 1919. He systematically subdued local resistance, and his success was due to the policy of indirect rule by which he governed the protectorate through the rulers who had been defected. On 1 January 1914, the two protectorates were amalgamated with Lagos, and it became a single entity known as the Colony and Protectorate of Nigeria under Sir Frederick Lugard as the Governor General.[9]

8. The colonial period in Nigeria witnessed incessant agitations by Nigerian Nationalist movements for increased political participation in the affairs of the country including increased powers both in the regions and at the centre. The increasing concessions afforded local participation resulted in more franchise and more seats in the Legislative Houses of the colony and dominance of the Legislative Houses by Nigerians, culminating in more intense agitation. Consequently, Nigeria gained independence in 1 October 1960. In 1963, Nigeria became a Republic sequel to the Republican Constitution of 1963.

9. The two United Nations Trust territories of the Northern and Southern Cameroon for which Britain was granted the control and administration became attached to Nigeria for administrative purposes since 1945.[10] A plebiscite organised and supervised by the United Nations for these two mandated territories in 1961 led to the election of the Northern Cameroon to be part of Nigeria, while the Southern Cameroon chose to reunite with the Republic of Cameroon.

10. Alhaji Tafawa Balewa became the Prime Minister, and Dr Nnamdi Azikiwe the first President under a Parliamentary system of government that was not to last. Disputes over the results of the 1962 and 1963 census, ethnic rivalry, high handedness of the ruling party, and the trial and imprisonment of prominent politicians in the opposition coupled with the widespread protest over the 1964 general election, led to pockets of civil unrest and acute violence in the old Western Region.[11] The result was a declaration of a state of emergency in that region by the central government and suspension of the regional government from office.[12] Consequently, there was a coup d'état on 15 January 1966, and a counter coup on 29 July 1966 in which the then Head of State, Major General Aguiyi Ironsi was assassinated, and Lieutenant Colonel Yakubu Gowon emerged as the Head of State.

9. Stock, R., *Nigeria, Microsoft Encarta 2006 [CD]* (WA Microsoft Corporation 2005).
10. Mbaku, J.M., *Decolonisation, Reunification and Federation in Cameroon*, in *The Leadership Challenge in Africa': Cameroon under Paul Biya* 31 (JM Mbaku & J Takougang eds, African World Press 2004).
11. Stock, R *supra* n. 9.
12. *Ibid.*

11. The counter coup of July 1966 was attended by the massacre of many Igbos in the northern part of the country where heavy casualties were recorded in human and material resources. This sad event and the constitutional imbalances resulted in the agitation by the then head of Eastern Military Government, Lieutenant Colonel Emeka Odumegwu Ojukwu, for more autonomy. The various peace moves including the Aburi peace talk did not calm the nerves of the Easterners, and the result was a declaration of Secession of the Eastern Region from the rest of the country under the name, 'Republic of Biafra',[13] and a counter reaction to guard the unity of the country followed leading to a civil war which lasted thirty months. Biafra surrendered to the Federal Military Government headed by General Yakubu Gowon in January 1970.

12. In July 1975, the government of General Yakubu Gowon was overthrown in a bloodless coup led by Brigadier Murtala Muhammed on allegation of corrupt practices, indiscipline, abuse of office and non-readiness to hand over the government to a democratically elected civilian government. Murtala Muhammed was subsequently assassinated in an unsuccessful coup attempt on 13 February 1976. He was succeeded by Lt General Olusegun Obasanjo who restored civilian rule and handed over to a democratically elected government on 1 October 1979 with Alhaji Shehu Shagari as the President under a presidential system of government as enshrined in the Constitution of the Federal Republic of Nigeria, 1979.

13. The general election of 1983 following the expiration of the four-year term of political office holders elected in 1979 were alleged to be marred with widespread irregularities, electoral fraud and violence and the charged atmosphere of insecurity and political turbulence resulting in another *coup d'état* by some military officers led by Major General Muhammadu Buhari on 31 December 1983 in which the civilian administration was overthrown.[14]

14. The regime of Muhammadu Buhari would be remembered for its condemnation of official corruption, battle against indiscipline and economic sabotage, but it soon became unpopular as a result of repressive governance and draconian laws. These unpopularity led to an overthrow of that government in another bloodless coup led by Major General Ibrahim Babangida in August 1985.

15. Babangida curiously adopted the title of president and commander in chief of the armed forces, and set 1990 as the target date for return to civil rule. His regime was responsible for the introduction of certain economic policies such as the Second Foreign Exchange Market, the Structural Adjustment Programme (SAP), and removal of Petroleum subsidy which did not translate into economic prosperity for the country. Babangida's regime was replete with corruption and abuse of office by his cronies. After an endless transition programme,[15] Babangida's regime finally

---

13. Nwechue, R., *Reflections on the Nigerian Civil War: Facing the Future* 6 (Trafford Publishing 2004).
14. Stock, R *supra* n. 9.
15. *Ibid.*

allowed general elections to hold on 12 June 1993 the result of which was later annulled before the release of the final figures. The annulment of results of an election which was widely acclaimed as the most free and fair in the history of Nigeria generated nationwide protests, resulting in political logjam which culminated in handing over power to an interim government after his broadcast to 'step aside'.

16. The interim national government made up of both civilian and military officers headed by Chief Ernest Shonekan did not last long as General Sani Abacha overthrew it three months after.

17. Abacha's regime is reputed to be the most oppressive and repressive regime that was second to none in the history of Nigeria. Apart from looting the country's treasury, there were gross human right abuses recorded during his era. Abacha died in office on 8 June 1998 and Major General Abdul Salam Abubakar took over.

18. Abdul Salam released all office holders detained by Abacha government and conducted general election in February 1999 resulting in the election of Olusegun Obasanjo (a former military ruler) as the country's president under the platform of the Peoples' Democratic Party. Obasanjo won a second term in a controversial re-election in April 2003, but unsuccessfully schemed for a third term in office.

19. In a general election in 2007, Umaru Musa Yar'Adua of the ruling party – the PDP, was elected as President. Again, that election was criticised by both local and international observers as massively rigged and far from being free and fair but was unsuccessfully challenged both at the Presidential Election Petition Tribunal and at the Supreme Court.[16] While the tenure of Musa Yar'Adua witnessed some positive changes in government policies towards socio-economic development, it was perceived as too slow in responding to major challenges and not sufficiently proactive to achieve the desired turn around in the economy. His ill health over a significantly long period of time caused the country major setbacks. Eventually, the National Assembly passed a resolution declaring the then Vice President Dr Goodluck Jonathan as Acting President. President Yar'Adua passed away on the night of 5 May 2010 and Goodluck Jonathan was sworn in as president pursuant to the provision of section 146(1) of the Constitution of the Federal Republic of Nigeria, 1999.[17]

20. The tenure of President Jonathan was another trying period for Nigeria. His tenure witnessed a catalogue of corrupt practices by some of his ministers, a manipulation of the Federation Account, embezzlement of public funds, and gross indiscipline. The massive killing and kidnapping by the Boko Haram sect and his inability to wield the State machinery and resources in combating the heinous

16. In December 2008, the Supreme Court of Nigeria, in a narrow split decision of 4–3 upheld the election of President Yar'Adua in the April 2007 presidential election.
17. That section provides that the vice president shall hold the office of the president if the office becomes vacant by reason of death, among other reasons.

crimes of the insurgents, added a hopeless state of insecurity to the misery and frustration of Nigerians. Many well-meaning Nigerians felt that change was the only option available to save the country from imminent disintegration and economic collapse. The attempt of President Goodluck Jonathan to secure a second term through the polls failed, and in a free, fair and credible election, Muhammadu Buhari (a former Nigerian Military Head of State) who was duly elected, was sworn in on 29 May 2015. Nigerians are hopeful that the new coalition which produced the new president would restore the lost confidence in governance and pilot the country to economic prosperity and social justice.

III. Economic and Social Values

21. Before the discovery of crude oil in the 1970s, agriculture was the mainstay of the country's economy with the regional governments during this period striving to maximise productivity in variety of food and cash crops.[18] Agriculture then accounted for more than 75% of the total export earnings of the country,[19] and food crops were cheap. With the discovery of crude oil in Nigeria and the subsequent boom in the sale in the international market, the oil sector became a major source of foreign earnings accounting for 99% of export revenue and 85% of government revenue.[20] It is reported that Nigeria is the eighth largest exporter of crude oil[21] and one of the largest in Africa.

22. The agricultural sector witnessed very serious setback and neglect consequent upon the oil boom with the country not being able to produce sufficient food stuff for the teeming population and consequently becoming an importer of food items to meet domestic demand.[22] Absolute reliance on crude oil brought about a chain of negative consequences: it led to a monetised economy with close to zero productivity in other sectors of the economy; it resulted in the rural-urban migration in search of the golden fleece with consequent unemployment, incessant pressure on infrastructure, and the emergence and proliferation of urban slums; it encourages and promotes official corruption in government including the oil sector; it paved way for external manipulation of the economy from the International Monetary Fund (IMF)[23] resulting in worsening poverty situation in the country.

18. For example, the North was known for the groundnut pyramid, the West for Cocoa, and the East for coal and Palm oil.
19. Stock, R *supra* n. 9.
20. The World Bank, Nigeria: Country Brief. Available at http//web.worldbank.org/ last assessed on 16 Apr. 2017.
21. OECD Report available at www.oecd.org/dataoecd/27/18/38562978pdf last assessed 14 Apr. 2017.
22. Ekpo, A.H. & Umoh, O.J., An Overview of the Nigerian Economic Growth and Development. Available at www.onlinenigeria.com/economics/.
23. This institution prescribed Structural Adjustment Programme (SAP) in 1986 and Trade liberalisation from 1995.

23. The introduction of privatisation in 1988[24] consequently resulting in the privatisation of major sectors of the economy such as oil refineries, telecommunications, power, airline, etc. for efficiency and rapid economic development, has not fulfilled the desired objectives; it has only benefited a few individuals.

24. Meeting the Millennium Development Goals in line with global economic objectives for sustainable economic growth and human development is a mirage in Nigeria. The target date for the realisation of 'the great vision' shifts from time to time[25] and despite the wind fall from the oil sector over the years, there is high level of poverty, inefficient delivery of social services, high rate of unemployment, poor infrastructure facilities and widespread insecurity. Incentive for agriculture is low due to poor access to land and non-availability of affordable credit facilities for farmers. The absence of social security system to reduce inequality and poverty has made life worthless for the poor masses.

25. While the Nigerian economy remains the second largest in sub-Saharan Africa and despite the huge earnings from crude oil, Nigeria remains highly underdeveloped. With a GDP per capita of less than USD 2.0,[26] poor governance and in depth corruption, the capacity of Nigeria to make a decisive effect on the African sub-region is waning.

26. The highest tier of Nigerian society is made up of wealthy politicians, businessmen, and the educated elite. These people, however, make up only a tiny portion of the Nigerian population. Many Nigerians today suffer under great poverty. The lower classes tend to have little chance of breaking from the vicious cycle of poverty. Poor education, lack of opportunities, ill health, corrupt politicians, and lack of even small amounts of wealth for investment all work to keep the lower classes in their place.

IV. Cultural Values

27. Nigeria is one of the most culturally diverse nations of the world. It is a multicultural nation with more than 500 ethnic groups identifying with very diverse socio-cultural system rooted in ethnic segmentation. While there are major ethnic groups associated with their language such as the Hausa, Igbo, and Yoruba, the significance of minority groups has not diminished.

28. Language is a key cultural identity, and all the ethnic and cultural groupings in the country have deep rooted traditional background and established oral traditions in proverbs which promote fundamental human values such as hardwork, honesty, discipline, and exemplary leadership. Every culture in Nigeria has unique diet,

24. This was initially introduced during the regime of Babangida but fully executed by the civilian administration of Obasanjo.
25. The initial date was 2010, then 2015, and currently 2030.
26. World Bank Report *supra* n. 20.

mode of dressing, mode of production, greetings, marriage, modes of socialisation, and rich history of political systems that could be harnessed for development.

29. In some Nigerian ethnic groups such as the Igbos, Ibibios, and the Yorubas, there is a form of caste system that treats certain members of the society as pariahs. The criteria for determining who belongs to this lower caste vary from place to place, but include being a member of a minority group, an inhabitant of a specific village, or a member of a specific family or clan. Members of the community will often discourage personal, romantic, and business contact with any of the affected group regardless of an individual's personal merits or characteristics. While this attitude may be unlawful[27] and even unconstitutional,[28] the practice continues in many communities in Nigeria.

30. Traditional marriages are of paramount importance in many Nigerian communities in spite of western culture, and most ethnic groups imbibe polygamy. Except in few Igbo communities where, for social reasons,[29] a woman may metaphorically marry another woman,[30] a marriage is taken to be a union between a man and a woman strictly, and same sex marriage is unknown.

31. For many Nigerian ethnic groups within the Igbo, Edo, and Hausa communities in Nigeria, inheritance is basically a male affair and women are seen as objects rather than subjects of inheritance.[31] This practice continues despite contrary and disapproving pronouncements of the Nigerian courts[32] and the negative disposition of international conventions in this regard.[33]

§2. Legal Background of the Country

I. Legal Family or Tradition

32. The Nigerian legal system exhibits the common law tradition in significant material particulars. For example, the English doctrine of precedent which requires the courts to treat like cases alike and enjoins lower courts to follow the decision of higher courts in the hierarchy is part of Nigerian law; the standard and burden of

27. *See*, e.g., Abolition of Osu system Law of Eastern Nigeria.
28. The Constitution of the Federal Republic of Nigeria 1999 as amended prohibits discrimination on the ground of sex, membership of a community or ethnic group, place of origin, religion, or political opinion: *See* s. 42 thereof.
29. A barren woman may take another woman for the husband to bear children for him.
30. Marriage here refers to formal acceptance of the woman into the household.
31. *See*, for example, *Nezianya v. Okagbue & Ors* (1963) 1 All NLR 352.
32. *Udensi v. Mogbo* (1976) 6 ECSLR 354; *Mojekwu v. Mojekwu* (1997) 7 NWLR (Pt. 512) 283; *Muojekwu v. Ejikeme* (2000) 5 NWLR (Pt. 657) 402 at 423–424; *Ukeje v. Ukeje* (2014) All FWLR (Pt. 730) 1323.
33. *See*, e.g., Convention on Elimination of all forms of Discrimination Against Women (CEDAW) GA Resolution 34/180 of December 1979 entry into force on 3 Sep. 1981.

proof in civil and criminal proceedings[34] follow the common law system; and the presumption of innocence entrenched in the Nigerian Constitution as a fundamental right[35] is rooted in the common law jurisprudence.[36]

II. Relation and Hierarchy Between Other Sources of Law

33. The Nigerian State owes its existence to a Federal Constitution.[37] Its provisions entrench the doctrine of separation of powers which defines the parameters and limitations of different organs of government;[38] provide fundamental objectives and Directive Principles of State Policy;[39] define qualifications for citizenship status;[40] and guarantee fundamental rights and freedoms of citizens.[41] The Constitution of the Federal Republic of Nigeria 1999 (the 1999 Constitution) is the basic law of the land and takes precedence over all other laws in existence;[42] and where there is any conflict between the Constitution and any other law, the Constitution shall prevail, and that other law shall, to the extent of its inconsistency, shall be void and of no effect.[43]

34. The Nigerian legal system consists of: (1) the indigenous Customary law[44] made applicable by the various High Court Laws meant to 'observe and enforce the observance of customary law which is applicable and not repugnant to natural justice, equity and good conscience, nor incompatible either directly or by implication with any law for the time being in force';[45] (2) Islamic law which was introduced into the northern part of Nigeria consequent upon the Fulani jihad of the nineteenth century and which consequently became super imposed on the pre-existing customary law of the area;[46] (3) the received English law comprising of the common law of England, the doctrines of equity and statutes of general application in force in England on 1 January 1900 introduced by the British consequent upon colonisation of the country, and subsequently made applicable as part of Nigerian law by the Law (Miscellaneous Provisions) Act Cap 80 Laws of the Federation of Nigeria and

---

34. In civil cases, the standard of proof is proof on balance of probabilities; in criminal matter, it is proof beyond reasonable doubt.
35. *Ibid.*, s. 36(5).
36. In civil law jurisdictions, the rule is the opposite; accused persons are presumed guilty until the contrary is proved.
37. The Constitution of the Federal Republic of Nigeria 1999 as amended provides in s. 2(2) that 'Nigeria shall be a Federation consisting of States and a Federal Capital Territory'.
38. *Ibid.*, ss 4, 5, and 6.
39. *Ibid.*, ss 13–24.
40. *Ibid.*, ss 25–32.
41. *Ibid.*, ss 33–46.
42. *Ibid.*, s. 1(1).
43. *Ibid.*, s. 1(3).
44. Customary law is unwritten, flexible, and varies from place to place. It is a question of fact to be proved by evidence unless judicial notice is taken of it: *See* ss 16, 17, 70, and 73(1) of the Evidence Act 2011.
45. *See*, for example, High Court Law of Lagos State Cap H3 Laws of Lagos State 2003, s. 26.
46. The effect of the Fulani jihad was total; it was meant to substitute the customs, traditions, and beliefs of the indigenous people of Northern Nigeria with the tenets of Islam.

Lagos, 1958 and applied by the Nigerian courts subject to local circumstances and situations;[47] (4) local legislations consisting of the Acts of National Assembly[48] including international treaties domesticated as part of Nigerian Law,[49] the Laws of the various State Houses of Assembly,[50] and various local government by-laws.[51]

35. All laws in existence before the 1999 Constitution including decrees and Edicts enacted by the previous military regimes were recognised as existing laws,[52] while certain laws were entrenched in the Constitution and cannot consequently be abrogated or amended through the normal legislative process, but in accordance with the constitutional amendment provisions.[53]

§3. Introduction to the Law of Property and Trust

I. Historical Origins and Evolution

36. The concept of property dates back to remote antiquity when man, conscious of his essence and existence, started appreciating the importance of control and management of resources for socio-economic reasons.[54] The recognition of the physical property accompanied by the right of dominium was the beginning of the evolution of claims under rudimentary rules of the ancient times. Early philosophers[55] saw it as an upshot of the natural law[56] regime with the attendant

---

47. The interpretation of principles of English common law is that given to it by the Nigerian courts even if it deviates from the interpretation in English cases, although where there are no Nigerian judicial authorities, English cases may furnish persuasive authority depending on the hierarchy of court that gave the decision.
48. The National Assembly (consisting of the senate and house of representatives) has powers to make laws for the peace, order, and good government with respect to matters included on the Exclusive Legislative List contained in Part I of the Second Schedule to the Constitution; matters contained on the Concurrent Legislative List as contained in Part II of the Second Schedule to the Constitution; and with respect to which it is empowered to make laws under the Constitution.: *See* ss 4(2) and (4) of the Constitution. The States cannot make laws with regard to the items on the Exclusive Legislative list: *See* s. 4(3) of the Constitution.
49. *See* Constitution of the Federal Republic of Nigeria 1999 as amended, s. 12.
50. The State Houses of Assembly shall make laws with regard to items on the Concurrent Legislative List as contained in Part II of the Second Schedule of the Constitution: *See* ss 4(6) and (7) of the Constitution.
51. For items on which the local government shall have power to make by-laws, *see* Fourth Schedule to the Constitution.
52. *Ibid.*, s. 315(4)(b).
53. *Ibid.*, s. 315(5)9(d).
54. In the primitive agrarian economy, property was seen as the main factor of production requiring protection while the nineteenth industrialisation ushered in various uses requiring management and control of property.
55. *See,* e.g., John Locke, Two Treaties of Government 358 (3rd ed. 1698).
56. The idea of natural law in the eighteenth century associated with natural rights in the sense of universal moral obligations or higher law to be applied, metamorphosed in the twentieth century to widespread acceptance of the existence of fundamental human rights built into the constitutional framework of modern democracies.

presumptions and presuppositions[57] while modern jurisprudence conceptualise it as a product of positive law.

37. The evolution of positive law simultaneously coincided with the development of property rights, and it has been said that 'law and property were born together and [must] die together'[58] suggesting that the existence, protection, use, enforcement, and termination of property rights are determined in modern times by positive law.

38. The concept of property encompasses the tangible and intangible, corporeal and incorporeal, ownership or title over them, and other interests in a thing less than ownership but nevertheless conferring certain rights in property.[59] In whichever sense the concept of property is construed, property law is designed to regulate the relation of persons to things thereby providing a secure foundation for the acquisition, enjoyment, and disposal of things or wealth.[60]

39. In Nigeria, property rights are products of the English common law,[61] rules of customary and Islamic law,[62] provisions of statutes[63] including the Land Use Act 1978,[64] the Constitution of the Federal Republic of Nigeria 1999 as amended,[65]and domesticated treaties such as the African Charter on Human and Peoples Rights.[66]

40. One of the ingenious devises of English law with respect to management of property is the trust concept. The trust concept is an English common law idea made applicable in Nigeria by the applicable reception statutes.[67] It is a fine development from the equitable jurisdiction of the common law courts, and has been said to remain to date, the greatest and most distinctive contribution of equity to English jurisprudence.[68] The trust grew out of the medieval concept of 'use' which enabled conveyance of property by a person (usually the owner) the *feoffor*, to another person the *feoffee*, for the benefit of named beneficiaries, the *cestui que* use.

---

57. The idea of right to property like other rights known to natural law is that it is inalienable as an inherent natural phenomenon existing independent of any human law.
58. Bentham, J., *The Theory of Legislation* 69 (Oceania Publications, Inc 1975) (1690).
59. *See,* e.g., *Donald v. Suckling* (1866) LR 1 QB 585.
60. *See* Paton, G.W., *Jurisprudence* Chap 21, 505 (3rd ed. Oxford 1972).
61. *See* the Law (Miscellaneous Provisions) Act 1964, s. 45(1); Law of England (Application) Law Cap 60 LWN 1959, s. 3. *See also* the various State High Court Laws.
62. *See* the various State High Court Laws in Nigeria.
63. *See,* e.g., the Statute of Frauds 1677, s. 4; Property and Conveyancing Law Cap 100 LWN 1959 applicable in the old western and mid-western states of Nigeria and adopted by the laws of those States; Property Laws of the various States in Nigeria; the various Land Instrument Registration Laws of the States; Landlord and Tenant Law applicable in the States, to mention but a few.
64. Cap L5 LFN 2010.
65. *See* Cap C23 LFN 2010.
66. Cap A9 LFN 2010.
67. *See* Interpretation Act Cap 123 LFN 2010, s. 45; s. 3 Laws of England (Application) Law Cap 60 Laws of Western Region of Nigeria, 1959 now applicable in Delta, Edo, Ekiti, Ogun, Ondo, Osun, and Oyo States of Nigeria carved out of the region. Also, the relevant provisions of various State High Court Laws in Nigeria.
68. Maitland Equity (Brunyate ed.) 1936 at 20.

41. While equity followed the common law to the extent that it recognised that legal estate in the property became vested in the feoffee upon conveyance of property real or personal, equity acted on his conscience by ensuring that the property was used for the benefit of the *cestui que* use as directed by the trust instrument. Thus, trust under the received English law has created a dual ownership system in property unknown to many other legal systems including the Nigerian customary law concept of trusteeship.[69] A trust has therefore been defined as 'the relationship which arises wherever a person called the trustee is compelled in equity to hold property, whether real or personal, and whether by legal or equitable title, for the benefit of some persons (of whom he may be one and who are termed *cestui que trust*) or for some objects permitted by law, in such a way that the real benefit of the property accrues, not to the trustee, but to the beneficiaries or other objects of the trust'.[70]

42. The recognition and enforcement of the 'use' by equity led to increased employment of the trust concept for various purposes ranging from the possibility of making it possible before the Statute of Wills 1540,[71] for intended beneficiaries under a will to take benefits under it, to circumventing statutory restrictions on transfers[72] by conveying property unto and to the use of third parties, and subsequently to the use of intended beneficiaries. In contemporary times, the institution of the trust continues to serve various functions[73] in the hands of property settlors, investors, and even the State.

II. The Concept of Ownership

Meaning

43. Ownership is the bundle of rights of a person over and above every other person or thing.[74] It is said that when the right of a claimant to possess, use and dispose of property is not subject to, or restricted by the superior right of another

69. *See* Jegede, M.I., *The Position of the Head of Family in Relation to Family Property* 21 Nigerian B.J. (1966).
70. Keeton, G.W. and Sheridan, L.A., *The Law of Trusts* 3 (12th ed. Law Publishers Ltd).
71. Prior to the Statute of Wills 1540, it was not possible to alienate land by Will since medieval land law regarded land tenure as a personal relationship that could not survive the owner of the property. Since the Will would not take effect until the death of the maker, the tenure of the land owner would be extinguished upon death.
72. The Statutes of Mortmain which culminated in the Statute De Viris Religionis, 1279 for example, prohibited conveyance of land to corporations and ecclesiastical foundations making it necessary when transfer was intended for the purposes of unincorporated associations, to transfer the land to some legal persons to hold it on their behalf.
73. For the functions served by the trust mechanism, *see infra* at para. 60.
74. *See* Pollock, F., *Jurisprudence and Legal Essays,* 98 (1961); *Abraham v. Olorunfunmi* (1990) 1 NWLR (Pt. 165) 53.

person, the right of ownership is said to be vested in him.[75]In the words of Tobi JCA (as he then was) in *Abraham v. Olorunfunmi*:[76]

> It [ownership] connotes a complete and total right over a property. The owner of the property is not subject to the right of another person. Because he is the owner, he has the full and final right of alienation or disposition of property, and he exercises his right of alienation and disposition without seeking the consent of another party because as a matter of law and fact, there's no other party's right over the property that is higher than that of his ... The owner of a property can use it for any purpose; material, immaterial, substantial, non-substantial, valuable, invaluable, beneficial or even for a purpose detrimental to his personal or proprietary interest. In so far as the property is his and inheres in him, nobody can say anything. He is the Alpha and Omega of the property. The property begins with him and ends with him. Unless he transfers his ownership over the property to a third party, he remains the allodial owner.[77]

44. However, the recognition of the private rights of others and the exigencies of physical planning for public good have resulted in imposition of some restrictions on the theoretical and pristine form of definition of ownership. For example, the common law claim in the tort of nuisance, the rule in *Rylands v. Fletcher*[78] and the regime of planning laws and regulations[79] have placed restrictions on the absolute and unconditional use of property.

45. It is also important to note that the owner of a thing is not necessarily the person who at a given time has the whole power of use and disposal since there is no such person; it suffices if the person has the residue of all such powers.[80] For example, a landlord of premises does not lose his right of ownership over the demised premises merely because he led a person into possession and use of the land as a tenant. The landlord still has a mediate right to possession and may come into occupation and put the premises to use by lawfully terminating the tenancy. Also, a bailor of goods does not cease to be the owner by merely placing chattels or goods in the possession of the bailee since he has a mediate right of possession and may lawfully terminate the contract of bailment in accordance with its terms.

---

75. *Ibid.*
76. *Abraham v. Olorunfunmi supra* n. 74.
77. *Ibid.*, at 74–75.
78. (1866) LR 1 Exch. 265.
79. *See*, e.g., Nigerian Urban and Regional Planning Act No. 88 1992 Cap N138 LFN 2010 applicable in the Federal Capital Territory Abuja and the Planning Laws of different States in Nigeria.
80. Pollock *supra* n. 74.

A. *Unity and Fragmentation*

46. Ownership under Nigerian law may be classified as:

(a) co-ownership and sole ownership;
(b) full and limited ownership;
(c) trust and beneficial ownership; and
(d) legal and equitable ownership

Co-ownership and Sole Ownership

47. Property may be owned by an individual acquiring same through purchase, grant, allotment, inheritance, or partition. But it may also be held by two or more persons. Under the Anglo-Nigerian law, such persons hold either as joint tenants or as tenants in common, while at customary law, they hold under communal or family ownership.

48. Co-ownership is ownership of the whole as opposed to several ownership of a part[81]either under the received English law or customary law, and it may be terminated by partition in which case, there is severance of interests and each portion becomes subject to sole ownership.[82]

Full and Limited Ownership

49. Full ownership is vested in the person, family, community, or the State exercising all the rights of an owner discussed earlier, while limited ownership flows as an abstraction from it. An example of limited ownership is the allotment to members of the family or community deriving their limited rights of ownership as abstractions from communal or family property. Also, under the Land Use Act 1978, the State Governor is said to be vested with radical title (full ownership) with respect to all parcels of land within the territory of a State,[83] while ownership rights of citizens have been streamlined in the form of rights of occupancy (limited ownership).

Trust and Beneficial Ownership

50. The trust concept recognises the trust and beneficial ownership coexisting in trust property such that a person called the trustee with trust ownership is under an obligation to use his ownership for the benefit of the other called the beneficiary with beneficial ownership. The true nature of the two types of ownership is brought out succinctly by Salmond on Jurisprudence[84] as follows:

---

81. *Olorunfunmi v. Asho* (2000) 2 NWLR (Pt. 643) 143.
82. *Ibid.*
83. *See* s. 1 of the Land Use Act 1978 Cap L5 LFN 2010.
84. 12th ed. 1966, pp. 256–257.

> The trustee is destitute of any right of beneficial enjoyment of the trust property. His ownership therefore, is a matter of form rather than of substance, and nominal rather than real. If we have regard to the essence of the matter rather than the form of it, a trustee is not an owner at all but a mere agent upon whom the law has conferred the power and imposed the duty of administering the property of another person. In legal theory however, he is not a mere agent but an owner. He is to whom the property of someone else is fictitiously attributed by the law, to the extent that the rights and powers thus vested in a nominal owner shall be used by him on behalf of the true owner. As between trustee and beneficiary, the law recognises the truth of the matter, as between these two, the property belongs to the latter and not the former. But as between the trustee and the third party, the fiction prevails. The trustee is clothed with the rights of his beneficiary and is so enabled to personate or represent him in dealings with the world at large.

51. Thus, the trust ownership of the trustee exists for the benefit of the beneficiary, the *cestui que trust*, and the former is bound to allow the beneficial enjoyment of the usufruct by the latter. The interest of the *cestui que trust* enures against every person except a bona fide purchaser for value without notice of the trust.

Legal and Equitable Ownership

52. Legal ownership is one rooted in the English common law, while equitable ownership is one emanating from the principles of equity. Legal ownership is good against the whole world while equitable ownership is good against all persons except a bona fide purchaser for value without notice. Legal ownership in property is usually protected by registration, while the interest of an equitable owner may be fortified by taking possession. Details of the distinction between legal and equitable ownership is undertaken later in this work. (*See* Chapters 2 and 3 of Part I *infra.*)

B. Immovable and Real Property

53. Nigeria has received into her legal system,[85] the English common law concept of property, and also its classification broadly into realty and personalty. Real property consists of immovable property such as land, things attached to, above and underneath land and incorporeal hereditaments. The general classification of land endorsed by jurists and adopted by case law and statutes in Nigeria are discussed fully in Chapter 1 of Part I infra.

54. Infringement of a right in real property such as unlawful dispossession from land gives the dispossessed owner a right in rem enabling him to recover the land as opposed to compensation for the loss.

---

85. Paton *supra* n. 60.

C. Movable and Personal Property

55. Other forms of property outside real property or immovable would qualify as personal property which is wide enough to cover not only movables such as goods or chattels, but also all forms of choses in action.[86] General classification of movable or personal property is discussed in Chapter 1 of Part II *infra*.

56. An infringement of a right in personal property gives the defendant a right in personam entitling him to damages for any loss or infringement. However, this classification is not watertight as leasehold interests created on land are regarded as 'chattels real'; the word 'chattels' indicating their true nature, and the word 'real' exhibiting their connection with land.

III. Estate and Patrimony

A. Unity and Fragmentation

57. *See* Part II of this monograph.

B. Trust and Fiduciary Mechanisms

58. Writers[87] have proposed various definitions of trust, but the most acceptable definition which has been adopted by Nigerian courts[88] is that given by Keeton.[89] Keeton defines a Trust as 'the relationship which arises where a person called the trustee is compelled in equity to hold property, whether real or personal, and whether by legal or equitable title, for the benefit of some persons (of whom he may be one and who are termed the cestui que trust) or for some object permitted by law, in such a way that the real benefit of the property accrues, not to the trustee but to the beneficiaries or other objects of the trust'.

59. Certain characteristics of a trust are discernible from this definition: first, the trust property is vested in the trustees not for their own benefit, but for the benefit

86. Choses in action are rights in intangible property which can only be realised through action in court. Examples are shares, debts, copyrights, etc.: *See Torkington v. Magee* (1902) KB 427 at 430.
87. *See* Lord Coke who defined trust as 'a confidence reposed in some other, not issuing out of the land but as a thing collateral thereto, annexed in privity to the estate of the land, and to the person touching the land for which the *cestui que trust* has no remedy but by subpoena in the Chancery': Co. Litt 276b; Sir Arthur Underhill defined trust as 'an equitable obligation binding a person (who is called the trustee) to deal with property over which he has control (which is called trust property) for the benefit of persons (who are called beneficiaries or *cestui que trust*), of whom he may himself be one and of whom may enforce the obligation'. *See* Underhill and Hayton: Law of Trusts and Trustees (14th ed.) 1 adopted by Bakibinga: Law of Trusts in Nigeria, Unilorin Press 1988, 18.
88. *Iwok v. University of Uyo* (2011) 6 NWLR 211 at 237; *Anuruba v. E.C.B. Ltd* (2005) 10 NWLR (Pt. 923) 237.
89. Keeton, G.W., *Law of Trusts* 9th ed. 3.

of the beneficiaries. Second, a trust may be created in respect of both real and personal property. Third, there can be a trust of an equitable interest such as where a beneficiary under a trust creates a trust of his equitable interest in favour of some other beneficiaries. Fourth, it is possible to have both the legal and equitable title vested in one person such as where the trustee holds a legal interest in trust for himself. Lastly, the donors purpose may not necessarily be limited to safeguarding the trust property and applying it in the manner directed, but may be made to serve some productive purposes such as investments, charity or other public purposes.

1. The Functions of Trust

60. The Trust is employed to save a transfer or a device to persons lacking the legal capacity to hold property such as an infant[90] or an unincorporated association.[91] It makes it possible to make provisions for dependents upon the death of parents, guardians, or other dependants where it would be necessary in certain circumstances to make secret or undisclosed provisions.[92] Where it is desirable to preserve property and ensure non-disposition in succession, a Trust is employed to secure successive benefits to many individuals.[93] To secure investments and ensure better returns on it, effective business arrangements could be put in place through devices such as unit trusts[94] and investment trusts.[95] Through the instrumentality of the trust, it is possible to make gifts for non-human objects such as the promotion of scientific and technological research and advancement.[96] The Trust provides an avenue for assuring employees on retirement or disablement of funds to fall back on through a scheme of mandatory contributions by the employer and employee into a fund held by trustees for the benefit of such employees upon retirement, or disablement during service. In Nigeria, such scheme has been instituted through the instrumentality of the Nigerian Social Insurance Trust Fund (NSITF) established under the NSITF Act[97] and the Pension Funds established under the Pensions Act.[98] The State has found the institution of Trust useful in making funds available for the

90. This position has been adopted by s. 7(a) of the Land Use Act 1978 Cap L5 LFN 2010.
91. Examples of unincorporated associations include societies, trade unions, churches, mosques, and non-governmental organisations. In Nigeria, the gaps and the attendant conveyancing difficulties engendered by lack of legal capacity have been abridged by the statutory requirement of registration of Trustees under Part C of the Nigerian Companies and Allied Matters Act Cap C20 LFN 2010.
92. Examples of such cases are where there are children born out of wedlock, or where it is desirable to make provision for a mistress. In Nigeria, where orphans are taken care of by relatives, a trust arrangement is a potent option to take.
93. There are advantages in this. For example, a protective trust such as this will protect the property from wastrels and preserve it in the event of the beneficiary's bankruptcy: *See* Adigun, O., Cases and Texts on Equity, Trusts and Administration of Estates, Ayo Sodimu (1987) 254.
94. *See* the Nigerian Investments and Securities Act, 1999, ss 124–145.
95. *See* generally, Part XI of the Nigerian Investments and Securities Act, 1999.
96. Examples abound all over the world of institutions such as the Ford Foundation established to promote research. In Nigeria, there is the TETFUND made available by government to all tertiary institutions to fund research projects.
97. No. 45 1992.
98. Cap P4 LFN 2010.

provision, sustenance, and enhancement of qualitative education and basic health-care needs of citizens, or for their protection against environmental hazards. In Nigeria, the Petroleum Trust Fund (PTF)[99] and the Education Trust Fund (ETF)[100] have such objectives.

2. The Applicable Law

61. The trust is an equitable concept, and the doctrines of equity apply in Nigeria by virtue of the various reception statutes.[101] In addition, statutes of general application that were in force in England on 1 January 1900 were received as part of the applicable English law[102]although these have been repealed and replaced in the States carved out of the old western and mid-western region of Nigeria.[103]

62. Nigerian Customary law to some extent recognises some forms of institutions that are somewhat similar to the trust.[104] An example is the issue of accountability of the family head and the position of head chiefs of the community vis-à-vis members of the community. But as pointed out earlier in this work, the English trust concept does not apply *stricto sensu* under customary law.[105]

63. The Nigerian case law and a number of local legislations are applicable. Regrettably, there is a dearth of case law in this area partly as a result of varying social factors, and the claim that 'many of its present day functions are adequately performed by the traditional extended family system'.[106] However, a number of enactments exist on the subject and they include the Trustees Investment Act,[107] Public Trustees Act,[108] the Property and Conveyancing Law,[109] the Trustees Laws,[110]the Administration of Estates Laws,[111] among others.

99. *See* Petroleum (Special) Trust Fund Cap P14 LFN 2010.
100. Cap LFN 2010.
101. *See* s. 45 of the Interpretation Act Cap 123 LFN 2010; s. 3 Laws of England (Application) Law Cap 60 Laws of Western Region of Nigeria, 1959 now applicable in Delta, Edo, Ekiti, Ogun, Ondo, Osun, and Oyo States of Nigeria carved out of the region. Also, the relevant provisions of various State High Court Laws in Nigeria.
102. *Ibid.*
103. *See* s. 3 Laws of England (Application) Law Cap 60 Laws of Western Region of Nigeria, 1959 now applicable in Delta, Edo, Ekiti, Ogun, Ondo, Osun, and Oyo States of Nigeria carved out of the region. Also, the relevant provisions of various State High Court Laws in Nigeria.
104. *See* paras 64–65 below.
105. *Ibid.*.
106. *See* Banire M, *The Nigerian Law of Trusts* 10 (Excel Publications 2002).
107. Cap T22 LFN 2010.
108. Cap 98 Laws of Nigeria 1958. The Public Trustees Act was omitted from the Laws of the Federation of Nigeria (LFN) 1990 and 2004, but applies in Lagos State and the former Western Region as Public Trustees Law with identical provisions.
109. Cap 100 Laws of Western Nigeria, 1959.
110. Cap 125 Laws of Western Nigeria, 1959.
111. Cap 1 Laws of Western Nigeria, 1959.

3. The Concept of Trust under Nigerian Customary Law

64. The customary land tenure system in Nigeria has always recognised family or communal ownership with a peculiar concept of trust as a confidence reposed in the head of the family or community holding the land for the use of the family or community, and thus, in a position analogous to that of the trustee in English law.[112] It is on this score that the family head for example, is said to be in charge and control of the family property with 'considerable and onerous duty to perform, varying in degree according to the size, wealth and importance of the family'.[113] Also, both the head chief of the community and the head of family are the agents through whom land transactions take place, to be dealt with as representing his and other interests affected,[114] and both, like the trustee, cannot use family funds to meet their personal needs.[115] It would appear also, following from the strength of judicial authorities on different customs in Nigeria,[116] that the family head is under obligations which are akin to those of trustees under English law.

65. However, it cannot be said that the family or community head is a trustee of the family or community land in the sense known to English law. For example, such head of the family or community is not vested with legal title unlike the English trustee, and any purported sale of family or communal land is voidable and does not vest valid title in the purchaser.[117] This is so notwithstanding that the sale involved a bona fide purchaser for value without notice which would validate a sale by the English trustee.[118] Under Nigerian customary law, members of the family may agree to remove the head and appoint another in his place, but the beneficiaries under the English trust cannot ordinarily remove a trustee.[119] Also, while the consent of the principal members of the family is required under customary law before the head can validly dispose of family property, beneficiaries under the English trust need not consent before trustees can alienate trust property.

66. Thus, while the Nigerian customary law recognises that persons in the position of the head of family or community is a fiduciary and a trustee of his powers to the extent that such powers shall not be exercised arbitrarily but only in the interest of other members of the family or the community, such head of the family or community does not qualify as a trustee in the strict sense under English law.

112. *See,* e.g., Viscount Heldane in *AmoduTijani v. Secretary, Southern Nigeria*(1921)AC 404 at 408.
113. Graham Paul C.J. in *Balogun v. Balogun* (1935) 2 WACA 299 at 299.
114. Viscount Heldane in *AmoduTijani v. Secretary, Southern Nigeria supra* n. 112.
115. *See* Robinson J in *Archibong v. Archibong* (1947) 18 NLR 117 at 123.
116. *See Archibong v. Archibong supra* n. 115 above; *Ozoma v. Ozoma* (1965/66) NMLR 88; *Akanbi v. Akande* (1966) NBJ 86; *Taiwo v. Dosunmu*(1966) NMLR 94.
117. *See Solomon v. Mogaji* (1982) 11 SC 1; *Salako v. Dosumu* (1997) 8 NWLR (Pt. 517) 371.
118. *Ibid.*
119. *Saunders v. Vautier* (1841) 10 LJ Ch. 354.

4. The Land Use Act and the Trust Concept

67. The Land Use Act[120] was enacted in Nigeria in 1978 for some socio-economic reasons[121] and with the main objective of making land available to Nigerians.[122] To achieve this main objective, section 1 of the Act vests title to land comprised in the territory of each State in the Federation of Nigeria in the Governor of the State to be held in trust for the use and common benefit of Nigerians. The appearance of the word 'trust' in that section poses the question whether the Governor of each State is a trustee as known to English law. In *Nkwocha v. Governor of Anambra State*[123] for example, Irikefe JSC commented that 'by this piece of legislation a legal trust affecting every inch of Nigerian land is created constituting every governor trustee in respect of the land within the limits of his State'.[124]

68. Section 1 of the Land Use Act no doubt separates the radical title vested in the Governor of the State from the beneficial enjoyment of interests in land by citizens in the form of rights of occupancy,[125] either granted by the Governor[126] or subject of deemed grant[127] but beyond this, a number of fundamental differences exist between the English trust and the trust created under the Land Use Act. In the first place, while the interest of the beneficiary under the English trust is equitable so that a disposition of property subject matter of trust to a bona fide purchaser for value without notice of the trust destroys the interest of the beneficiary and vests a valid title in the purchaser, a holder of a right of occupancy actual or deemed holds in law and a subsequent grant by the Governor will not confer a valid title on the subsequent grantee even if he gave consideration for the grant and had no notice of the subsisting interest.[128] Second, the Governor unlike the English trustee, is not under any of the onerous duties imposed by equity on trustees,[129] owes no fiduciary duties to the holder of a right of occupancy, and cannot be called to render account to them. Third, most of the remedies available to the beneficiary against the trustee in the event of a breach of trust are not available against a Governor under the Land Use Act, and most of the obligations imposed on the Governor under the Act are not enforceable by the courts in the same manner as the obligations of the trustee under

---

120. Cap L5 LFN 2010.
121. The pre-Land Use Act regime was replete with issues of insecurity of title to land; problem of fraud and land speculation prevalent in the urban centres; fragmentation of land making it difficult to access sufficient land for agricultural and industrial purposes; challenges facing government acquisition of land for housing and other economic development; etc. *See* Smith, I.O., *Practical Approach to Law of Real Property in Nigeria* 469–471 (Ecowatch Publications 2013).
122. *See* Preamble to the Act.
123. (1984) 6 SC 362.
124. *Ibid.*, 364.
125. Rights of occupancy are rights to occupy and use land subject to the provisions of the Land Use Act.
126. *See* s. 5(1) of the Act.
127. *See* ss 34 and 36 of the Act.
128. *See,* for example, *Dzungwe v. Gbishe* (1985) 2 NWLR (Pt. 8) 528; *Dantsoho v. Mohammed* (2003) 6 NWLR (Pt. 817) 457; *Ibrahim v. Mohammed* (2003) 6 NWLR (Pt. 817) 615.
129. For the duties imposed on trustees, *see* paras 563–578 *infra.*

English law can be enforced. The obligations imposed on the Governor were by no means fiduciary and incomparable to the extensive fiduciary duties of the English trustee.

69. Thus, 'trust' in the context of section 1 of the Land Use Act is no more than an obligation on the part of the Governor to exercise the powers of control and management of the land over which radical title is vested in him for the benefit of Nigerians. It is used in the 'higher sense' as opposed to the 'lower sense' of true trust which the courts would enforce.[130] Judicial authority for this conclusion can be found in the decision of the court in *Tito v. Waddell.*[131] In that case, a claim by the inhabitants of Ocean Island that the Crown as their trustee had failed in its fiduciary duty to them by receiving on their behalf, royalties less than the proper rates, failed on the ground that the word 'trust' used in the relevant documents and in the Mining Ordinances should be construed as meaning no more than a governmental obligation, the breach of which the courts were powerless to remedy.

5. Trust Distinguished from Other Legal Relationships

70. The characteristics of a trust are better appreciated when distinguished from other legal relations such as contract, bailment, agency, office of personal representatives, and power of appointment.

6. Trust and Contract

71. While an agreement is an essential element in the formation of a contract and also forms the basis of many trusts, the two relationships differ in some respects:

(a) A contract creates legal obligation; a trust is equitable in nature.
(b) While an agreement is essential for the creation of a contract, it is not essential for the creation of trust since a trust may be created by way of grant without the agreement of either the trustee or the beneficiary.
(c) The right to enforce a contract is a right *in personam* to the extent that action can be brought against the other contracting party or parties; a trust creates a right in rem and in the event of a breach of trust, property is recoverable not only from the trustee, but also from the third party to whom he has transferred the property except a bona fide purchaser for value without notice of the trust.
(d) The rule of privity of contract enables only a party to a contract to sue on it; a beneficiary under a trust can enforce a trust even though he is not a party to its creation.
(e) Consideration is a crucial element of a contract unless made by deed; a beneficiary under a trust may enforce a trust even though he is a volunteer so long as the trust is completely constituted.

---

130. Per Megarry V.C. in *Tito v. Waddell* (No. 2) (1882) 7 AC 619 at 625.
131. *Ibid.*

7. Trust and Bailment

72. Bailment is an arrangement whereby a person known as the bailee is given possession of chattels by another person known as the bailor for a specific purpose after which the property is returned either to the bailor, or according to his direction. To the extent that both the bailee and the trustee have an obligation to take good care of the property, they could be said to be holding upon a kind of trust, but there are certain differences between them in the following respects:

(a) Whereas the trust relationship is equitable, that of bailment is legal.
(b) Only chattels can be bailed, whereas any kind of property can be the subject matter of a trust.
(c) A trustee is generally the legal owner of the trust property and has the 'general property' in the subject matter of the trust which enables him to pass a good title to the bona fide purchaser for value without notice of the trust; whereas, a bailee has only a special property in the chattels bailed, the general property remaining in the bailor, and cannot therefore pass a good title in it to third party, not even to a bona fide purchaser for value without notice.

8. Trust and Agency

73. While agents and trustees must act personally and cannot delegate their responsibilities; are accountable for profits made in the discharge of their obligations and owe fiduciary duties to the principal and the beneficiaries respectively, the following differences exist:

(a) Trust relationship is equitable while agency relationship is legal.
(b) Whereas agency is founded on a contract between principal and agent, in most cases, there is no contractual relationship between trustees and beneficiaries.
(c) Whereas an agent does not own his principal's property though he is able to dispose of it and pass good title to a third party by virtue of the authority conferred on him either by his principal or by law, a trustee is the legal owner of the trust property.
(d) While an agent is bound to act in accordance with the authority conferred on him by his principal or by law, a trustee acts in the best interest of the trust and he is not subject to the control of the beneficiary.

9. Trust and Administration of Estates

74. Both the trustees and personal representatives are vested with properties which they are under an obligation in equity to deal with for the benefit of others and except where a contrary intention appears, the fiduciary duties of personal representatives are similar to those of trustees.

75. Generally, a personal representative may be a trustee under a Will, and in the old western and mid-western regions of Nigeria, he was always a trustee for sale and the notional doctrine of conversion would operate upon sale, to convert real property (i.e., land) to personal property (i.e., money) where the deceased died intestate.[132] However, the Trustees Act 1893 and the Trustees Laws applicable in different States of Nigeria, extend the meaning of the term 'trust' to the duties incidental to the office of the personal representatives and define 'trustee' as including, where the context so admits, a personal representative.[133]

There are however, notable differences between them as follows:

(a) The trustee has a primary duty to hold trust property while the personal representative has a duty to distribute it.
(b) While two trustees or a trust corporation is required to give a valid receipt for the proceeds of sale of land, such rule does not apply to personal representatives.
(c) Whereas the authority of trustees is always joint; that of personal representatives is joint in respect of land, but joint and several in respect of pure personalty. Thus, while one of several personal representatives may validly dispose pure personalty and pass a good title to a bona fide purchaser, one trustee without the authority of other trustees cannot pass a good title to pure personalty upon disposition to a bona fide purchaser.
(d) The provisions of the Trustees Act 1893 and the Trustees Law applicable in the various States in Nigeria relating to the appointment and retirement of trustees do not apply to personal representatives.[134]
(e) In the old western and mid-western states of Nigeria,[135] personal representatives in the case of intestacy are necessarily trustees because they hold on a statutory trust for sale.
(f) While the period of limitation in respect of actions against trustees and personal representatives is six years, the limitation period in respect of personal estate of the deceased is twelve years although where the action is for arrears of interest on legacies, it must be brought within six years.[136]

10. Trust and Power

76. The basic distinction between 'trust' and 'power' is that a trust is imperative in the sense that there is an intention to impose an obligation, while a power is discretionary to the extent that if the donee of the power fails to exercise it, he cannot be compelled to do so. Whereas in the event of failure of a donee of a power to exercise the power, an object of the power cannot claim any share in the property which

---

132. Administration of Estates Law Cap 1 Laws of Western Nigeria, 1959, s. 37.
133. Trustees Act 1893, s. 2; Trustees Law, Laws of Western Nigeria, Cap 125 1959, s. 2.
134. *See,* for example, Cap 125 Laws of Western Nigeria, 1959, ss 24 and 26.
135. *See,* for example, Administration of Estates Law Cap 1 Laws of Western Nigeria, 1959, s. 39.
136. *See,* for example, Limitation Act 1966, s. 31; Limitation Law of Lagos State Cap 118 Laws of Lagos State 2003, s. 32(1).

will pass to whoever is entitled in default of appointment, in the case of trust, the court will enforce a trust to divide property among a class.

77. However, there could be a power in the nature of a trust thereby creating a trust in favour of the beneficiaries, so that if the donee fails to exercise the power, the court will divide the property, subject matter of the trust, among the objects equally on the basis that 'equality is equity'. The question whether a power is a mere power or a trust power is one of intention of the settlor as ascertained from a proper construction of the instrument. For example, if it can be shown that the settlor intended the benefit of the property to go to a class of beneficiaries in any event, then the disposition is a trust, otherwise it may be treated as a mere power. Also, where there is a gift over in default of appointment, the power is a mere power,[137] but when there is no gift over in default of appointment, the power may be coupled with a trust[138] provided that there are other indications of an intention to benefit the class.[139]

78. A trust is valid only when the object is certain whereas, certainty of object is not an essential requirement for a valid power. If there is no one to enforce a trust, this may be fatal to its validity, whereas the validity of a power does not depend upon the existence of someone capable of compelling its exercise.

11. Powers and Duties of Trustees

79. The trustee has powers to deal with the trust properties in accordance with the terms of the trusts as contained in the trust instrument. A trustee also derives his power from duties imposed on him under the law, but while the trustee must carry along the beneficiaries in the performance of his duties, this is not a requirement for the valid exercise of his power.[140]

12. Capacity to Create Trusts

80. A person who has the capacity to hold and to dispose a legal interest in property can create a trust and be appointed a trustee.

Minors

81. Since an infant cannot hold a legal estate in land,[141] it follows therefore that he cannot create a trust in respect of the legal estate in realty; but he can hold equitable interest in personalty.

---

137. A residuary gift in favour of the donee of the power is not a gift over for this purpose.
138. *Burough v. Philcox* (1840) 5 My & Cr. 72.
139. *Re Weeks Settlement* (1897) 1 Ch. 289.
140. *Ademola v. Sodipo* (1994) 7 SCNJ (Pt. 11) 417.
141. *See* the Land Use Act, Cap L5 LFN 2010, s. 7; Property and Conveyancing Law, Cap 100 LWN 1959, s. 35 and corresponding provisions in the Property Laws of the various States.

Persons of Unsound Mind

82. A person of unsound mind or person suffering from mental incapacity can neither create a valid trust nor be a trustee. Most of the cases decided by the Nigerian courts are those related to testamentary trust.[142]

83. Trust created by a person suffering from mental incapacity will be declared void particularly where such a person is unable to understand that he was creating a trust or being appointed as a trustee.[143]

Corporate Bodies

84. A company registered in Nigeria under the Companies and Allied Matters Act[144](CAMA) is a corporate entity and as such, can create a trust of its property as contained in the company's objects clause in the Memorandum of Association; but an unregistered company cannot.

13. Classification of Trusts

85. Trusts may be classified as follows:

a. Express, Implied or Resulting, or Constructive Trusts

Express Trusts

86. Express trusts are trusts created by the acts of the owner of property either inter vivos such as a declaration of trust by the settlor; or by conveyance of property to trustees; or by Will.

Implied or Resulting Trusts

87. This is a trust that arises from the presumed intention of the owner of the property. Instances where a resulting trust may arise are as follows:

(a) Where an express trust fails.
(b) Where the beneficial interest under an express trust is not fully disposed or exhausted.
(c) Where there is a purchase in the name of another or where a person makes a voluntary conveyance of his property to another.[145]

---

142. *See Johnson v. Maja* (1950/51) 13 WACA 290; *Adebajo v. Adebajo* (1973) 3 E.C.S.C.R 544.
143. *Re Beaney* (1978) WLR 770.
144. *See* Companies and Allied Matters Act No. 3 2020.
145. In *Ezennah v. Attah* (2014) 17 WRN 31, Tobi JSC held that: 'The best example of a trust implied by law is where property is purchased by A in the name of B, that is to say, A supplies the purchase money and B takes the conveyance title. In the absence of any explanation, such as an intention to

Constructive Trusts

88. These are trusts imposed by equity irrespective of the intention of the owner of the property. Circumstances that can give rise to constructive trust are as follows:

(i) Unauthorised profit by trustees and other fiduciaries in the execution of their duties will be held on a constructive trust for the beneficiaries or other persons entitled.
(ii) A stranger intermeddling with trust property holds the property on constructive trust.
(iii) A vendor of land becomes a constructive trustee between execution of the contract of sale and completion.
(iv) A mortgagee who has sold mortgage property pursuant to his power of sale is a constructive trustee of the proceeds of sale after paying off the principal, interest, and cost of sale.
(v) Acquisition of the property by fraud or misrepresentation.[146]

b. Private and Public Trusts

89. Private trusts are trusts created for the benefit of the individual, group, or class of persons or for some private purpose, while public trusts are meant for the benefit of the public at large. An example of public trusts are charitable trusts meant for the promotion of scientific, educational, or public welfare.[147]

c. Perfect and Imperfect Trusts

90. A trust of perfect obligation is one with human beneficiaries who have the capacity to compel performance of same by the trustee. A trust of imperfect obligation which is also referred to as 'purpose trust' are trusts not enforceable by human beneficiaries and are generally void, except that in the case of trusts for charitable purposes, they are considered to be of perfect obligation since they are enforceable by the Attorney General. However, following English decisions on the point, Nigerian courts may not prevent the enforcement of a trust of imperfect obligation if the trustees wish to carry it out.[148]

---

give the property to B, Equity presumes that A intended to hold the property in trust for him': *See Ukatta v. Emembo* (1963) 7 ENLR 137; *Re Obabunmi Pedro* (1961) LLR 127; *Ughutewbe v. Shonowo* (2004) 6-7SC 24–26.

146. *Marques v. Edematie* (1950) 19 NLR 75; *Ayorinde v. Scott* CCHCJ/2/72; *Onuruba v. Ekeke* (2005) 10 NWLR 14–15; *Kotoye v. Saraki* (1994) 7 NWLR (Pt. 357) 414; *Ushutevbe v. Shonowo* (2004) 16 NWLR (Pt. 989) 300; *Anuruba v. E. C. B Ltd* (2005) 10 NWLR (Pt. 933) at 237; *Ibekwe v. Nwosu* (2011) 4 SC (Pt. 11) 125.

147. *Iyanda v. Ajike* (1948) 19 NLR 11; *Phillips v. Phillips* (1967) All NLR 204 *Adeseye v. Williams* (1964) All NLR 459.

148. *See,* e.g., *Adeseye v. Williams* (1964) 2 All NLR 37.

d. Completely and Incompletely Constituted Trusts

91. A trust is completely constituted when the necessary steps have been taken to vest the trust property in the trustee for the benefit of the beneficiaries. This happens when the settlor either declares himself to be a trustee of the property by simple declaration, or where he transfers the property to trustees on trust declared by him. Pending compliance with the necessary formalities, the trust is incompletely constituted. Trusts created under Wills are regarded as completely constituted trust, while a covenant with trustees to settle property in the future or where conveyance to the trustees is defective are examples of incompletely constituted trust.

92. A completely constituted trust can be enforced by any beneficiary including a volunteer, while an incompletely constituted trust can be enforced only by those who furnished the settlor with consideration.[149]

93. There are exceptions to the rules relating to constitution of trusts:

(i) It does not apply to property given by Will since in the event of the death of the testator, his property vests in the executors of the Will who are bound to carry out the provisions of the Will in favour of volunteer beneficiaries.
(ii) The court may perfect an imperfect voluntary transfer of property upon the fulfilment of the requirements of a valid *donatio mortis causa* namely: that the donor made the gift in contemplation of death; that the completion of the gift is made conditional upon the death of the donor; and the donor has physically delivered to the donee either the subject matter itself or the means of getting at it. Where these conditions are met, the court will compel the donor's personal representatives to perfect the gift.
(iii) An imperfect gift to a donee who later becomes executor or administrator of the donor's estate is considered perfected by the vesting of the legal title to the property in the donee as personal representative.[150]
(iv) By the doctrine of proprietary estoppel, a donor of an imperfect gift to a donee who made improvements on the subject matter to his knowledge is estopped from asserting his title to it, and may be compelled to perfect the gift.[151]

C. Express Private Trusts

1. Formalities for Creation of Express Trusts

94. The general rule is that there must be an intention to create a trust and such intention may be construed from the provisions of the trust instrument, the oral declaration of the settlor, and the circumstances of the situation. While there are

149. Equity will not assist a volunteer: *See Jefferys v. Jefferys* (1841) Cr. & PL 738.
150. This is the rule in *Strong v. Bird* (1874) 18 Eq. 315.
151. *See Dillwyn v. Llewelyn* (1862) 4 De Cr. F&J 517.

generally no legal formalities required for the creation of a trust, there are basic statutory requirements for the creation of trust of land.

Trust of Land to Take Effect Inter Vivos

95. An intention to create a trust of personalty requires no formality; it may be created orally, in writing, or by implication. However, where trusts are in respect of land to take effect inter vivos, the trust must be created and made in writing with written evidence signed by the settlor.

96. Section 7 of the Statute of Frauds 1677 (being statute of general application) requires that any declaration of trust relating to land must be evidenced by a memorandum in writing signed by the party creating the trust. Section 78(1)(b) of the Property and Conveyancing Law applicable in the States of the former western and mid-western regions provides as follows:

> 'Any declaration of trust respecting land or any interest therein must be manifested and proved by some writing signed by some person who is able to declare such trust or by his will.'

97. Where there is a failure to comply with these provisions, the trust is unenforceable but not void, since writing is not necessary to create a trust but only to evidence the creation of trust.[152] The writing need not be in any particular form provided it contains all the material terms of the trust. It must however contain the signature of the settlor himself and not that of his agent. It may be noted also that the requirement of writing does not apply to resulting and constructive trust of realty since such trusts are implied by law once the conditions prescribed by equity for their existence are present.[153]

98. Apart from the requirement of writing for the creation of trust of land for evidential purposes, it is essential that a disposition of an equitable interest such as the interest of beneficiaries under a trust shall be in writing signed by the person disposing of the same or by his agent otherwise, such disposition will be void.[154] But where the trustees conveys the legal estate to a third party, there is no disposition within the provisions of statute,[155] and if the property constituting the subject matter of the trust is personalty, writing is not necessary.[156]

---

152. *Forster v. Hale* (1798) 3 Ves 696.
153. *Rochefoucauld v. Boustead* (1897) 1 Ch. 196.
154. Section 9 Statute of Fraud 1677 and s. 78 (1)(c) Property and Conveyancing Law Cap 100 1959 make writing essential for the disposition and not mere evidence of the disposition, and these provisions apply whether the property subject of disposition is realty or personalty: *See Grey v. IRC* (1960) AC 1.
155. *See* n. 154 above.
156. *Vanderwell v. IRC* (1967) AC 29.

Trusts Created by Will

99. Where a trust is created by testamentary disposition, it is the requirement of the law that such trust must be in writing. The provision of section 9 of the Will Act 1837 and section 6 of the Wills Law applicable in the various States of the Federation[157]provides that no Will shall be valid unless it is in writing, signed on the face of it by the testator, or some person in his presence and by his direction and the signature is attested by two witnesses in the presence of the testator. A Will that fails to comply with these requirements is void and cannot devise or bequeath any interest.

100. However, since the provisions of the above statutes were designed to prevent fraud, equity will not allow them to be used as an 'engine' of fraud. Therefore, a person who has obtained property by reason of his promise to hold it as trustee though, such promise is not in writing, will not be allowed by equity to subsequently deny the trust because there is no written evidence. The intervention of equity allows a party to enforce such disposition in certain circumstances notwithstanding non-compliance with the provisions of the Wills Act or Wills Laws. This is achievable under secret trust. The donee is regarded as holding such a gift as a constructive trustee, and the secret beneficiary takes his interest 'dehors' (i.e., outside) the Will.

D. Secret Trusts

101. Secret trusts are trusts appearing in Wills but which do not disclose the identity of the beneficiaries. There are two types namely: fully secret trusts and half-secret trusts.

102. Under the fully secret trusts, the Will contains no reference to a trust at all; the gift generally appearing to be beneficial on the face of it. For example, a provision in the Will that: 'I give the sum of =N=250,000 to Bassey' creates a fully secret trust and enforceable by the secret beneficiary where the identity of the beneficiary has been communicated to the donee during the testator's lifetime[158] and the donee has accepted the trust and has promised the testator to hold the property on trust for the named beneficiary.[159]

157. *See*, e.g., Wills Law of Lagos State Cap W5 Laws of Lagos State 2015, Cap 170 Laws of Oyo State 2000; Cap 37 Laws of Abia State 1999; Cap 143 Laws of Akwa Ibom State 2000; Cap 144 Laws of Adamawa State 1997.

158. Where there is no communication, donee holds on resulting trust: *See Re Boyes* (1884) 26 Ch.D 531. A delivery to the donee an envelope containing the beneficiaries name is sufficient communication: *See Re Keen* (1937) Ch. 236.

159. *McCormick v. Grogan* (1869) LR 4 HL 82.

103. Where the property is devised to two or more co-owners and only one of them promises to hold the property on trust, he is bound and the others take beneficially, but where the gift is joint, and a promise is made before or at the time of making of the Will, it binds the others.[160]

104. Failure to comply with the requirements of a fully secret trust disentitles the supposed secret beneficiary to the gift and the donee holds the property on a resulting trust.[161]

105. In the case of the half-secret trust, the Will states that the trustee is to hold on trust but does not express the objects of the trust.[162] For example, a clause in the Will making a gift of =N=250,000 to Falilat 'on trust declared' creates a half-secret trust which the secret beneficiary can enforce if the identity of the beneficiary was communicated to the donee by the testator before or during the making of the Will, with the said donee promising to hold the property on trust, and the Will makes it clear that communication has already taken place.[163] Failure to comply with the requirements of a half-secret trust disentitles the secret beneficiary to the gift and the donee holds the property on a resulting trust.

1. Creation of Express Trusts: The Three Certainties

106. For a trust to be valid there must be certainty of words or intention; certainty of subject matter which encompasses certainty as to property and as to beneficial interests; and certainty of objects.

Certainty of Words or Intention

107. Words employed under a trust must depict the intention of the settlor. To create a trust, words must be clear without any ambiguities. Failure of a trust on the ground of uncertainty of the settlor's intention entitles the donee of the property to take absolutely as no binding trust is created.

Certainty of Subject Matter

108. There must be certainty as to the property subject matter of the trust in the sense that it must make clear what property must be bound by the trust, failure which the trust would fail as there is no trust of any property.

109. The beneficial interests to be taken by each beneficiary must be certain, otherwise, there would be a resulting trust for the settlor or in the case of a testamentary devise, for the residuary legatee or devisee under the Will.[164] There is no failure

160. Kodilinye, G., *An Introduction to Equity in Nigeria* 70–71 (Sweet & Maxwell 1975).
161. *Re Boyce* (1884) 26 Ch.D 531.
162. *Blackwell v. Blackwell* (1929) AC 38.
163. *Ibid.*
164. *Boyce v. Boyce* (1849) 6 Sim 476.

for uncertainty however, where the trustees are given a discretion as to the precise amount that each beneficiary is to receive; these are valid as discretionary trusts. Where property is given on trust for a principal beneficiary, subject to the rights of other beneficiaries to an uncertain part of the property, the uncertain trusts fail and the principal beneficiary is entitled to the whole. In any case, the court may apply the maxim 'equality is equity' and divide the property equally between the beneficiaries in the case of uncertainty as to beneficial interests.

Certainty of Objects

110. The identity of the beneficiaries must be described and indicated with precise accuracy. For example, there will not be a valid trust where property is given to a vague class of beneficiaries such as 'dependants' or 'near relations'. Where there is failure of trust for uncertainty of objects, there will be a resulting trust for the settlor or the testator's estate.

E. Express Public or Charitable Trusts

111. Public or charitable trusts are those meant for the alleviation of poverty,[165] advancement of education[166] or religion[167]or other charitable purposes beneficial to the community.[168]

112. Charitable trusts are becoming increasingly popular in view of the worldwide movement in support of poverty alleviation and the promotion of beneficial scientific research and social welfare. It has the following advantages:

(a) Unlike a private trust, charitable trust will not fail for uncertainty of objects. Provided it is shown that the donor intended the property to be applied for charitable purposes, failure to specify the particular objects to be benefited is not fatal, for in that case, the court will direct a scheme for the application of the property.[169]
(b) A purpose trust will be valid if it is charitable, otherwise, it will be void for being a trust of imperfect obligation.[170]
(c) Charitable trusts unlike private trusts are, in some cases, exempt from the rule against perpetual trusts, and may therefore exist for an indefinite period.[171]
(d) While charitable trusts like private trusts are generally subject to the rule against perpetuities and the trust property must therefore vest in the donee within the

165. *Re Scarisbrick* (1951) Ch. 622.
166. *Incorporated Council of Law Reporting for England and Wales v. AG* (1971) 3 All ER 1029 at 1046.
167. *Re Moon's Will Trusts* (1948) 1 All ER 300.
168. *Re Jones deceased* (1918) NLR 80.
169. Fabunmi J.O., *Equity and Trust in Nigeria* 168 (University of Ife Press Ltd. 1986).
170. *See,* for example, *Iyanda v. Ajike supra* n. 147.
171. *Re Marlette* (1945) 2 Ch. 284.

perpetuity period[172] (lives in being and twenty-one years after), once the gift is so vested, the trust may be perpetual.[173] Also, where there is a gift to one charity followed by a gift over to another charity, the gift over would be valid beyond the perpetuity period.[174]

(e) Certain special taxation privileges and exemptions are accorded charitable trusts, and certain taxation inducements are offered to persons to confer benefits on charitable institutions.[175]

113. For an intended charitable trust to be valid, it must benefit the community or public. Thus a bequest that benefits certain individuals in a locality or community,[176] or that defined by a test of relationship to a particular individual or body[177] is not charitable. But a trust is nonetheless charitable where it is for the benefit of a section of the public as for example, gift to a locality,[178] or for those of a particular denomination.[179] Where it is meant for the relief of poverty, it is charitable even though defined by a relationship to an individual or body,[180] or the employees of a particular employer.[181]Also, a gift is charitable if made to a person whose office is charitable;[182] the person is irrelevant if the purpose is indicated and that purpose must be exclusively charitable.

114. A trust is not charitable unless the objects are exclusively charitable.[183] But the fact that a charitable gift incidentally promotes other purposes which are not charitable will not invalidate it.[184]

172. *Re Green's Wills Trust* (1985) 3 All ER 455.
173. *Chamberlayne v. Brochett* (1872) LR 8 Ch App 218.
174. *Re Tyler* (1893) 3 Ch. 252; *Royal College of Surgeons v. National Provincial Bank* (1952) AC 631. But the exception will apply neither to a gift over to a charity from a non-charity: *See Re Mills Declaration of Trust* (1952) All ER 506; nor to a gift over from a charity to a non-charity: *Re Engels* (1943) All ER 506.
175. Section 21(5)(c) of the Companies Income Tax Act Cap 21 LFN 2010 makes donations made by a company for a charitable purpose deductible from the company's income for purposes of computing its tax liability, while s. 17 of the Capital Gains Tax excludes certain specified properties donated or bequeathed to charitable institutions from Capital Transfer Tax.
176. *Iyanda v. Ajike supra* n. 147.
177. *Re Crompton* (1945) Ch. 123.
178. *Re Jones deceased* (1918) NLR 80.
179. Kodilinye, G. *supra* n. 160 at 103.
180. *Re Scarisbrick* (1951) Ch. 622.
181. *Gibson v. South American Stores* (1950) Ch. 177.
182. *Re Flinn* (1948) Ch. 241.
183. *Chicester Diocesan Fund v. Simpson* (1944) AC 341; *Re Diplock* (1948) Ch. 465; *Re Eades* (1920) 2 Ch. 353.
184. For example, it has been held that an institution for the furtherance of the study and practice of surgery was a charitable one even though it might incidentally promote the professional interest of individual surgeons: *See Royal College of Surgeons v. National Provident Bank* (1952) AC 631.

115. Ordinarily, in the case of a private trust, there will be a resulting trust of the unexhausted trust property or the surplus to the original settlor, in the case of charitable trust, such property may be applied cypres, i.e., to some other charitable purpose resembling as closely as possible the purpose specified by the settlor, provided that the settlor or testator has a general charitable intent.[185]

F. Implied or Resulting Trusts

116. It has been suggested that the aim of the courts in enforcing implied and resulting trusts is to carry out the presumed intention of the testator or settlor.[186] In implied or resulting trusts, it is not the intention of the testator or settlor to declare a trust, but the law implies a trust from the conduct of the parties.[187] Thus, both the Statute of Frauds[188] and the Property Law of different States in Nigeria[189] exclude resulting, implied, and constructive trusts from the requirements of writing, since the requirement of writing would defeat the purpose meant by law. In implied or resulting trusts, their objects need not be immediately identifiable, and although an infant cannot be an express trustee, he can be a resulting trustee.

117. A resulting trust may occur in the following circumstances:

(1) Where an express trust fails for failure of the object[190] or for any other reason,[191] there will be a resulting trust in favour of the donor or his estate.
(2) Where the beneficial interest under an express trust is not fully disposed of or exhausted, a resulting trust occurs.[192] However, where there is no indication that the donor intended to retain any interest in the property and there is no indication that the beneficiaries shall take the surplus, the property becomes bona vacantia and passes to the State.[193]
(3) A transfer into and purchase in the name of another raises a presumption of resulting trust in favour of the real purchaser[194] provided the latter raised money as purchaser and not as a lender.[195] This presumption may be rebutted where the law would make a presumption of advancement such as where a husband purchased property in the name of the wife,[196] but not otherwise;[197]

185. *Re Davies* (1902) 1 Ch. 876.
186. Keeton, G.W., *Law of Trusts* 9th ed. at 176.
187. *Akwei v. Akwei* (1943) 9 WACA 111; *Registered Trustees of Islamic Missionary Society v. Bello Abasi* (1958) WRNLR 117.
188. Section 8 thereof.
189. Section 78(2) thereof.
190. *Re Ball* (1947) Ch. 228; *Re Ames Settlement* (1946) Ch. 217.
191. *Re Obabunmi Pedro* (1961) LLR 127.
192. *Re Obabunmi Pedro supra* n. 191.
193. Re West Sussex Constanbulary's Benevolent Fund Trusts (1971) Ch. 1.
194. *Ukatta v. Emembo* (1963) 7 ENLR 137.
195. Kodilinye *supra* n. 160 at 88.
196. *Silver v. Silver* (1958) 1 All ER 523.
197. *Mercier v. Mercier* (1903) 2 Ch. 98.

or where a father purchases property in the name of a legitimate child;[198] or a purchase was made by a person to whom the purchaser stands in loco parentis.[199] The presumption of a resulting trust or of advancement may be rebutted by evidence of purchaser's or donor's real intention.[200]

G. Constructive Trusts

118. The concept of constructive trust derives not from the intention express or implied of the settlor, but from the equitable notion of what is conscionable and equitable from the circumstances of the case before the court. The law imposes a trust in a variety of different relationships some of which are discussed below:

(1) A person in a fiduciary position is regarded as a constructive trustee of any profits made out of the property in his custody,[201] for the benefit of the person entitled to the property.
(2) Where a person receives trust property with actual or constructive notice that it is trust property, or though receives the trust property innocently, but subsequently deals with it in a manner inconsistent with the trust, or assists the trustee in dealing fraudulently with the trust property, he becomes a constructive trustee of the settlor.
(3) Upon exchange of a valid estate contract, the vendor becomes a constructive trustee of the land for the purchaser until completion.[202] He holds the title on trust for the purchaser and owes an obligation not only to take care of the property, but also to refrain from doing anything which may be prejudicial to the equitable interest of the purchaser.
(4) A mortgagee who enters into possession of the mortgage property is a constructive trustee for the mortgagor with regards to all rents and profits accruing from the property;[203] and when he exercises power of sale regarding the mortgage property, he is a constructive trustee of the surplus in his hand after paying the principal, interest and cost of sale of the property.[204]
(5) A mortgagor who creates an equitable mortgage by deposit of title deeds is a constructive trustee of the legal estate for the mortgagee and the agreement to create a legal mortgage is one for which a court will make an order of specific performance.[205]

---

198. But not where purchase is by the mother: *See Bennet v. Bennet* (1879) 10 Ch.D 479.
199. *Ojule v. Okoya* (1968) 2 All NLR 42.
200. *Shephard v. Cartwright* (1955) AC 431.
201. *Marques v. Edematie* (1950) 19 NLR.
202. *Lysaght v. Edwards* (1876) 2 Ch.D 499.
203. *Re Prytherch* (1889) 42 Ch.D 590.
204. *See* Conveyancing Act 1881, s. 21(3); Property and Conveyancing Law Cap 100 Laws of Western Nigeria 1959, s. 127.
205. *Russel v. Russel* (1783) 1 Bro. C.C 269.

(6) A person who acquires property by fraud may be compelled to hold it as constructive trustee against whom an action for unjust enrichment may be brought.[206]

IV. Possession and Title

119. In property law parlance, claims to property are usually denoted by the word 'title'. Title connotes the existence of facts from which the right of ownership or possession could be inferred limitation being in terms of time.[207] It is said to be the degree of control, use, and enjoyment that are recognised and protected by law. Title may be absolute in which case it is synonymous with ownership, or restrictive in which case, it is tantamount to possession.

120. A claim to title may be original or derivative. An original title creates a right de novo usually acquired by the first settlor in the case of real property, or the first to acquire personal property. A derivative title is acquired usually through transfer or assignment either absolutely or subject to conditions. A mere occupational right or custody without more does not amount to title.

121. Possession is the direct physical relationship of a person to a thing. Possession may take the form of physical control of property mainly, otherwise known as *de facto* possession i.e., custody or occupation which is a question of fact; or it may be coupled with animus possidendi, which is singular and exclusive, thereby constituting *de jure* or legal possession.[208]

122. Possession in law is exclusive possession or nothing. Exclusive possession is characterised not only by the continuous acts of uninterrupted possession, but also by the exclusion of all other persons from possession. Legal possession includes constructive possession such as where a servant is let into possession by the master or where a bailee of goods or chattels has the key to the door or receptacle of the place where they are kept.[209]

123. Possession may be lawful or wrongful: it is lawful where it is exercised as a right of ownership or by grant, and wrongful where it is neither. A wrongful possession is nonetheless protected by law as it is good against the whole world except the true owner. Thus, an intervention with such wrongful possession without lawful justification may give rise, in the case of real property, to an action for recovery of

206. Kodilinye *supra* n. 160 at 96.
207. *See Ogunleye v. Oni* (1990) 2 NWLR (Pt. 135) 784.
208. *Buraimoh v. Bamgbose* (1989) 3 NWLR (Pt. 109) 352 at 355.
209. *Ward v. Turner* 28 ER 275.

the land or premises,[210] and, in the case of chattels, to an action in the tort of conversion.[211] It is no defence that ownership is vested in a third party.[212]Exclusive possession gives rise to possessory rights ranging from exclusion of intruders and trespassers,[213] to presumption of ownership until the contrary is proved.[214]

Right of Prescription

124. Prescription is a common law doctrine by which certain incorporeal rights such as easements and profits can be acquired over the land of others.[215] It is the acquisition of a right through long use or enjoyment such that the law presumes that the right was lawfully granted.[216] Whether the right is acquired at common law,[217] by lost modern grant[218] or under the Prescription Act 1832,[219] the use must be without force, without secrecy, and without permission (*nec vi, nec clam, nec precario*). It must be a use by or on behalf of a freeholder owner against another freehold owner; and the use must be one that could have been lawfully granted by deed.[220] The benefit of all interests subsisting including easements and profits subsisting for the benefit of an estate vests in the registered proprietor of a registered estate. Thus easement arising at common law or under the lost modern grant are legal interests and the purchaser of that unregistered burdened land is bound by such legal interests. Where the burdened land is registered, it constitutes an overriding interests capable of binding successive registered proprietors.

Adverse Possession

125. As opposed to the right of prescription which is enjoyed as a right traceable to a grant in cases of incorporeal hereditament at common law, the doctrine of adverse possession rests on wrongful possession rather than any presumption of right. Unlike prescription, adverse possession operates within the provisions of the statute of limitation,[221] and it is concerned with title to the land itself rather than an

210. This may take the form of action for declaration of title or recovery of possession, trespass, and injunction.
211. The tort of conversion is the denial of the claimant's title to goods by a defendant asserting either his own title or that of a third party: *Kuwait Airways Corporation v. Iraqi Airways Corporation* (Nos 4 and 5) (2002) 2 AC 883 at 995.
212. *Wilson v. Lombank* (1963) 1 WLR 1294.
213. *Apatira v. Igbo* (1941) 16 NLR 28.
214. *Ozokpo v. Paul* (1990) 2 NWLR (Pt. 133) 494 at 518.
215. C. Harpum, S. Bridge, and M. Dixon, *The Law of Real Property*, 8th ed. Sweet & Maxwell (2012) 1457 para 35-002.
216. *Ibid.*
217. Initially prescription at common law could be traced to use from the time immemorial and later fixed for 1289 within living memory.
218. The lost modern grant is the presumption of law that upon acquisition of the right for a period of twenty years or more, it could be presumed that the grantee of the right had a conveyance containing the grant which was lost.
219. A claim under the Prescription Act 1832 allows a party to claim an easement after a period of twenty years of continuous use without interruption.
220. *Bakewell Management Ltd v. Brandwood*(2004) UKHL 14.
221. See the Limitation Act 1966 applicable in the Federal Capital Territory of Nigeria, s. 16, and corresponding provision in the Limitation Law applicable in the federating States.

incorporeal hereditament. Unlike prescription which operates positively like a conveyance, adverse possession operates negatively by eliminating the claim of a person having a superior title without transfer from that person.[222]

126. Where the actual owner of land is dispossessed of, or has discontinued with possession without taking steps to recover possession from the adverse possessor for a period prescribed by the statute of limitation, his title becomes extinguished in favour of the adverse possessor.[223] By extinguishing the right of the owner to recover the land in favour of the adverse possessor, the latter's possession becomes impregnable giving him a title superior to all other persons.[224]

127. To qualify as an adverse possessor for purposes of acquisition of title under the statute of limitation, a person must have entered into peaceful and exclusive possession of land with the intention to possess (animus possidendi),[225] and must have been exercising an open and continuous adverse possession of land without the permission of the real owner.[226]

128. However, the doctrine of adverse possession does not apply to customary land tenurein Nigeria, and a customary landowner may bring an action for recovery of land or premises outside the limitation period[227] except where the defendant has been in continuous and undisturbed possession for many years to the knowledge of the customary land owner, and has, in the believe that he has a valid title, expended money, or altered his position.[228]This exception was drawn based, not on 'any provision of English law as to the limitation of actions, but simply on the grounds of equity, on the ground that the court will not allow a party to call in aid principles of native law, and least of all principles, which ... were developed in and are applicable to a state of society vastly different from that now existing merely for the purpose of bolstering up a stale claim.'[229] While the doctrine of adverse possession as encapsulated in the statute of limitation of actions does not apply under Islamic law in Nigeria, the principle of 'standing by' applies under Islamic law as it does under customary law,[230] with some variation. The rule which is known as *Hauzi* under Islamic law states that where a person has been in undisturbed possession of land for a period of ten years or more while the true owner stands by and does nothing to claim his property, and the parties are not related by blood or marriage, the person in possession acquires title to the land.[231]

---

222. C. Harpum, S. Bridge, and M. Dixon (n. 215) 1458; Bu*ckinghamshire County Council v. Moran*(1990)] Ch. 623 at 644.
223. *Majekodunmi v. Abina* (2002) 1 SC 92.
224. *Buckinghamshire County Council v. Moran* (1990) Ch. 623 at 644 para B.
225. *Pye (Oxford) Ltd v. Graham (2003) 1 AC 419 HL.*
226. *Roy v. Lagona* (2010) VSC 250 para 35*; Mount Camel Investments Ltd v. Peter Thurlow* (1988) 1 WLR 1078.
227. *Mora v. Nwalusi* (1962) 1 All NLR 681; *Olohunku v. Teniola* (1991) 5 NWLR (Pt. 192) 501 at 513.
228. *Awo v. Cookey Gam* (1913) 2 NLR 100.
229. *Ibid.*, 101.
230. *See* para. 128 above.
231. *Yaro Ningi v. Dan Katsina* (1991) 3 NWLR (Pt. 177) 76.

Part I. Immovable Property and Real Property

Chapter 1. General Classification

§1. INTRODUCTION

129. Classification of real property or immovables such as land by Nigerian law may follow from its natural content, in which case, the topsoil, the subsoil, and things growing thereon are basic elements;[232] or from the legal content encompassing not only the basic elements of the natural content, but also everything above and below the surface of the earth,[233] things attached to land through the use of capital and/or labour,[234]and incorporeal hereditaments such as easements, rents, and profits.[235]

§2. LAND AS THE EARTH SURFACE

130. This consists of the topsoil i.e., all that surface of the earth which is not covered by the sea,[236] appearing in different forms and serving different purposes. In Nigeria, about nine categories of land existed under customary and Islamic law, the general law, the State Lands Law,[237] and the Federal Capital Territory Act[238]

232. *See Unilife Development Company Ltd v. Adeshigbin* (2001) 4 NWLR (Pt. 704) 609. To this list of basic elements of the natural content is the inclusion of 'water', which is considered to be a specie of land such that an action to recover possession of a pool or rivulet of water must proceed as an action to recover land covered with water.
233. This is represented by the maxim: 'the owner of land owns everything above it to the sky and everything beneath it to the depths' and was captured by the Court of Appeal in *Ibrahim v. Yola* (1986) 4 CA (Pt. 1) 98 at 115.
234. This is known by the maxim *Quicquid plantatur solo solo cedit* i.e., everything affixed to land becomes part of the land and is captured by the Supreme Court of Nigeria in *NEPA v. Amusa* (1976) 12 SC 99.
235. *See,* for example, Property and Conveyancing Law Cap 100 LWN 1959, s. 2 applicable and adopted in States carved out of the former western and mid-western region of Nigeria.
236. *Salami v. Gbodoolu*(1977) 4NWLR (Pt. 277) at 287.
237. *See,* for example, State Lands Law Cap S11 Laws of Lagos State, 2003.
238. No. 6 1976 Cap F6 LFN 2010.

before the advent of the Land Use Act in 1978[239] (the Act) and these are preserved by the Act,[240] subject to its provisions. They are as follows:

131. Stool Land (Amiriyya Land) This is the seat of traditional rulers and enures for so long as there is heir to the throne.[241] A traditional ruler has no more than a life interest in the land and cannot claim the land as his own or as representing his family property held in trust for himself and other members of the family.[242] While the palace remains and is being used as the official residence of the traditional ruler, the responsibility for maintenance or repair rested with the community in early times, and now in the State government.[243] Where the said land ceases to be stool land, it reverts back to the family or community initially having title over same.[244]

Communal and Family Land

132. Communal land exists for the benefit of the whole community with the head chief holding it in trust for the use of members of the community.[245] Also, family property which evolves through intestacy[246] has corporate existence as title is vested in the family as opposed to the individual. The individual member of the community or family enjoys user rights[247] mainly and cannot alienate his allotted portion or devise same by Will without the consent of the community or family.[248] However, an act of partition put an end to the joint ownership and vests the individual member with title.[249]

Land Cultivated by the Individual Members of the Community or Family (Mamluk Land)

133. The right of the individual to cultivate and use communal land is recognised under customary and Islamic law.[250] The use of land for agriculture by members of the community, or neighbouring community under customary tenancy, and the need to allow such land to lie fallow for purposes of recuperation of the soil, have been recognised since time immemorial as an important system of land tenure in Nigeria.

---

239. Cap L5 LFN 2010.
240. *Ibid.*, ss 4 and 48.
241. *Akodu v. Omidiji* (1927) 8 NLR 55.
242. *Oyekan v. Adele* (1952) 14 WACA 209.
243. *See,* for example, s. 3(3) of the Obas and Chiefs Law of Lagos State Cap O2 Laws of Lagos State, 2003.
244. Smith, I.O., *Practical Approach to Law of Real Property in Nigeria* 12 (Revised ed. Ecowatch Publications Nigeria, Ltd. 2013).
245. *Amodu Tijani v. Secretary, Southern Nigeria* (1921) AC 399.
246. *Olowosago v. Adebanjo* (1988) 4 NWLR (Pt. 88) 275.
247. *Lewis v. Bankole* (1908) 1 NLR 82.
248. *Akeju v. Suenu* (1925) 6 NLR 87.
249. *Olorunfunmi v. Asho* (2000) 2 NWLR (Pt. 643) 143.
250. Smith, I.O. *supra* n. 244 at 13.

Virgin Bush or Waste Land (Mawat Land)

134. The right of the individual to acquire any part of the virgin bush and do as he pleases to sell, lease, or pledge without any family restrictions or inhibition is a notable system of land tenure in Nigeria.[251] The children of such individual may inherit the property as family property, unless he disposes of it otherwise in his lifetime or by Will.[252]

Beach Land

135. Beach land belongs to the whole town, village, or community within the boundaries of which it lies.[253] Unless it is the subject matter of an extension of a grant of communal land, no individual, family, or household has any right over same, and the grantee cannot alienate the portion or any other portion at that.[254]

Foreshores

136. Foreshores or any reclaimed land belongs to the State subject to any existing customary usage and rights by natives within the contiguous local community.[255] Such customary usage include access to the water, landing, embarking, mooring and hauling up of canoes, placing or storing things thereon,[256] etc. Under the various State Land Laws[257] in Nigeria, a grant under the law shall not, unless otherwise expressly provided therein, confer any right to the foreshore.

Private Land Subject of the Old Conveyance by Fee Simple

137. Some parcels of land in popular towns and cities in Nigeria hitherto subject to the regime of customary and Islamic law have been vested in individuals through deeds of conveyance in English form by the mid-twentieth century.[258] Such deed of conveyance vested absolute interests in the purchasers independent of all customary or Islamic law principles.

State Lands

138. Apart from the foregoing categories of land under the English, Customary and Islamic law, State lands have been known. State lands evolved from the combination of Crown lands as defined by the Crown Lands Ordinance 1918[259] as amended[260] and land acquired by the various State governments in Nigeria pursuant

251. Elias, T.O., *British Colonial Law* 236–237 (Sweet & Maxwell 1962).
252. *Ibid.*
253. *Chief Young Dede v. African Association Ltd* (1910) 1 NLR 130; *Henshaw v. Henshaw & Ors and Company Francais* (1927) 8 NLR 77.
254. *Henshaw v. Henshaw & Ors and Company Francais supra* n. 240 above.
255. *Attorney General, Southern Nigeria v. John Holt & Ors* (1910) 2 NLR 1 at 11.
256. *Ibid.*
257. *See,* for example, State Land Law of Lagos State Cap S11 Laws of Lagos State of Nigeria, 2003.
258. *See Oshodi v. Balogun* (1936) 2 ALL ER 1632.
259. *See* s. 2 of Cap 45 of the Laws of the Federation of Nigeria and Lagos 1958.
260. The Law was subsequently amended in 1935, 1941, 1945, 1947, 1954, and 1955.

to the Public Lands Acquisition Law.[261] State lands in Nigeria are found in major towns in Nigeria under the designation Government Reservation Areas (G.R.A).

Federal Lands

139. Federal lands exist in some parts of Nigeria with history of Federal presence,[262] and basically in the Federal Capital Territory of Abuja pursuant to the Federal Capital Territory Act 1976.[263]

§3. Surface Water Covering a Parcel of Land Forms Part of the Land

140. Under Nigerian law, surface water forms part of the land surface.[264] Surface water in this regard is distinct from waters of a natural stream, lake or river, ownership of which is vested in the Federal Government[265] and navigable waterways, inland waterways, rivers, ports, and internal waterways which are under the management and control of the National Inland Waterways Authority.[266]

§4. Everything above the Earth Surface to the Sky

141. The common law principle that everything above the earth surface to the sky is land, forms part of Nigerian law.[267] However the height approved by law is that which 'is necessary for the ordinary use and enjoyment of the land and the structures upon it for above that height, the owner has no greater rights in the airspace than any other member of the public'.[268]Also, everything beneath the earth to the depths is said to form part of it. An example is the percolating or subterranean water which may be a source of water supply, or subsoil of different texture which qualifies as building materials. Minerals are however excluded under Nigerian law as ownership of the resources is vested in the Federal Government under Nigerian Law,[269] and the owner of land above the minerals cannot lay claim to ownership of

261. *See,* e.g., Public Lands Acquisition Act 1917 Cap 167 LFN 1958.
262. An example is the case of Lagos as the former Federal Capital Territory.
263. No. 6 1976 Cap F6 LFN 2010.
264. *Amachree v. Kalio* (1914) 2 NLR 108; *Adigun v. Aina* (1964) 1 All NLR 12; *Elf Nig Ltd v. Sillo* (1994) 6 NWLR (Pt. 350) 258.
265. *See* s. 1 of the Minerals and Mining Act Cap M12 LFN 2010.
266. National Inland Waterways Authority Act Cap N47 LFN 2010, s. 11; *Gani-Tarzan Marine Enterprises Ltd. v. Caravelle Resources and Investment Ltd* (2011) 14 NWLR (Pt. 1266) 125. But note that the Law recognises the right of owners of land adjoining, abutting, or encompassing waterways, rivers, and streams to settle and erect structures on the bank of the waterways and rivers and to extract rent from others seeking to use the land. Violation of the right entitles owners of the land to compensation: *See Braide v. Adoki* (1931) 10 NLR 15*; Adesina v. Lemonu* (1965) 1 All NLR (Pt. 1) 233; *Elf Nig Ltd v. Sillo*(1994) 6 NWLR (Pt. 350) 258*; Nigerian National Petroleum Corporation v. Sele* (2004) 5 NWLR (Pt. 866) 379 at 427–428.
267. *Kelsen v. Imperial Tobacco Co Ltd* (1957) 2 QB 334; *Ibrahim v. Yola* (1986) 4 CA (Pt. 1) 98 at 115.
268. *Bernstein of Leigh (Baron) v. Skyviews& General Ltd* (1977) 3 WLR 136.
269. *See* s. 18 of the Interpretation Act Cap 123 LFN 2010 which defines land to exclude Minerals.

it, but is entitled to compensation under the Minerals and Mining Act[270] upon revocation of his right of occupancy under the Land Use Act.[271]

§5. Things Attached to Land

142. Nigerian law recognises things attached to land as forming part of the land and subject of the same rights of property as the soil itself (*Quicquid plantatur solo solo cedit*).[272] Thus, where X builds on Y's land without the latter's approval and in the absence of laches on his part, the building automatically becomes subject of Y's ownership along with the land.

143. The applicability of the rule of *quicquid plantatur solo solo cedit* generally under the customary land tenure system is not in doubt,[273] although the institution of customary tenancy may not allow for its application for the simple reason that the understanding of parties usually is that the customary tenant shall put the land of the overlord to use and hold same in perpetuity subject to good behaviour.[274]

144. Under Islamic law, a person has no title to buildings erected on his land by a trespasser, but may require that the land be restored back to its original state or claim compensation for the restoration. Ownership of building attached to land or crops or trees planted on land are separate from the land itself and are commonly held by a separate title so that the maxim *quicquid plantatur solo solo cedit* does not apply.[275]

Exceptions to the Quicquid Plantatur Rule

145. The Supreme Court of Nigeria in the case of *NEPA v. Amusa*[276] identified exceptions to the rule. In the words of Fatayi-Williams JSC:

> [t]his general rule of law is subject to any contract entered into by the parties and also the doctrines and rules of equity … [and] as defined in specified statutes … .[277]

From the above, three exceptions have been identified as exceptions to the age long rule of the English common law received as part of Nigerian law. They are as follows:

---

270. Cap M12 LFN 2010.
271. For provisions of the Act relating to revocation of rights of occupancy, *see* s. 28.
272. *NEPA v. Amusa* (1976) 1 FWLR 242 at 249; *Orinawo v. Okene* (2002) 14 NWLR (Pt. 786) 157; *Unilife Development Co. Ltd v. Adeshigbin* (2001) 4 NWLR (Pt. 704) 609 at 625.
273. *See Alao v. Ajani* (1989) 11 WACA 81; *Okoiko v. Esedalue* (1974) 3 SC 15.
274. *Etim v. Eke* (1941) 16 NLR 43.
275. *See* generally, Quadri, A.A., *Islamic Jurisprudence in the Modern World, 316* (1999) Taj Publishers.
276. *NEPA v. Amusa supra* n. 272.
277. *Ibid.*, at 115.

Contract

146. Where parties expressly or by necessary implication exclude applicability of the rule in their contract, it does not apply. An example of this is found in lease agreements where parties agree that the lessee shall be entitled to remove fixtures or accretions at the end of the lease, or where a particular rule of customary or Islamic law provides not only for the terms of a relationship, but also the rights and liabilities of both contracting parties and remedies for breach of contract.[278]

Rules and Doctrines of Equity

147. The rule will be excluded where the owner of land is guilty of laches, acquiescence or standing by,[279] or where the owner is precluded by equitable or proprietary estoppel from going back on a promise or resiling from a representation which encouraged an adverse possessor[280] to expend money on improvements without apprising him of his intention to dispute the land.[281]

Statutes

148. A number of statutes could be identified as creating exceptions to the rule:

(a) Section 11 of the State Lands Act[282] and its States' counterparts[283] provides that on the determination of a lease granted under it, any building thereon passes to the State, unless the lease is for a term not exceeding thirty years in which case, the lessee is entitled to remove the building if the government is not willing to buy them.[284]Thus, the rule does not apply to improvements made on State land subject to a term of lease not exceeding thirty years as the allottee is entitled to remove them upon the expiration of the lease.
(b) Section 15 of the Land Use Act[285] vests in the holder of a Statutory right of occupancy the right to, and absolute possession of improvements made on the land, notwithstanding that the radical title to land, the subject of statutory right of occupancy, is vested in the Governor.
Ownership of mineral deposits in land is vested in the Federal Government, pursuant to the relevant provisions of the Mines and Minerals Act[286] and not in the holder of a right of occupancy over the land.
(c) Section 14 of the Recovery of Premises Act provides that a tenant who, 'with the previous consent in writing of the landlord executed in his accommodation any improvements, he shall be entitled, at the termination of the tenancy, on quitting his accommodation, to receive compensation from his landlord in

278. *Anene v. Okororie* (1977) IMSLR 268.
279. *Okoh v. Olotu* (1953) 20 NLR 123; *Ude v. Nwara* (1993) 2 NWLR (Pt. 278) 638 at 660; *Ibrahim v. Yola* (1986) 4 CA (Pt. 1) 98 at 117–118.
280. *Ibrahim v. Yola* (1986) 4 CA (Pt. 1) 98 at 117–118.
281. *Ude v. Nwara supra* n. 279.
282. Cap 45 Laws of the Federation of Nigeria and Lagos 1958.
283. *See,* e.g., Laws of Lagos State Cap S 11 2003.
284. *Ude v. Nwara supra* n. 279 at 660.
285. Cap L5 LFN 2010.
286. Cap M12 LFN 2010.

respect of any such improvement'. This provision which has been re-enacted in the various States' Rent Control Laws constitutes an exception to the rule of *quicquid plantatur solo solo cedit.*

(d) Section 24(2) of the Lagos State Agricultural Holdings Law 1986[287] provides that on the determination or revocation of a temporary occupation licence or the grant or allocation of an agricultural holding under the law, the holder or allottee 'may harvest his crops and remove his unexhausted improvements, chattels and fixtures on the land'.

§6. Incorporeal Hereditament

149. An incorporeal hereditament is defined as 'an inheritable right existing on land which is not the object of sensation, can neither be seen nor handled but which is a creature of the mind and exist only in contemplation of the law'.[288] They consist in such intangible rights such as easements, licences, profits. These rights are recognised both at customary law and under Islamic law in Nigeria. For example, the rights of fishing inhabitants of a locality to dry their nets on adjoining land,[289] or a right of free passage over all public thoroughfares[290] are rights known to customary law, while the right of passage, the right to let flow or to pour out water, or the right to draw water are rights recognised under Islamic law.[291]

150. All land vested in the Governor of each State by virtue of the Land Use Act[292] include incorporeal rights such as easements and licences. Thus, the Governor is vested with the power to grant easements appurtenant to statutory rights of occupancy[293] or to grant licence to any person to enter upon any land which is not the subject of statutory right of occupancy, or of a mining lease, mining right, or exclusive prospecting licence granted under the Mineral Act or any other enactment, and to remove or extract building materials.[294]

287. No. 18 of 1986.
288. Blackstone Commentaries, vol. II 17.
289. *Mercier v. Denne* (1905) 2 Ch. 338.
290. *Obasa v. Baruwa & Ors* (1931) 10 NLR 104.
291. *See* generally, Schacht, J., *An Introduction to Islamic Law* 142 (Clarendon Press).
292. Cap L5 LFN 2010.
293. *Ibid.*, s. 5(1)(b).
294. Minerals and Mining Act Cap M12 LFN 2010; s. 12.

Chapter 2. Legal Interests

§1. Introduction

151. Interests in land in Nigeria may be legal or equitable. Legal estate is a full and absolute interest, complete and perfect so far as regards the apparent right of ownership and possession, while an equitable interest is an interest recognised in equity as available to a person, in contrast with a legal interest.[295] While legal interests developed from the rules of the common law as subsequently streamlined by local statutes in the various States of Nigeria, equitable interests resulted from the rules of equity permeating various rules of common law, acting on conscience, enforcing sanctity of agreements, and forestalling the desire to use provisions of statutes as engine of fraud.

§2. Nature of Legal Interests

152. A legal interest is a product of positive law which states the requirements for its creation and the essential formalities for vesting same in law.[296] Failure to meet the requirements renders the creation void or the vesting of same ineffectual. It could be absolute such as where there is a grant, or an outright assignment; it could be restrictive such as where a lease is created; it could flow from the main grant such as easements or restrictive covenants; it could be subject to qualification as in the case of the trust or creation of interest in succession.

153. A legal interest in land is a right in the land itself so that whoever acquires the land is bound by that right whether he knew of it or not.[297] One significant feature of a legal interest is that it is good against the whole world and any purchaser of property the subject matter of a legal interest takes subject to it. It may subsist concurrently with or subject to any other legal interest in the same land.[298]

154. Legal interests rank in priority according to the time of creation[299] and may defeat a prior equitable interest where the holder is a bona fide purchaser for value without notice of the prior equitable interest.[300]

---

295. Halsburys Laws of England 4th ed. vol. 16 para. 1317 at 885.
296. For example, the requirements of writing, consent, stamping, and registration of interest in Nigeria.
297. Baker, P.V., *Megarry's Manual of the Law of Real Property* 56 (5th ed. Stevens & Sons Ltd. 1975).
298. *See,* for example, Cap 110 Laws of Abia State 2005; Cap 100 Laws of Akwa Ibom State 2000; Cap 122 Laws of Bauchi State 2006; Cap 106 Laws of Katsina State 1991; Cap 121 Laws of Kaduna State 1991; Cap 114 Laws of Kebbi State 1996; Cap P10 Laws of Kwara State 2007; Cap 100 Laws of Ogun State 1978; Cap 98 Laws of Ondo State 1978; Cap 132 Laws of Osun State 2001 among others.
299. *Auta v. Ibe* (2003) 13 NWLR (Pt. 837) 347; *Dantsoho v. Mohammed* (2005) 6 NWLR (Pt. 817) 457.
300. *Animashaun v. Olojo* (1990) 6 NWLR (Pt. 154) 111; *Kachalla v. Banki & 2 Ors* (2006) 2–3 SC 41.

§3. LEGAL INTERESTS WHICH MAY BE CREATED

155. Legal interests may be created at common law using prescribed formalities[301] or under statute. In Nigeria, the various property legislations in the States[302] define legal interest as 'a right, interest or charge, in or over land (subsisting or created at law) which is by law authorised to subsist or to be created as a legal interest'.[303]

156. The laws have codified legal interests cognisable in land as follows:[304]

(i) Right of occupancy
(ii) Sublease
(iii) Underlease
(iv) Sub-underlease
(v) A charge by way of legal mortgage
(vi) Right of entry or re-entry exercisable over or in respect of any of the interests in (i), (ii), (iii), and (iv) above.

All other interests not falling within the itemised categories take effect as equitable interests mainly.[305]

I. Right of Occupancy

157. A right of occupancy may be granted under the Land Use Act 1978[306]either by the Governor in the form of a statutory right of occupancy over land whether or not in an urban area, or by the local government in the form of customary rights of occupancy, but only in respect of land in non-urban areas.[307] In the Federal Capital Territory (FCT), the whole area is classified as urban and consequently, only a statutory right of occupancy may be granted by the Minister on behalf of the President of the Federal Republic of Nigeria,[308] the whole parcels of land in the FCT having been vested in the Federal Government of Nigeria before

301. This is usually done by deed registered as an instrument.
302. *See,* for example, s. 1(1) Cap 100 Laws of Akwa Ibom State of Nigeria 2000, Cap 128 Laws of Kwara State of Nigeria 1994; s. 3(1) Cap 114 Laws of Sokoto State of Nigeria 1996, Cap 114 Laws of Kebbi State of Nigeria 1996.
303. Cap 100 Laws of Akwa Ibom State of Nigeria, s. 19(1) and corresponding provisions in the Laws of other States.
304. *Supra* n. 302.
305. *See* subs. (2) to the laws cited in *supra* n. 302.
306. Cap L5 LFN 2010.
307. *Ibid.,* s. 6(1).
308. *Ona v. Atenda* (2000) 5 NWLR (Pt. 656) 244.

the advent of the Land Use Act.[309] Also, the minister may, on behalf of the Federal Government, grant a statutory right of occupancy with regards to Federal Government land in the States.[310]

158. Statutory right of occupancy granted by the Governor which includes other interests such as easements, appurtenants,[311] 'shall be for a definite term and may be granted subject to the terms of any contract which may be made by the Governor and the holder not being inconsistent with the provisions of the Act'.[312]

159. Pre-existing rights on land in urban areas are converted to statutory rights of occupancy deemed granted by the Governor, while land rights in non-urban areas are converted to customary right of occupancy deemed granted by the local government.[313] However, no deemed grant exists in the FCT.[314]

160. Right of occupancy whether actual or deemed have similar tenurial implications under the Land Use Act[315] except that actual grants by the Governor are limited to term of years.[316]

161. An actual grant whether statutory or customary cannot be made to override existing deemed rights, customary or statutory;[317] the effect of such inconsistent right is to render the subsequent grant a nullity.[318]

162. The Governor may issue a certificate of occupancy under his hand as evidence of grant when granting a statutory right of occupancy;[319] or when any person in occupation of land under a customary right of occupancy applies in the prescribed manner;[320] or when any person is entitled to a statutory right of occupancy.[321] A certificate of occupancy with regards to Federal land can only be issued by the Federal Government and not by the Governor of the State where the land is situate.[322] Also, a local government cannot issue a certificate of occupancy.[323]

---

309. *See* s. 1 of the FCT Act 1976. This is confirmed by s. 49(1) of the Land Use Act Cap L5 LFN 2010 and entrenched in the Nigerian Constitution by virtue of s. 297(1) of the Constitution of the Federal Republic of Nigeria 1999 as amended.
310. Section 49(1) of the Land Use Act Cap L5 LFN 2010 as amended.
311. *Ibid.*, s. 5(1).
312. *Ibid.*, s. 8.
313. *Ibid.*, ss 34 and 36.
314. The FCT Act 1976 Cap F6 LFN 2004 swept away all pre-existing land rights customary or otherwise: *See* s. 1 of the Act.
315. *Savannah Bank (Nig) Ltd v. Ajilo* (1989) 1 NWLR (Pt. 97) 305.
316. Land Use Act Cap L5 LFN 2010; s. 8.
317. *Kyari v. Alkali* (2001) 11 NWLR (Pt. 724) 412; *Dansoho v. Mohammed* (2003) 6 NWLR (Pt. 817) 457; *Ibrahim v. Mohammed* (2003) 6 NWLR (Pt. 817) 615.
318. *See* cases in n. 317 above.
319. Land Use Act Cap L5 2010, s. 9(1)(a).
320. *Ibid.*, s. 9(1)(b).
321. *Ibid.*, s. 9(1)(c).
322. Control and management of such land is vested in the Federal Government pursuant to s. 49(1) of the Land Use Act Cap L5 LFN 2004. *See also* s. 47(1) of the Act.

163. A certificate of occupancy does not cure defect in title, and when the title of the holder is in issue, proof of title is required by law.[324]

164. The holder of a statutory right of occupancy shall, during the term of the occupancy, have exclusive possession of the land subject to right of occupancy against all persons except the Governor.[325] The holder also has the sole right to, and absolute possession of all the improvements on the land, and may transfer same with the prior consent of the Governor.[326]

165. A right of occupancy shall not be alienated by assignment, mortgage, sub-lease, transfer of possession or otherwise howsoever, without the consent of the Governor in the case of a statutory right of occupancy[327] or where the property in a non-urban area is to be sold pursuant to an order of court;[328] and in all other cases, without the consent of the local government first had and obtained.[329] Failure to obtain Governor's consent renders any transaction purporting to transfer the right of occupancy void.[330]

166. A right of occupancy may be revoked generally by the Governor for over-riding public interest[331] and where this happens, compensation shall be paid in appropriate circumstances,[332] but only in respect of the unexhausted improvements.[333]

167. It is important to note with regard to Federal Government land in the States or in the Federal Capital Territory, that the powers of the Governor under the Act (i.e., to grant statutory right of occupancy, issue a certificate of occupancy, give consent, etc.) shall be exercisable by the president or any minister designated for the purpose.[334]

II. Sublease or Underlease and a Sub-underlease

168. These interests are capable of being created as estates in hierarchy and like a chain, anchored on the superior interest leaving for the holder of such superior

---

323. Under both ss 6 and 36 of the Land Use Act, a local government is empowered to *register* a person as a holder of a customary right of occupancy; it has no power to issue a certificate of occupancy.
324. *Ogunleye v. Oni* (1990) 5 NWLR (Pt. 152) 745.
325. Cap L5 LFN 2010 s. 14.
326. *Ibid.*, s. 15.
327. *Ibid.*, s. 22.
328. *Ibid.*, s. 21.
329. *Ibid.*
330. *Savannah Bank (Nig) Ltd v. Ajilo* (1989) 1 NWLR (Pt. 97) 305; *Union Bank plc & Anor v. Ayodare & Sons (Nig) Ltd* (2007) 13 NWLR (Pt. 1052) 567.
331. *Ibid.*, s. 28.
332. *Ibid.*, s. 29.
333. *Ibid.*
334. *Ibid.*, s. 51(2).

interest, a reversionary right which enures for the duration of the interest subsumed.[335] These categories of leases may be created either to run concurrently with the pre-existing lease (a lease of reversion), or to run only at its expiration (a lease in reversion or a reversionary lease).

169. It is noteworthy however, that a future lease creates no estate as it were, but only a right to possession known as *inter esse termini* with its implications.[336] The rule of inter esse termini is now abolished in the States covered by the Property and Conveyancing Law[337] (namely, Oyo, Osun, Ondo, Ekiti, Ogun, Edo, and Delta States), as well as in the various States with landlord and tenant legislation.[338] In those States, a lease is capable of taking effect at law or in equity according to the estate or powers of the grantor, from the date fixed for commencement of the term without actual entry.

A Charge by Way of Legal Mortgage

170. This is a form of statutory charge over property but without an assignment per se of a term of years. A legal chargee in this case has the rights and remedies applicable to a legal mortgagee.

III. A Right of Entry or Re-entry Exercisable over or in Respect of Any of the Interests above

171. The right of entry or re-entry otherwise known as a reversionary right is available to the holder of a right of occupancy or headlessor with lesser interests created thereunder. It is a proprietary right which not only entitled the holder to possession, but also gives the right to protect the property from depreciation or injury to its appurtenances. Except otherwise prescribed by statute, in the case of forfeiture, it gives the holder the right to take physical possession and put an end to the lease.

IV. A Right, Easement or Privilege in or over Land Equivalent to Any of the Interests Above

172. These are generally incorporeal hereditaments such as easements and profits, usufructs, licences, and the likes. They are encumbrances attaching to proprietary interests which enure for the benefit of a third party and may constitute overriding interests of some sorts.

---

335. These are interests carved out of a right of occupancy which, from the tenor of the Land Use Act, is a lease.
336. The lessee of an *inter esse termini,* unlike a lessee of reversion, is neither entitled to the benefit nor subject to liability of covenants running with the reversion. He is however entitled to sue in trespass to protect his right to possession.
337. Cap 100 LWN 1959, s. 163(1).
338. *See* s. 115(1)(2) Cap 75 Laws of Rivers State 1999, Cap 79 Laws of Bauchi State 2006; s. 112 Cap 75 Laws of Sokoto State 1996, Cap 75 Laws of Kebbi State 1996 and corresponding provisions in other States where the Law exists.

Chapter 3. Equitable Interests

§1. Nature and Scope

173. All other interests outside the categories listed by local statutes would take effect as equitable interests. Being generally rights in personam,[339] equitable interests are enforceable against certain persons except a bona fide purchaser of the legal estate for value without notice[340] or somebody claiming through such person in which case, the equity is destroyed and the purchaser takes free of it.

174. Equitable interests range from the interest of the beneficiaries under a trust, to others such as the mortgagor's equity of redemption evolving after the date set for the repayment of a loan has passed,[341]equitable right to enforce restrictive covenants against successors in title of the covenantor[342] and the right of a purchaser under an estate contract before the legal estate of the vendor is conveyed to him.[343] Many other equitable interests corresponding to legal estates and interests in land exist in leases, mortgages, easements, etc. and shall be considered later.

§2. Mere Equities

175. It is necessary to distinguish equitable interests from 'mere equities'. Equities are rights having priority over the right of an assignee of property, or rights effective against a trustee in bankruptcy even after process has commenced.[344] Examples include the right to rescind a contract or transfer for fraud or misrepresentation,[345] the right to rectify a contract or deed for mistake,[346] and the right to set-off in equity.[347]

176. While such equities have the appearance of a right in rem enforceable in appropriate circumstances, unless and until the right is exercised, it is more akin to

339. A right *in personam* is a right enforceable against specifically determinate person or persons as opposed to rights enforceable against indeterminate number of persons, that is, a right in rem. However, the right of a beneficiary under a trust is said to lie also in rem, subject only to the right of a bona fide purchaser for value without notice. *See* Megarry, R. & Wade, W., *The Law of Real Property* 114 (5th ed. Sweet & Maxwell 1984). This is so because the equitable doctrine of tracing trust property permits the beneficiary to follow the trust property, either in its original or converted form, into the hands of the trustee and other indeterminate number of persons except the bona fide purchaser of the legal estate for value without notice.
340. Megarry, R. & Wade, W. *supra* n. 339 above at 114 citing Maitland, Equity 114, 115.
341. *Fairclough v. Swan Brewery Co Ltd* (1912) AC 565; *Yaro v. Arewa Construction Ltd* (2007) 17 NWLR (Pt. 1063) 333.
342. *Tulk v. Moxhay* 14 ER 1143.
343. An enforceable estate contract vests an equitable interest in the purchaser which he can devise by Will, charge, or sell.
344. *Re Eastgate* (1901) 1 KB 465; *Tilley v. Bowman Ltd* (1916) 1 KB 745.
345. *Car and Universal Finance Co. Ltd v. Caldwell* (1965) 1 QB 525.
346. *Phillips v. Phillips* (1862) 45 ER 1164.
347. *Hanak v. Green* (1958) 2 QB 9.

a personal right against the other party and may be defeated if not exercised promptly, or where the property is acquired by a bona fide purchaser of the legal title without notice of the equities.

§3. Priority of Interests

177. Interests in land; legal or equitable, may arise at different times and under different circumstances in the same property. Situations such as this have made it imperative for the courts to develop rules of priority in order to appropriately rank the competing interests. The doctrine of priority evolved under the maxim: *qui prior est tempore portior est jure* – 'he who is first in time is stronger in law'. This maxim of English law is part of Nigerian law and is being applied by Nigerian courts. Thus, where two parties claim their root of title from the same grantor, the interest of the parties will, prima facie, generally rank in order of creation.[348]

178. The following principles have developed in relation to doctrine of priority over the years:

(1) Where there are two legal interests created on the same land, the first in time in the order of creation has priority.[349] Where both legal interests are registered, each takes effect from the date of registration, and not from the execution of the deed of transfer.[350]A registered legal interest has priority over another that is not registered.
(2) A legal interest created before an equitable interest takes priority over the equitable interest unless and until it is set aside.[351]
(3) Where an equitable interest was created before the legal interest, the holder of the legal interest has priority only if it is shown that he obtained the legal interest for value without notice of the equitable interest.[352] This is the situation for example, where the holder of the equitable interest was not in possession.[353]
(4) Where both parties hold equitable interests, the first in time in order of creation, has priority. The rule is that where the equities are equal and neither of the parties hold a legal estate, the first in time prevails.[354]

---

348. *Kachalla v. Banki & 2 Ors supra* n. 300; *Gege v. Nande* (2006) 10 NWLR (Pt. 988) 256; *Ashiru v. Olukoya* (2006) 11 NWLR (Pt. 990) 1; *Ugwunze v. Adeleke* (2008) 2 NWLR (Pt. 1070) 148; *Eleran v. Aderonpe* (2008) 11 NWLR (Pt. 1097) 50.
349. *Dansoho v. Mohammed* (2005) 6 NWLR (Pt. 817) 451; *Ibrahim v. Mohammed* (2005) 6 NWLR (Pt. 817) 615; *Auta v. Ibe supra* n. 299.
350. *Amachreev. Zankley* (1963) 2 SCNLR 223; *Ashiru v. Olukoya supra* n. 348; *Tewogbade v. Obadina* (1994) 4 NWLR (Pt. 388) 326.
351. *Teniola v. Olohunku* (1999) 5 NWLR (Pt. 602) 280 at 298; *Dabo v. Abdullah* (2005) 7 NWLR (Pt. 923) 181 at 204.
352. *Animashaun v. Olojo supra* n. 300; *Kachalla v. Banki& 2 Ors supra* n. 300.
353. *Aminu v. Ogunyebi* (2004) 10 NWLR (Pt. 882) 457; *Etajatu v. Ologbo* (2007) 16 NWLR (Pt. 1061) 554.
354. *Okoye v. Dumez (Nig) Ltd* (1985) 1 NWLR (Pt. 4) 783; *Owie v. Ighiwi* (2005) 5 NWLR (Pt. 917) 184; *Kachalla v. Banki supra* n. 300.

179. The doctrine of *nemo dat quad non habet* – 'a man cannot give what he does not have or no longer possesses' – is not applicable to deny the holder of a legal interest of his priority over an earlier equitable interest where it is shown that at the time of creating the legal interest, the vendor had possession of the property in question. The principle is only applicable where both parties hold legal interest or equitable interest.[355]

180. Sale of land under customary law is complete when the purchaser pays money and is led into possession by the vendor, and a deed of assignment is not necessary to convey title. Thus, if the land is subsequently assigned to a purchaser under a deed of assignment, a claim that the first party's interest was an equitable interest cut-off by the latter bona fide purchaser will not be upheld by the court as the latter purchaser takes subject to the interest of the first.[356]

181. The doctrine of priorities under Benin customary law has been settled in a number of cases and in this regard, the following principles may be distilled:

(a) When there are competing titles to a piece of land, the question to be asked is who has made out a better title and not who first obtained the Oba's approval which is a single though culminating step in the whole chain of events and conditions to be strictly fulfilled by a prospective purchaser.
(b) Where two allocations have been made by the same ward Plot Allotment Committee, the first one takes priority. If two Plot Allotment Committees allocate a piece of land, the issue of priority does not arise. One person in the case of such a dispute will not get title just because he got approval first. It is the person that obtained allocation from the Ward Allotment Committee which has control over the area of location of the land in issue that gets title.[357]

182. A question of priority will only arise where both parties derived title from the same source and to the same land. Priority is between two possibly good titles and not between one good title and another which was initially a bad one.[358]

183. Also, there can be no priority of acquisition of land where the parties are not ad idem about the particular land that is the subject of acquisition; where the land claimed by the parties are different, the issue of priority does not arise.[359]

---

355. *Dansoho v. Mohammed supra* n. 349.
356. *Ogunbambi v. Abowaba* (1951) 13 WACA 222; *Okoye v. Dumez (Nig) Ltd supra* n. 354; *Clay Industries (Nig) Ltd v. Aina* (1993) 8 NWLR (Pt. 516) 208 at 236 paras B–D.
357. *Okeaya v. Inneh* (1970) 1 All NLR 1, *Gold v. Osaseren* (1970) 1 All NLR 125, *Aigbe v. Edokpolo* (1977) 2 SC 1, *Bello v. Eweka* (1981) 1 SC 101, *Arase v. Arase* (1981) 5 SC 33, *Awoyegbe v. Ogbeide* (1988) 1 NWLR (Pt. 73) 659, *Ugbo v. Aburime* (1994) 8 NWLR (Pt. 360) 1, *Enabulele v. Agbonlahor* (1999) 4 NWLR (Pt. 598) 166, *Ojo v. Azama* (2001) 4 NWLR (Pt. 702) 57.
358. *Gankon v. Ugochukwu Chemical Industries Ltd* (1993) 6 NWLR (Pt. 297) 55, *Badaru v. Bisiriyu* (1997) 5 NWLR (Pt. 504) 290, *Usman v. Joda* (1998) 13 NWLR (Pt. 582) 374 and *Okhuarobo v. Aigbe* (2002) 9 NWLR (Pt. 771) 29.
359. *Aduke v. Obiareri* (2002) 4 NWLR (Pt. 758) 537.

I. Bona Fide Purchaser of the Legal Estate for Value Without Notice

184. A bona fide purchaser for value without notice has been defined as a person who purchased property for valuable consideration without notice of any prior right or title which, if upheld, will derogate from the title which he has purported to acquire.[360]As against a person who had acquired a prior equitable interest over property, a subsequent bona fide purchaser of the legal estate without notice takes priority. It is said that 'it is the absence of notice of the prior equitable interest that provides a haven which serves to protect the interest of the subsequent purchaser from the eroding forces of the knowledge of the prior purchaser's equity'.[361]

185. The definition of the term bona fide purchaser of the legal estate for value without notice has been broken down by Obaseki JSC in *Animashaun v. Olojo*[362] as follows:

> What is the meaning of a 'bona fide purchaser of the legal estate for value without notice'? Bona fide is defined as 'in good faith, honesty, without fraud, collusion or participation in wrong doing'.
> Purchasing for value – 'Purchaser' in its technical sense does not necessarily imply purchaser for value. 'For value' are included to show that value must be given to earn the immunity from equitable claims. Value means any consideration in money, money's worth (e.g. other lands, stocks and shares and shares or services or marriage ….)
> Of a legal estate – As courts of equity break in upon the common law, when necessity and conscience require it, still they allow superior force and strength to a legal title to estate. …
> Without Notice – He must have no notice of the existence of equitable interest. He must have neither actual notice nor constructive notice or imputed notice. A person has actual notice of all facts of which he had actual knowledge however that knowledge was acquired. … .
> Constructive Notice – The Court of Chancery insisted that purchaser should inquire about equitable interest with no less diligence about legal which they could ignore only at their own peril. The motto of English conveyance is caveat emptor; the risk of encumbrances is on the purchaser who must satisfy himself by a full investigation of title before completing his purchase. A purchaser would be able to plead absence of notice only if he had made all usual and proper inquiries and had still failed to detect the equitable interest. …
> Imputed Notice – There is a third category of notice known as imputed notice. If a purchaser employs an agent, such as a solicitor, any actual or constructive notice … which the agent receives is imputed to the purchaser. … .

360. *Best (Nig) Limited v. Blackwood Hodge (Nig) Ltd* (2011) 5 NWLR (Pt. 1239) 95.
361. *Animashaun v. Olojo supra* n. 300 at 122.
362. *Supra* n. 300 at 122–123.

186. A bona fide purchaser of the legal estate for value who had notice[363] of a prior equitable interest takes subject to it. This is so, where he had knowledge, actual or constructive of the presence of the holder of a prior equitable interest working thereon,[364] or where there was a building occupied by tenants existing on the land at the time of acquiring interest in it.[365]

187. The plea of bona fide purchaser for value presupposes a valid transfer of the property to the party raising the plea, and where the transfer is void or confers no estate or interest, no such plea can be entertained.

---

363. Notice which may be actual or constructive must be in relation to matters which might affect the efficacy of the title of the vendor: *See Jaffar v. Ladipo* (1969) 1 All NLR 165; *Bank of the North Ltd v. Bello* (2005) 7 NWLR (Pt. 664) 244; *Ohiaeri v. Yusuf* (2009) 6 NWLR (Pt. 1137) 207.
364. *Clay Industries (Nig) Ltd v. Aina supra* n. 356.
365. *Briggs v. The Chief Lands Officer of Rivers State of Nigeria* (2005) 12 NWLR (Pt. 938) 59.

Chapter 4. Limited Interests

§1. Usufruct

188. The concept of usufruct, a medieval Latin word meaning 'use and enjoyment', derives from Roman law referring to the right to enjoy the use and advantages of another's property short of the destruction or waste of its substance.[366] Examples of usufruct under Nigerian law are the right of easement and profit a prendre. The scope and application of these concepts are discussed extensively in §6 *infra*.

§2. Building and Planting Rights

189. *See* §5 under use and habitation/occupation.

§3. Leasehold Interests: Chattels Real

190. Leasehold interests in Nigeria provide individuals and corporate bodies who cannot afford a purchase of real property, the opportunity to access residential or commercial premises at either a fixed or a periodic rent commensurate with affordability. The high cost of acquiring land through purchase, the unaffordable mortgage conditions coupled with the cut-throat interest rates have made it difficult to own houses and have made leases and tenancies more attractive.

I. Nature of Leasehold Interests

191. A holder of a right of occupancy[367] actual[368] or deemed[369](the lessor) may demise a lesser interest in the land subject of that right to another person (the lessee) under an agreement – oral or in writing – for a term of years or for such other periodic term as may be agreed by the parties to the agreement. An intention to create a lease through consensus ad idem is crucial to the existence of a lease, while lessor's exclusive possession, certainty of the parties, property to be demised, the duration of the lease, and the terms of the lease are essential for its validity.[370] A lease may take effect without the necessity of actual entry provided an agreed rent is reached between the parties.[371]

366. Black's Law Dictionary 6th ed. 1544.
367. A right occupancy is the main interest enjoyed by Nigerians on land since the commencement of the Land Use Act, 1978, radical title having been vested in the Governor of the State: *See* s. 1 of the Land Use Act Cap L5 LFN 2010.
368. Land Use Act Cap L5 LFN 2010, s. 5(1).
369. *Ibid.*, ss 34 and 36.
370. *UBA v. Tejumola* (1986) 4 NWLR (Pt. 38) 815; *Odutola v. Papersack (Nig) Ltd* (2006) 18 NWLR (Pt. 1012) 470.
371. *Opara v. Schlumberger (Nig) Ltd* (1995) 4 NWLR (Pt. 390) 440.

II. Creation of a Lease

192. A lease may be created by parole, or by a memorandum in writing or by deed.[372] To create a legal estate in favour of the lessee, the lease has to be by deed except leases taking effect in possession for a term not exceeding three years at the best rent obtainable.[373]

193. However, in equity, an oral lease of any duration above three years including one of incomplete memorandum in writing is enforceable if followed by sufficient acts of part performance. Thus, if on the strength of a parole agreement for a lease, a lessee is put in possession and pays rent, or does acts for the benefit of the property, or by reason of his occupation alters his position, an order of specific performance may be made by a court of competent jurisdiction. Also, a lease which is void at law for want of a deed is enforceable under the rule in *Walsh v. Lonsdale*[374] if the plaintiff can show that its essential terms have been reduced into writing sufficiently to satisfy the provisions of statute on the requirement of written memorandum.[375] The rule in *Walsh v. Lonsdale* which is applicable in Nigeria is that an agreement for a lease is as good as a lease. Thus, where there is an agreement for a lease under which possession has been taken, the tenant is deemed to hold in equity as if a lease had actually been granted. This rule has some limitations: where an agreement is not such that the court will make an order of a specific performance,[376] or where the right may be created on a grant of legal estate only,[377] or where there is an assignment to a third party,[378] or where the interest of a bona fide purchaser for value without notice of the equity is involved.[379]

194. A party seeking to enforce an agreement for a lease if the defaulting party fails to perform his obligation can sue for specific performance, or damages or both.[380]

III. Perfection

195. The Land Use Act makes it mandatory for the holder of a statutory right of occupancy to seek and obtain Governor's consent for a valid lease to be created.[381]

372. *Odutola v. Papersack.*
373. Statute of Frauds 1677, s. 3; Property and Conveyancing Law Cap 100 Laws of Western Nigeria 1959, s. 79(1).
374. (1882) 21 Ch. 9.
375. *Savage v. Sarrough* (1937) 13 NLR 141.
376. For example, where the Plaintiff has contravened a clause in the covenant contained in the agreement: *See Coatsworth v. Johnson* (1886) 55 LJ QB 220.
377. *See* the Conveyancing Act 1882, s. 6; and the Property and Conveyancing Law 1959, s. 87(1).
378. *Innih v. Ferado Agro Consortium* (1990) 5 NWLR (Pt. 152) 604.
379. *Ajose v. Oshinlaja* (1925) 6 NLR 98.
380. *Bata Shoe Company v. Melikan* (1956) 1 FSC 110.
381. Land Use Act 1978 Cap L5 LFN 2010, s. 22(1).

Any instrument purporting to create a leasehold interest without the requisite consent is void.[382] An agreement for a lease is an agreement to grant a lease in favour of the lessee, and to the extent that it does not transfer any interest to the lessee, it does not require the Governor's consent.[383]

196. A lease attracts ad valorem stamp duty,[384]and an agreement for a lease is charged with duty as if it were an actual lease for the term and consideration mentioned.[385]A lease for a term of more than three years must be registered.[386] An unregistered lease is not void but inadmissible in evidence and has no priority as against a subsequent registered lease.[387] However, where the tenant is in possession of land by virtue of a registrable instrument which has not been registered and paid rent to the landlord, he acquires an equitable interest therein which is as good as a legal estate and can only be defeated by a bona fide purchaser of the legal estate for value without notice of prior equity.[388]

IV. Types of Tenancy

197. Generally, tenancy in Nigeria is classified as contractual tenancy and statutory tenancy.[389] Contractual tenancy may further be classified into periodic tenancy and fixed tenancy. Periodic tenancy has been further divided into weekly tenancy, monthly tenancy, quarterly tenancy, half-yearly tenancy,[390] yearly tenancy, and other forms of periodic tenancy that may be recognised by law or created by the landlord and the tenant – such as tenancy at will.[391] Each of the types and subdivisions will now be looked at in details.

V. Contractual Tenancy

198. In *Farajoye v. Hassan*,[392] the court defined a contractual tenancy as 'the usual or common one that involves agreement between the landlord and the tenant, written or oral on the terms and conditions of the tenancy'. A contractual tenancy is

382. *Ibid.*, s. 26. But an agreement for a lease does not require governor's consent: *See Awojugbagbe Light Industries Ltd v. Chinukwe* (1995) 4 NWLR (Pt. 390) 379.
383. *Sanni v. Ogunbode* (2001) 8 NWLR (Pt. 714) 74.
384. Stamp Duties Act Cap S8 LFN 2010, ss 66–68.
385. *Ibid.*, s. 68(1).
386. *Osibamowo v. Khawam* (1972) NMLR 88 at 89. In Lagos State, a grant or sublease of State land exceeding five years shall be registered: *See* Lagos State Lands Registration Law No. 1 2015, s. 8.
387. Registration Act, No. 36 1924 ss 15 and 16.
388. *Okoye v. Dumez supra* n.354.
389. *African Petroleum Limited v. Owodunni* (1991) 8 NWLR (Pt. 210) 391; (2004) All FWLR (Pt. 208) 771, Per Karibi-Whyte in *Farajoye v. Hassan* (2006) 16 NWLR (Pt. 1006) 463–468.
390. Section 13 of the Tenancy Law of Lagos State 2011 statutorily recognises half-yearly tenancy for the first time.
391. Tenancy at will is a form of contractual tenancy, but not fall under any of the classification into periodic and fixed tenancies. It will appear to be sui generis because it is neither of fixed tenure like fixed tenancy nor of successive certain tenures as periodic tenancy.
392. (2006)16 NWLR (Pt. 1006) 487.

a conscious effort of the landlord and the tenant which must involve all the elements of a valid contract such as offer, acceptance, consideration, and intention to create legal relation. It is purely a contract between the landlord and the tenant. It is a contract of tenancy, which if written, usually contains the terms and conditions of the tenancy, together with the rights and obligations of both the landlord and the tenant.

199. A contract of tenancy may also be orally made. Where this is the case and the terms and conditions of the tenancy are not expressly spelt out, the law will not presume that parties agree on covenants that are ordinarily expected to be expressly stated in a tenancy agreement if so desired by the landlord and the tenant. The rule that the court will not make a contract for the parties will come to play.[393] However, covenants that are implied by law will at all times be interpreted to be part of the oral tenancy agreement. Such covenants include, on the side of the tenant, obligation not to commit waste, tenant-like use of the demise premises; and on the side of the landlord, allowing tenant quiet enjoyment of the premises, warranty as to fitness for habitation, and not to derogate from his grant.

200. A tenancy contract cannot derogate from terms, conditions, and/or covenants recognised by statute as forming part of any tenancy agreement, whether or not such terms are contained in the written or oral agreement between the tenant and the landlord.

VI. Fixed Tenancy

201. A tenancy is said to be fixed when there is certainty as to the commencement and the expiration of the tenancy. It is for a fixed duration, which means that upon the expiration of the duration, the tenancy determines naturally by effluxion of time. A fixed tenancy does not enjoy presumption of automatic renewal like a periodic tenancy. It is a tenancy for a term certain, and the certainty of the term is known to and agreed on by both parties right from the beginning. In *Joseph v. Adole*,[394] the Court of Appeal construed a fixed tenancy as follows: The position of the law is that a lease or tenancy for a fixed term automatically determines when the fixed term expires. Quit notice is usually obviated in the case of a fixed tenancy since the term of expiration is normally known unlike periodic tenancies that continues automatically from period to period until it determines by a notice to quit. *See Nweke v. Ibe* (1974) 4 ECSLR page 54.

202. A fixed tenancy, after its effluxion, can be converted to a periodic tenancy where the tenant enters into a new periodic tenancy agreement with the landlord; or

393. *Tominas Nigeria Limited v. Chigbu* (2006) LPELR-11924 (CA).
394. (2010) LPELP-CA/A/198/2007, Per Aboki, J.C.A. at 16, paras B–C.

to a statutory tenancy where the tenant holds over without the consent of the landlord; or to a tenancy at will where the tenant holds over with the consent of the landlord on condition that either of the parties may terminate the tenancy at their pleasure.

VII. Periodic Tenancy

203. A periodic tenancy is one that begins and ends at a particular period, but which renews automatically at the end of that particular period for another successive period of equal length. Unlike a fixed tenancy, a periodic tenancy enjoys automatic renewal at the end of one period – the renewal of which is presumed to be on the same terms and conditions as the expired period. It is not for a term certain, as the very end of it cannot be ascertained by the landlord and the tenant as at the time of entering into the contract.

204. A periodic tenancy is a form of a contractual tenancy, and it may be for one week, one month, six months, one year or more, depending on the relevant law and the agreement between the parties.

VIII. Tenancy at Will

205. Tenancy at will arises where a tenant, after the expiration or effluxion of his tenancy, holds over with the consent of the landlord, but on condition that either the landlord or the tenant may terminate the tenancy at their pleasure. It is devoid of certainty of term when the tenancy will be determined. Tenancy at will is also a form of contractual tenancy because it involves a decision reached ad idem by the landlord and the tenant.

206. Construing the nature of a tenancy at will, the Court of Appeal in a very recent case of *Oyegbesan v. Oyegbesan*[395] held as follows:

> A tenancy at will has built into the mutual understanding that both the tenant and the landlord can terminate the tenancy when any of them likes or at any time convenient to any of them.

207. In Nigeria, many of the recovery of premises statutes fix the length of notice required to terminate a tenancy at will at seven days;[396] the same length of notice required to determine a weekly tenancy.

395. (2014) LPELR-23358(CA) Per Ndukwe-Anyanwu, J.C.A. (pp. 10–11, paras G–C).
396. *See,* for example, s. 13(1)(a) Lagos State Tenancy Law No. 14 2011.

IX. Tenancy at Sufferance

208. A tenancy at sufferance is one in which the original grant by the landlord to the tenant has expired, usually by effluxion of time, but the tenant holds over the premises without the assent of the landlord.[397] A tenant at sufferance therefore is 'one who comes in by right and holds over without right'. If the landlord for any reason agrees to the tenant remaining on the premises, the tenancy at sufferance becomes converted into tenancy at will,[398] and where rent is paid and accepted or if an agreement to pay is entered into, regular tenancy will be created.[399]

209. Two major features differentiate a tenancy at sufferance from a tenancy at will: a tenancy at sufferance is a common law concept like a tenancy at will, but unlike a tenancy at will, it is no longer known to and applicable in any tenancy relationship in Nigeria;[400] and the tenant in a tenancy at sufferance holds over just like a tenant in a tenancy at will, but he holds over without the consent of the landlord.[401]

210. A tenancy at sufferance can be differentiated from a statutory tenancy even though both of them have one major feature in common: holding over without the consent of the landlord. The Supreme Court succinctly captures the distinction between tenancy at sufferance and statutory tenancy in *African Petroleum Ltd v. Owodunni*[402] as follows:

> Whereas a tenancy at sufferance is a concept of the common law in areas where there are no statutes designed to protect tenants who are holding over after their contractual tenancies have come to an end, the statute, where such exist, performs the same function in the case of a statutory tenant.[403]

X. Tenancy by Estoppel

211. Where a lease of property in respect of which the lessor has no title is granted, a tenancy by estoppel is granted and both the lessor and lessee are precluded from denying the existence of the landlord and tenant relationship. A tenancy by estoppel has all the attributes of a true tenancy and both parties are bound by covenants in such lease. It becomes a true tenancy when the lessor subsequently acquires title to the property.

397. *African Petroleum Ltd v. Owodunni* (1991) 8 NWLR (Pt 210) 139.
398. *Turner v. Bennott* (1842) 9 M & W 643.
399. *Mann v. Lovejoy* (1826) Ry & M 355.
400. *African Petroleum Ltd v. Owodunni supra* n. 397.
401. *Ibid.*
402. *Ibid.*
403. Per Nnaemeka-Agu, JSC, at 795 (paras A–B).

XI. Statutory Tenancy

212. This is a tenancy that is brought about by operation of law, as distinct from one brought about by the conscious effort or the consensus ad idem of the landlord and the tenant. It is a tenancy that the law presumes to result after the original contractual tenancy has expired as in the case of a fixed tenancy or has been determined as in the case of a periodic tenancy, but the tenant holds over or fails to give up possession of the demised premises.

213. The concept of statutory tenancy in Nigeria is a judicial coinage rather than an unequivocal legislative recognition.[404] It is a creation of the court which is drawn majorly from the incidents of the obligations imposed on the landlord by the Recovery of Premises Laws of the respective States in Nigeria in the event that the landlord seeks to recover premises from the tenant after the determination or expiration of the contractual tenancy.

214. By its nature, a statutory tenancy has the following features:[405]

(a) It is a tenancy that results by operation of law after the expiration of an earlier contractual tenancy between the landlord and the tenant.
(b) It is deemed to have been recognised by a statute as distinct from an oral or express contractual tenancy agreement entered into between the landlord and the tenant.
(c) It is usually an incident of obligations vested by a statute on the landlord towards recovery of the premises being occupied by the tenant.
(d) It allows the tenant to hold over the possession of the premises without the consent or willingness of the landlord until appropriate legal action has been taken against him or possession is voluntarily yielded up by him.
(e) It allows the tenant to be entitled to and claim all the benefits in the enabling statute and in the original contract between him and the landlord.
(f) It confers no estate on the tenant but gives him right of possession equal to that of a tenant with estate.[406]
(g) It creates a tenancy only within the ambit of the enabling statute.
(h) Termination can only be in accordance with the manner and length of term of the original grant between the landlord and the tenant.
(i) It creates an anomalous legal entity which will not ordinarily be described as a tenancy.
(j) It creates a tenancy where the tenant cannot be regarded as a trespasser until he is properly served the statutory notice(s) and same has expired.

---

404. *African Petroleum Ltd v. Owodunni supra* n. 397; *Pan Asian African Co. Limited v. National Insurance Corporation Limited* (1982) 9 SC 1; *Sule v. Nigerian Cotton Board* (1985) 2 NWLR (Pt. 5) 17; *Oduye v. Nigerian Airways Limited* (1987) 2 NWLR (Pt. 55) 126; *Adeponle v. Saidi* (1956) NSCC 71.

405. *Ibid.*

406. The right of possession is personal only to the statutory tenant. It extinguishes with the death of the tenant and does not pass or transfer to his successor whether or not the statutory tenancy has been determined. *See Adeponle v. Saidi supra* n. 404.

XII. Covenants in Leases

215. Covenants in every contractual relationship operate as terms and conditions of a contract that must be observed by parties to the contract in other to respect the sanctity of the contract. Covenants are usually enforceable upon breach, by the party who suffered from the breach occasioned by the other party. It is the covenants in themselves that make up the contract.

216. Covenants represent the set of promises to do or not to do certain acts.[407] Where, therefore, parties to a tenancy agreement have covenanted to restrain from doing certain acts,[408] the doing of such act will amount to a breach of contract which is actionable against the party that breaches the covenant. In the same manner, the landlord and the tenant usually covenant to do certain acts, and failure to do same will amount to a breach by the erring party.[409] On the importance and bindingness of the terms and conditions of a contract, the Supreme Court held in *Isheno v. Julius Berger* (Nigeria) Plc,[410] as follows:

> It is settled law that parties to an agreement or contract are bound by the terms and conditions of the contract they signed, in this case, exhibit H, and cannot operate outside its terms and conditions.[411]

217. The sanctity of covenants in a contract is not only applicable to written agreement signed by the landlord and the tenant, but will also apply to contracts orally entered into by the parties,[412] especially when the terms are clearly spelt out. The Court of Appeal has emphasised that:

> It is in the public interest that the sanctity of tenancy agreements like all contracts be protected and the rule of law upheld at all time.[413]

218. Three fundamental questions are involved in considering covenants in leases namely:

(1) Who are bound by covenants?
(2) What are these covenants?
(3) What are the remedies for breach?

---

407. Black's Law Dictionary, 9th ed. 419.
408. For example, the landlord is usually restrained from interfering with the quiet and exclusive possession of the tenant while the tenant is usually restrained from parting with the landlord's reversion or denying the landlord's title.
409. A good example of this is where the landlord covenanted to pay the necessary charges payable in law by the owner of the demised premises and where the tenant also covenanted to insure the premises demised.
410. (2008) All FWLR (Pt. 415) 1633 at 1653.
411. Per Akintan, JSC at 1653 paras H–A.
412. *Robinet Nigeria Ltd v. Shell Nigeria Gas Ltd* (2013) LPELR-22144(CA).
413. *Amakeze v. Onwudiwe*Suit No. CA/E/159/2008 delivered on 22 Mar. 2013.

XIII. Persons Bound by Covenants

219. As between the original parties to a lease, there is privity of contract and privity of estate hence, the covenants run with the land and the reversion and either the landlord or the tenant can enforce the covenant whether or not it touches or concerns the land, personal or collateral.

220. Where there is an assignment of the lease or reversion, there is privity of estate between the original landlord and assignee of the lessee, and notwithstanding the absence of privity of contract, either party can enforce covenants in the lease which touch and concern the land i.e., covenants which affect the nature, quality, or value of the demised property, or the mode of using or enjoying it,[414] as opposed to personal or collateral covenant, such as covenant to purchase the reversion; covenant to pay a sum of money to another; covenant that lessor shall not open another beer or spirit house within half a kilometre radius of the demised premises. Covenants which touch and concern the land include covenant to pay rent or taxes; to repair; to renew the lease, etc., which affect landlord qua landlord and tenant qua tenant.

221. In the case of a sublease, there is neither privity of contract nor estate and so, neither the sub-lessee nor the headlessor can enforce any form of covenant (touching and concerning the demised premises, personal or collateral) against one another.[415]

XIV. Types of Covenant

222. Generally, covenants can be classified broadly into three namely: express covenants; implied covenants, and usual covenants.

223. Express covenants are the ones that are unequivocally stated, agreed upon, and/or clearly spelt out by the parties to a tenancy relationship. Where the law does not imply a covenant, it has to be expressly stated in the agreement otherwise, the law will not imply it. Examples of express covenants are covenants to pay rent; covenant to pay rates and outgoings; covenant not to assign or sublet (sometimes without a licence); covenant as to use; covenant to renew; covenant to purchase, etc.

224. Implied covenants are those, the existence of which the law presumes or implies and incorporates into the tenancy agreement between the parties. The presumption and incorporation of implied covenants into the tenancy agreement by law are made either to ensure that parties do not exclude vital covenants meant for the preservation or reasonable enjoyment of the demised premises,[416] or to protect the

---

414. Per Russel LJ in *Horsey Estate Ltd v. Steiger&Petrifite Co. Ltd* (1899) 2 QB 79 at 89.
415. *Nigerian Properties Co. Ltd v. Doherty* (1958) WNLR 85.
416. Examples are lessors covenant for quiet enjoyment, fitness of premises for habitation or non-derogation from grant; or lessee's covenant to effect tenantable repairs or not to commit waste.

interests of parties to a lease or tenancy agreement where there are no express covenants or where the covenants in existence are inadequate.[417]

225. Usual covenants are species of implied covenants either necessary for the actualisation of parties' intention in the lease or tenancy agreement[418] or recognised as relevant and/or popular or common in relation to a type of lease or tenancy.[419]

226. Under the Tenancy Law of Lagos State 2011, the above-mentioned express, implied, and usual covenants have now been recognised as rights and obligations of the landlord and the tenant respectively.[420] This will appear to be novel and in particular, to the Lagos Law alone. The implication of this is that where a tenancy agreement entered into in Lagos State does not contain express covenants or does not expressly exclude the relevant provisions of the Lagos State Tenancy Law 2011 on the rights and obligations of landlord and tenant, the court will imply the rights and obligations of the parties under the Law as their covenants under the agreement.

XV. Implied Covenants

A. For the Lessor

Quiet Enjoyment

227. The lessee shall be entitled to recover damages if his enjoyment of the demised premises is substantially disturbed by the acts of either the lessor or somebody claiming under the lessor. This is so for example, where the lessor, with a view to ejecting the lessee, removes doors, and windows of the demised premises.[421]

Fitness of Premises for Habitation

228. A covenant that the premises shall be fit for habitation is an implied warranty in the nature of a condition and this applies not only at the commencement of the lease, but for a reasonable time thereafter. An example of this type of covenant is a warranty that there is nothing on the demised premises which shall affect either the health or general well-being of the lessee,[422] or the absence of the physical condition of the premises which would make it generally unhabitable for the lessee.

---

417. A good example can be found in the catalogue of covenants implied contained in ss 6, 7, and 8 of the Tenancy Law of Lagos State 2011.
418. A good example is the covenant to sublet or assign in a development agreement creating a term of years in favour of the developer since that is the only way the developer can recoup the cost of development.
419. Examples are covenant to pay rent, rates, and outgoings, covenant to repair, covenant to insure and others that are usually expressly made by parties to lease or tenancy agreements.
420. *See* ss 6, 7, 8, and 9 of the law.
421. *Lavender v. Betts* (1942) All ER 72.
422. *Collins v. Hopkins* (1921) 2 KB 617.

Non-Derogation from Grant

229. This covenant assures the lessee that the lessor shall not frustrate the use of the land for the purposes for which it was let. For example, a lease to X for residential purposes is frustrated where the lessor admits of anything which causes noise pollution on the premises.[423]

B. For the Lessee

Obligation to Use the Premises in a Tenant-Like Manner

230. A lessee owes an obligation to use and deliver up the premises in a tenant-like manner and keep the premises in a state of repair. This entails doing everything on the premises which a reasonable lessee must do to keep the premises in a good state of repair. Such acts like mending the electric light when it fuses, unstopping the sink when it blocks, or maintaining the walls to ensure they do not fall apart are examples of discharge of lessee's obligation under this covenant[424] and failure to discharge those obligations amounts to a breach of covenant.

Obligation Not to Commit Waste

231. A lessee for a fixed term or a periodic tenant is liable for both voluntary[425] and permissive[426] wastes. A tenant at will who commits voluntary waste immediately brings the tenancy to an end and becomes liable in trespass.[427]

XVI. Usual Covenants

232. Parties to a lease may agree that 'the lease shall contain all usual and proper covenants and provisos' and the question whether particular covenants are usual is a question of fact for the court to decide by evidence.[428] In determining what covenants are usual, the courts will be guided by the general conveyancing practice, the type of lease in question, the custom of the locality in which the premises is situated or the usage of trade for the purpose of which they are let or other circumstances prevailing at the time.[429] Many of the covenants that qualify as usual covenants under statutes in Nigeria are the popular express covenants in leases such as covenant to pay rent; to keep and deliver up the property in good repair; to pay

423. *Birmingham Dudley & District Banking Co v. Ross* (1888) 38 Ch. 295 at 313.
424. Per Denning L.J in *Warren v. Keen* (1954) 1 QB 15 at 20.
425. Altering the structure of the house is an example.
426. An example is the negligence or omission of the lessee in allowing the building to fall or rot away for want of necessary repairs.
427. *Countess of Shrewbury's case* (1600) 5 Co. Rep. 13.
428. *Flexman v. Corbett* (1930) 1 Ch. 672.
429. *Ibid., See also* s. 33(2) Landlord and Tenant Law Cap 75 Laws of Rivers State of Nigeria, 1999; s. 35(2) Cap 71 Laws of Akwa Ibom State of Nigeria 2000, Cap 79 Laws of Bauchi State of Nigeria 2006.

taxes, etc.,[430] while covenants relating to forfeiture or re-entry upon lessee's bankruptcy;[431] not to assign without licence;[432] to leave lease instrument with lessor's solicitor for registration,[433] etc. are examples of covenants held not to be usual covenants. While the court will take judicial notice of usual covenants prescribed by statutes, a party relying on a particular covenant which is usual 'having regard to the type of lease contemplated and the area in which the demised property is situated', must prove the existence of such usual covenant by evidence.

XVII. Express Covenants

233. Express covenants are covenants which the court will not imply in a lease and which may not qualify as usual covenants as defined above. While implied or usual covenants may be expressed in writing, covenants required to be in writing cannot be implied by law. The following are some of the popular express covenants in leases:

Covenant to Pay Rent

234. Since payment of rent is not one of the prerequisites for a valid lease,[434] express covenant for payment of a certain rent is required, otherwise none is presumed by law.[435] Rent may be paid in money or money's worth in accordance with the parties' agreement, and except the agreement stipulates payment of rent in advance, the law presumes that rent is payable in arrears.[436] Arrears of rent may ground an action for re-entry or forfeiture only when there is a demand of such rent by the lessor[437] and failure or refusal of the lessee to pay accordingly.[438] Where an accommodation is regulated by the Rent Control Legislation,[439] it is unlawful to charge a rent in excess of the standard rent prescribed by Law,[440] and any claim for possession based on unlawful rent increase is a nullity and the lessee may counterclaim for recovery of the unlawful rent.[441]

430. *See* s. 34(1) Law of Landlord and Tenant Cap 75 Rivers State 1999, Cap 71 of Akwa Ibom State 2000, Cap L4 of Kwara State 2007.
431. *Hyde v. Wardon* (1877) 5 Exch. D 72.
432. *Henderson v. Hay* 29 ER 738.
433. *Brookes v. Drysdale* 3 CPD 52.
434. A tenant at Will is nonetheless a tenant despite non-payment of rent.
435. *See,* for example, s. 73 Landlord and Tenant Law Cap 75 Laws of Rivers State of Nigeria 1999, Cap L4 Kwara State 2007; s. 75 Cap 76 Laws of Anambra State 1991.
436. *G.B Ollivant v. Alakija* (1950) 13 WACA 63; ss 75(1) 76(1) Landlord and Tenant Law Cap 75 Laws of Rivers State of Nigeria 1999, Cap L4 Kwara State 2007, Cap 71 Akwa Ibom 2000.
437. Unless there is a clause in the lease dispensing with the need for a formal demand.
438. *Da Rocha v. Shell (Nig) Ltd* (1938) 14 NLR 1; *Dawodu v. Odulaja* (1976) 6 UILR (Pt. 3) 373.
439. Various States in Nigeria have the Rent Control Legislation: *See* s. 4(1) Cap R3 Laws of Cross River State of Nigeria 2004; s. 16(1) Cap 146 Laws of Oyo State 2000, to mention but a few. *See also Agbaje v. Bankole* (1971) 1 All NLR 275.
440. *Ibid.*
441. *Akpiri v. Oluwa* (1972) 11 CCHCJ 85.

Covenant to Pay Rates and Outgoings

235. Normally, rates and outgoings are payable by the owner of a tenement and not by the lessee unless the latter has covenanted to pay. Where the lessee is obligated to pay but fails to pay, the lessor can sue for it and seek an order for possession for breach of covenant;[442] but the lessor cannot appropriate money meant as rent or other purpose by the lessee for payment of rates and outgoings.[443]

Covenant Not to Assign or Underlet

236. Ordinarily, a lessee may assign or sublet the demised premises unless restrained by express provision in a lease.[444] This covenant may be absolute in which case, the lessor may refuse to accede the lessee's request to assign or sublet without giving any reason for refusal; or it may be qualified i.e., subject to lessor's consent in which case, consent shall not be refused in the case of a responsible and respectable assignee or sub-lessee.[445] A covenant not to assign does not restrain the lessee from underletting and vice versa.[446] A covenant not to assign or sublet is not broken by assigning or subletting a part of the premises.[447] A covenant not to part with possession of the premises or any part thereof is not broken by the grant of a licence to place advert callings on the wall of the demised premises since the lessee is not thereby deprived of legal possession.[448] Where an assignment or subletting is prohibited without lessor's consent, granting of consent cannot be conditional upon payment of a fine or other charges unless otherwise provided in the lease agreement, as this is prohibited by law.[449]

442. *Olorunnimbe v. Lucas* (1963) 2 All NLR 189.
443. *Ibid.*
444. *Keeves v. Deen* (1924) 1 KB 685.
445. *Theodorou v. Bloom* (1964) 1 WLR 1152.
446. *Sweet & Maxwell v. Universal News Services* (1964) 2 All ER 30.
447. *Cook v. Shoesmith* (1951) 1 KB 752; *Ishola-Williams v. Hammond Projects Ltd* (1988) 1 NWLR (Pt. 71) 481 at 499–502; *Olaniyan v. Shokunbi* (1997) 6 NWLR (Pt. 509) 447.
448. *Stening v. Abrahams* (1931) 1 Ch. 470; *Enigbokan v. Akinosho* (1957) SCNLR 9.
449. Conveyancing Act 1881, s. 3; Property and Conveyancing Law 1959, s. 159. *See Obasuyi v. Mandilas & Karaberis Ltd* (1962) WNLR 51.

Covenant as to Use

237. Leases of residential or business premises may contain a covenant by the lessee restricting their use. Such covenant, where they exist, may be enforced by injunction, or breach of them compensated by damages, or, if there is a right of re-entry, forfeiture may result.[450] A covenant in a lease restricting the form of use of the land must be clearly and unambiguously prohibitive to be enforceable; a covenant merely declaratory of the specific use to which premises may be put does not show that the use of the premises was restricted to the specific purpose only.[451]

Covenant to Renew

238. An option to renew clause in a lease is a lessor's covenant enforceable by the lessee against the lessor or the assignee of the reversion. An option to renew clause must be clear and certain leaving no consideration for determination in the future otherwise, it will be void for uncertainty.[452] The condition stated for the exercise of the option by the lessee (e.g., notice in writing) must be duly complied with for the option to be exercisable;[453] but this condition is waived where the lessor accepted rent covering a period outside the current term thereby acquiescing to renewal under an option to renew.[454] An option to renew is an offer which must be accepted in total; a written request by the lessee containing new terms must be accepted by the lessor otherwise, the option lapses.[455] An option to renew until exercised does not constitute a demise of the optional term but being an interest in land, it is capable of assignment even by a trustee in bankruptcy, and devolves on the death on the lessee's personal representatives.[456]

Covenant to Repair

239. Covenant to repair and the extent of repairs required may be a lessor's or lessee's covenant depending on the agreement between the parties. Normally, the obligation to carry out internal repairs is that of the lessee under the general implied obligation of using the premises in a tenant-like manner and liability for waste committed; and same follows for short leases. In the case of long leases or where the repairs concern the main structure such as the roof, wall, the lessor has an obligation to effect repairs.[457] A covenant to repair in a lease agreement is subject to two major limitations: first, it is not enforceable where a legal estate has neither been effectively conveyed to the lessee, nor a valid agreement on which an order of specific performance could be made, entered into.[458] Second, where the covenant excluded fair wear and tear or damage arising from natural causes, the lessee is

450. Halsbury's Law s of England 3rd ed. vol. 23 620 Art. 1320.
451. *Dawodu v. Odulaja* (1976) 10 OYSHC (Pt. 1) 65.
452. *Ayinke v. Osunsedo* (1973) 8 CCHCJ 5.
453. *Ibid.*
454. *Moukarzel v. Hannah* (1947) 12 WACA 125.
455. *International Institute of Tropical Agriculture v. Khawam* (1975) WSCA 158.
456. *Kuforiji v. PZ Co. Ltd* (1959) LLR 57.
457. *National grindlays Ltd v. Panater* (1965) EALR 648.
458. *Chidiak v. Coker* (1954) 14 WACA 506.

relieved from liability to repair if the disrepair or dilapidation resulted from the operation of fair wear and tear or of natural causes.[459] While the lessee may bring the defect requiring repairs to the knowledge of the lessor and bring an action for specific performance of the covenant or sue for damages upon failure of the lessor to carry out the necessary repairs, the lessee cannot withhold rent or relinquish possession consequent upon lessor's failure or inability to carry out repairs.[460]

Covenant to Insure

240. This is of necessity in building leases and others of long duration to protect the reversionary interest of the lessor by protecting the demised premises against losses and damages caused by fire and other hazards. The covenant will usually require the lessee to insure the property with a reputable insurance company or one approved by the lessor at any time during the duration of the term and pay premium for the full value of the property. It is a breach of the covenant where the premises are left uninsured for any part of the term however short and notwithstanding that no hazard occurred, or that a proper insurance had been effected afterwards.[461] A breach of this covenant is a continuing one but may be waived if the lessor received rent after and with notice of the omission to insure before the rent became due.[462]

Covenant to Build in a Workmanlike Manner

241. Covenant to erect building in a workmanlike manner is a usual covenant in a building lease, and where there is a structural defect, the lessee is liable in damages[463] while the lessor can rescind the contract for a fundamental breach of the agreement.[464]

Option to Purchase the Reversion

242. A covenant to purchase the reversion is not one that touches and concerns the land so as to be enforceable between the assignee of the lessee and the original lessor. An assignee of the lessee who intends to enforce the covenant can only do so where the benefit of the covenant has been specifically assigned to him.[465] Where a lease agreement contains a covenant to purchase the reversion and the lessor attempts to sell the reversion, the court may, upon application by the lessee, set aside the sale.[466]

---

459. *Saidi v. Trezise* (1961) LLR 135.
460. *Oke v. Salako* (1972) 11 CCHCJ 88; *Demuren v. Plastic Manufacturing Co. Ltd* (1974) 6 CCHCJ 689.
461. *Penniall v. Harborne* (1848) 11 QB 368.
462. *Doe v. Gladwin* (1845) 6 QB 53.
463. *Coward v. Gregory* (1866) LR 2CP 153.
464. *Kennedy v. Panama Royal Mail Co. Ltd* (1867) LR 2QB 580.
465. *Re Button's Lease* (1963) 3 WLR 903.
466. *Owosho v. Dada* (1984) 7SC 149.

Covenant to Deliver Up Possession

243. This covenant is an assurance that the lessee shall deliver possession to the lessor upon the expiration of the lease. Delivery of possession by the lessee is done by relinquishing possession and delivering the keys to the lessor who accepts them with the intention of changing possession.[467] The effect of a breach of the covenant is the tenant's liability in damages which will include the rent of the premises during which time the lessor is kept out of possession, the reasonable damages and cost incurred by the lessor in respect of claims against him naturally arising out of the lessee's failure to deliver possession, and where a sub-lessee is in possession, the cost of an action brought against him to recover possession.[468]

XVIII. Remedies for Breach of Covenant

244. The remedies open to the lessor upon breach of covenant depends on whether the covenant is for non-payment of rent; assignment, subletting, or parting with possession of the premises; and other covenants.

XIX. Covenant to Pay Rent

245. The lessor's remedy for breach of covenant may be in the form of distraint for the rent, action for arrears of rent, or an action for forfeiture.

Distress for Rent

246. The lessor's right to distrain for rent is available under the Landlord and Tenant Law of the old western region of Nigeria applicable in Ekiti,[469] Ogun,[470] Ondo,[471] Osun,[472] and Oyo[473] States in respect of non-residential accommodation. In those States, the lessor in person or through a duly certified bailiff can distrain for rent on any goods or chattels of the owing lessee within six months after the determination of the tenancy.[474] A lessee who has distrained for rent may proceed to sell the goods or chattels seized after serving upon the lessee or leaving on the demised premises a notice setting forth the amount due; particulars of goods seized, the place where the goods have been impounded, and the date and time when the goods will be sold.[475] Where distraint for rent is levied by a bailiff, he shall, in addition to the information required by law to be contained in the notice, include the

467. *Asoropa v. Orelaja* (1976) 5 CCHCJ 1405.
468. *Hill and Redman's Law of Landlord and Tenant* 593 para. 456 (13th ed.).
469. Cap L4 2010.
470. Cap 55 Laws of Ogun State of Nigeria, 1978.
471. Cap 75 Laws of Ondo State of Nigeria, 2006.
472. Cap 65 Laws of Osun State of Nigeria, 2001.
473. Cap 71 Laws of Oyo State of Nigeria, 2000.
474. *Ibid.*, s. 8.
475. *Ibid.*, s. 20(1).

fees charges and expenses prescribed by the rules.[476] Where the arrears of rent remains unpaid for five days after the distraint, the lessor or any bailiff employed by him shall sell the goods or chattels so distrained towards the satisfaction of the rent to which the goods and chattels were distrained, as well as the fees, expenses, and charges lawfully incurred in such distraint.[477] In the other States outside the old western region of Nigeria, the power of distraint is only available to the lessor executing a court judgment for arrears of rent in accordance with the Sheriff and Civil Process Law,[478] or pursuant to a court order on being satisfied that a lessee has defaulted in paying the standard rent fixed by the court. Save in such circumstances, any act of distraint is wrongful and may amount to trespass.[479]

Action for Arrears of Rent

247. An action for arrears of rent lies against the lessee or his personal representatives upon demand by the lessor and refusal to pay by the lessee. In an action for arrears of rent, the lessee shall be entitled to all defences open to him in an action under an ordinary contract including the Statute of Limitation.[480]

Action for Forfeiture

248. The lessor may re-enter the premises in the event of a breach of covenant to pay rent by the lessee; but no action in forfeiture lies in the absence of a forfeiture clause in a lease agreement.[481] The lessor must, as a prelude to re-entry consequent upon lessee's failure to pay rent, make a formal demand for the rent[482]except where the rent is in arrears for six months and the distrainable goods on the demised premises are not sufficient to satisfy the amount of the arrears,[483] or where the lease agreement contains the words 'whether formally demanded or not' in the covenant.[484]

249. A right of re-entry for breach of covenant to pay rent cannot override the processes for the recovery of premises prescribed by the various recovery of premises statute in Nigeria.[485] Thus, it is unlawful under the recovery of premises statutes to seek to take possession forcefully using self-help rather, an action to recover

476. *Ibid.*, s. 20(2).
477. *Ibid.*, s. 24.
478. *See*, for example, Cap 113 Ondo State 1978; Cap 118 Ogun State 1978; Cap 115 Oyo State 2000; Cap 127 Adamawa 1997; Cap 127 Taraba State 1997; Cap 134 Sokoto State 1996; Cap S6 Lagos State 2003.
479. *Eliochin (Nig) Ltd v. Mbadiwe* (1986) All NLR 1.
480. Limitation Law Cap L67 Laws of Lagos State 2003; Cap 70 of Osun State; Cap 76 of Oyo State 2000; Cap 89 of Kwara State 1994; Cap 84 of Bauchi State 1991; Cap 80 of Sokoto State 1996; Cap 80 of Kebbi State 1996 among others.
481. *Koya v. Babayale* (1980) 20 OYSHC (Pt. 1) 342.
482. *Dawodu v. Odulaja* (1976) OYSHC 65.
483. Section 210 Common Law Procedure Act, 1852.
484. *Thomson v. Chama* (1962) LLR 86.
485. *See*n. 482.

possession may be brought, and such action when brought, is equivalent to actual entry for enforcement of the forfeiture clause.[486]

250. Since an action for forfeiture for non-payment of rent is regarded in equity in the character of a penalty and as a means of enforcing the payment of rent, and as the injury arising from the breach of such conditions admits of compensation, the court may grant relief against forfeiture on payment or tender of the amount due.[487] But relief will not be granted where the premises in question is used for immoral purposes.[488]

XX. Covenant Against Assignment, Subletting or Parting with Possession

251. A breach of the covenant against assignment, subletting or parting with possession by the lessee entitles the lessor to either damages for breach of the covenant or forfeiture of the lease. A lessor bringing a claim for damages must show that he has suffered or would suffer pecuniary loss from the breach otherwise, he is entitled to nominal damages only.[489] However, where the lessee shows that the assignment, subletting or parting with possession was consequent upon the lessor unreasonably withholding consent, he is not liable in damages.[490]

XXI. Other Covenants

252. A breach of other covenants apart from covenant to pay rent empowers the landlord to sue for damages, or injunction, or specific performance of the covenant or forfeiture of the lease. The requirements for forfeiture for breach of covenants other than covenant for payment of rent and covenant against assignment, subletting or parting with possession of the demised premises are prescribed by section 14 of the Conveyancing Act 1881 and section 161 of the Property and Conveyancing Law 1959. The laws provide that:

(a) A lease is subject to forfeiture only when there is some provision to that effect in the lease.
(b) A lessor cannot re-enter the premises unless he served on the lessee a notice specifying the particular breach complained of and if the breach is capable of remedy, requiring him to remedy the breach within a reasonable time or otherwise make compensation in money.

486. *See* Lambo J. in *Thompson v. Chama* (1962) LLR 86.
487. *Davis v. Best* 12 Ves 475.
488. *Egerton v. Esplanade Hotels Ltd* (1947) 2 All ER 88.
489. *Olagbaju v. L.D Alberto & Co. Ltd* (1979) 20 OYSHC (Pt. 2) 187.
490. *Stirling Astaldi Ltd v. Idowu.*

253. In an action for forfeiture, the lessor must prove:

(i) that the service of the notice was made known to the lessee himself; or
(ii) to an underlessee holding under the sublease; or
(iii) to the person who last paid the rent.

254. In the proceedings, the lessee may apply for relief and the court, after reviewing the circumstances of the case and the conduct of the parties, may refuse such relief or grant it upon such terms as to costs, expenses, compensation, penalty, damages, etc. as it thinks fit. But the discretion will not be exercised in favour of a lessee who knowingly suffers the premises for illegal purposes.[491]

255. A lessor is said to have waived his right to forfeiture where, upon having knowledge of the breach committed by the lessor, condones it and collects rent from the lessee.[492]

XXII. Termination of Leases

256. A lease may be terminated by surrender, effluxion of time, notice to quit, merger, and frustration.

XXIII. Surrender

257. Where a lessee surrenders lease to his immediate lessor who accepts the surrender, the lease merges in the lessor's reversion and is extinguished. Surrender may be by act of parties having the express intention of effecting a surrender, or by operation of law such as where one party to a lease does and the other assents to an act inconsistent with the continuance of the lease.[493]

258. Every express surrender is void unless it is made by deed or writing, and it must be to the immediate lessor; a surrender to a superior lessor does not amount to a surrender but operates merely as an assignment of the lease.

XXIV. Effluxion of Time

259. The expiration of a fixed term put an end to the relationship of lessor and lessee unless there is an agreement or statutory provisions to the contrary.[494] Where

491. *Egerton v. Esplanade Hotels Ltd supra* n. 488.
492. *Mathews v. Smallwood* (1910) 1 Ch. 777 at 786; *Ajao v. Haightons (West Africa) Ltd* (1972) 9 CCHCJ 82; *Udih v. Izedomwen* (1990) 2 NWLR (Pt. 132) 357.
493. *Ohochukwu v. Attorney General River State* (2012) 6 NWLR (Pt. 1295) 53 at 81; *Nwafile v. Ossai* (1972) 2 ECSLR (Pt. 2) 579.
494. *Ogualaji v. Attorney General Rivers State* (1997) 6 NWLR (Pt. 508) 209.

the lessee remains in possession at the expiration of the lease, the lessor shall issue and serve on him, a Notice of owner's intention to recover possession (i.e., seven-day notice), and subsequently bring an action for possession on legally recognised grounds.

XXV. Notice to Quit

260. Notice to quit may be required under the lease agreement to bring an end to a periodic tenancy and where this is the case, the length of notice is that required under the lease agreement as opposed to one prescribed by statute. To determine a periodic tenancy under statute, a statutory notice is required, and the nature and length of the notice requires is prescribed by statute. The provisions of the various Recovery of Premises Statutes in the States[495] including the Tenancy Law of Lagos State 2011[496] require a week's notice in the case of a tenancy at will or weekly tenancy; a month's notice for monthly tenancy; a three-month notice for a quarterly tenancy; and six-month notice for yearly tenancy. In addition to this, the Tenancy Law of Lagos State[497] prescribes a three-month notice for half-yearly tenancy. The nature of the tenancy shall, in the absence of any evidence, to the contrary, be determined by reference to the time when rent is paid or demanded.[498] Where a statutory notice is issued and served, payment and acceptance of rent upon the expiration of the notice does not amount to a waiver. The status of the lessee upon the expiration of the notice as a statutory tenant gives a right to continue in occupation subject to his performing in favour of the lessor all contractual obligations under the lease including payment of rent.[499] The issuance of a statutory notice to quit by the solicitor shall be preceded by a letter of instruction by the landlord to the solicitor instructing the latter to recover possession of premises on the landlord's behalf. This requirement is very strict and any such notice issued either without or before the letter of instruction is issued is null and void and of no effect.[500]

XXVI. Merger

261. At common law, a lease is terminated when the term of years (i.e., the lease) and the reversion merge and this happens where, in law, the landlord transfers his reversion to the tenant. For a merger to occur, the same person must have

495. *See,* for example, s. 8(1) Recovery of Premises Law Cap 118 Laws of Adamawa State of Nigeria; s. 6(1) Recovery of Premises Law Cap 109 Laws of Rivers State of Nigeria, 1999; s. 13(1) Tenancy Law of Lagos State of Nigeria 2011.
496. Lagos State Tenancy Law 2011, s. 13(1).
497. *Ibid.,* s. 13(1) (d).
498. Subsection (2) of the Laws cited in n. 495 except Lagos State. For Lagos State, *see* subs. (6) thereof. There is a corresponding provision in the Recovery of Premises Laws of other States in Nigeria.
499. *Chelsea Investment Property Ltd. v. Federal Commissioner of Taxation* (1966) 115 CLR 1 at 6; *Akpiri v. Oluwa* (1972) CCHCJ 98.
500. *Ayiwoh v. Akorede* (1951) 20 NLR 4; *Coker v. Adetayo* (1992) 6 NWLR (Pt. 249) 612 paras C–D.

acquired title to the lease and the reversion in the same capacity. A person is not acquiring title to the lease and the reversion in the same capacity and there is no merger if, for example, he holds the lease as his private property and acquires the reversion as a trustee, executor, or administrator. In equity however, the question whether there is a merger or not would depend on the intention of the parties, and in the absence of direct evidence of intention, the presumption in equity is that despite the two interests becoming united in the tenant, merger is not intended if it is to the interest of the tenant, or only consistent with the tenant's duty that merger should not take place. This is so where there is a mortgage of the tenancy because otherwise, the mortgagee would lose his security.[501]

XXVII. Frustration

262. A lease may be frustrated by a supervening event or a force majore for which neither party has control. In *Araka v. Monier Construction Company (Nig) Ltd*,[502] a yearly tenancy was created in favour of the respondent. One of the conditions of the grant was that only the respondent's expatriate engineers would reside in the house. The period of the tenancy coincided with the period of the Nigerian civil war and government ordered all expatriates to leave the area. When the war ended two years later, the landlord claimed rent for the period and the tenant contended that the government order to vacate the area frustrated the tenancy. The Supreme Court of Nigeria held that the tenancy was frustrated by the war and that the landlord was not entitled to the rent claimed.

§4. Emphyteusis and Rent Charge

263. Not applicable in this jurisdiction.

§5. Use and Habitation/Occupation

264. The right to use and occupy land exist in Nigerian customary law under family land holding and customary tenancy.

I. The Concept of Use and Occupation under Family Land Holding

265. Ownership of family property is vested in the family as a whole; the individual having a right of use only. Under customary law, family means the direct offshoot of the founder i.e., the children.[503] 'Children' is generally held to refer to both male and female children.[504]

501. *Capital Counties Bank Ltd v. Rhodes* (1903) Ch. 631.
502. (1978) 9 & 10 SC 9.
503. *Lewis v. Bankole supra* n. 247.
504. *See Ricardo v. Abal* (1927) 7 NLR 58.

266. The right to reside in the family property is one of the most fundamental incidents of family property. A member of the family is entitled to be allotted a portion of the family property for his exclusive use and enjoyment. A member is entitled to exclusive enjoyment of his allotment for the purpose for which it was granted, and any attempt by the head of family to disturb his quiet enjoyment may be actionable in trespass.[505] He may build his house on the land as well as farm on it. The right springs from unity of possession which exists from the nature of the title held by the family. Once the land is allotted to him he holds the land to the exclusion of any other member of the family.[506]

267. A member of the family does not enjoy ownership rights; he has a mere occupational right to use the property during his life time. Ordinarily, his children are allowed to continue with the use and occupation of the land after his demise, but this is not as of right and the family may, if it is not convenient for them, reallocate another portion to the children.

268. The member's right to be allocated land and to live, farm, and enjoy the allocated land cannot be disturbed even by the family. The member cannot sell or dispose of the land allocated to him from the family property as he has only the right of use.[507] He cannot also use the property as collateral for his personal debt.[508]

269. Any improvements made on family land by a member of the family belong to the family. In *Shelle v. Asajon*,[509] it was held that where a member of the family replaced old thatched roof of the family house which she occupied with corrugated iron sheets, she did not thereby become the owner of the house. The law is that no matter how long the allottee of family property may have stayed on the land and regardless of any improvements carried out on it, the occupational right granted to him can never ripen into full ownership.[510] Also any alienation of such improvements to a stranger is void or at best voidable. As Savage J puts it in *Mosanya v. The Public Trustees*,[511] 'Yoruba law leans against destruction. Family property under Yoruba law belongs to the family as distinct, perpetual legal entity. It is clear from the following cases: *Adagun v. Fagbola*,[512] and *Oshodi v. Aremu*[513] that the fact that this type of property is vested in a body corporate implies that no transaction affecting interest therein is valid unless done by or with the consent of the family itself.' It was further held that 'the principle or maxim *quicquid plantatur solo solo cedit* applies under customary law where there has been improvement on the land which has been created without permission of the owner or owners'.

---

505. *Agbloe v. Sappor* (1947) 12 WACA 187, *See also Okoh v. Olotu.* (1953) 20 NLR 123.
506. *Okoh v. Olotu supra n. 505.*
507. *Akeju v. Suenu* (1925) 6 NLR 87.
508. *Jacobs v. Oladuni Brothers* (1935) 12 NLR 1.
509. (1957) 2 FSC 65 at p. 67.
510. Per Craig, JSC in *Bamgbose v. Oshoko* (1988) 2 NWLR (Pt. 78), 509 at 519; *Shelle v. Asajon; Adagun v. Fagbola* (1932) 11 NLR 110; *Salako v. Oshunlami* (1961) WNLR 189 p. 192.
511. (1980) 4–6 CCHCJ 254; (1980) FNR 261.
512. (1932) 11 NLR 10.
513. (1954) WACA 83.

270. The right of members of the family as regards ingress to and egress from the family house was examined in In *Lewis v. Bankole*.[514] For this purpose, members of the family were considered in two different categories: those that are actually residing in the family house and those not so residing. It was held that with respect to members of the family who were not resident in the family property, no such right was established. Also in *Thomas v. Thomas*,[515] it was held that resident members had a reasonable right of ingress and egress to the family house and except for purposes of attending family meetings or other business of the family, non-resident member had no such right.

II. The Concept of Use and Occupation under Customary Tenancy

271. Customary tenancy involves a grant of land by a person, family, or community known as the overlord to another known as the customary tenant, to possess and use the land upon certain terms and conditions agreed with the overlord including payment of tribute. It affords the customary tenant the opportunity to remain in possession in perpetuity subject to good behaviour.

272. The concept of customary tenancy is peculiar to Nigerian customary law and has no equivalent in English law. Its true nature is captured by the Supreme Court in *Aghenghen v. Waghoreghor*[516]as follows:

> In customary land law parlance, the customary tenants are not gifted the land; they are not 'borrowers' or 'lessees'; they are grantees of land under customary tenure and hold, as such, a determinable interest in the land which may be enjoyed in perpetuity subject to good behaviour.

273. Unlike the English-type lease, customary tenancy has no certainty of term and its creation requires no formality beyond the handing over of the land by the grantor to the grantee in the presence of witnesses. It creates however, the relationship of landlord and tenant between the parties and is not in the nature of a mere occupational licence which confers no interest in land.[517]

274. It is the main incident of a customary tenancy that a customary tenant pays tribute[518] to the overlord and enjoys his holding in perpetuity subject to good

---

514. *Supra* n. 503.
515. (1932) 16 NLR 5.
516. (1974) SC 1.
517. *Jinadu v. Esurombi-Aro* (2005) 14 NWLR (Pt. 944) 142; *Bassey v. Bassey* (2009) 12 NWLR (Pt. 1156) 617.
518. Tribute may be in the form of money or money's worth such as rendering some services in the grantor's farm, or in consideration of the harvest or produce derived from the use of the land being shared between the grantor and grantee in mutually agreed proportions: *See Akintola v. Oyelade* (1993) 3 NWLR (Pt. 282) 379.

behaviour[519] and failure by a customary tenant to pay his tribute to the overlord as and when due, is a good ground for forfeiture of the customary tenancy.[520] But non-payment of tribute is not inconsistent with the creation or existence of customary tenancy as payment of tribute could be overlooked by the overlord as a result of long association between the parties or consequent upon the tenant's good behaviour.[521]

275. Upon creation of customary tenancy, full possessory rights are conveyed to the customary tenant. The customary tenant has exclusive possession of the land granted, and except the tenancy so permits or the tenancy is lawfully determined, the overlord has no right to enter the land without the tenant's permission.[522] The customary tenant can therefore maintain an action for damages in trespass against the overlord or any third party at that, for interfering with his possession, and an injunction to restrain further interference.[523] The customary tenant's right to exclusive possession avails against a purchaser of the overlord's reversion and others claiming through him.[524]

276. The customary tenant owes an obligation not to deny the overlord's title. The right to exclusive possession of the customary tenant does not in any way vest right of ownership; the tenant has mainly a right of use which is subject to the overlord's right of reversion and the right of re-entry exercisable when the cause arises.[525] Consequently, the tenant cannot dispose portions of the land, or name the land after him or acquire title by length of stay. Where he engages in any act tantamount to a denial of the overlord's title, the overlord is entitled to exercise his right of forfeiture and may re-enter the land accordingly.[526]

277. The customary tenant owes a duty not to alienate or attempt to alienate his interest without the overlord's permission as any such alienation is void, and an attempt is evidence of tenant's denial of overlord's title either of which makes the tenancy liable to forfeiture.[527]

278. Also, where the customary tenant uses the land for a different purpose from that agreed at the commencement of the tenancy without the consent of the overlord, it amounts to a breach of obligation for which the overlord may seek forfeiture of the tenancy.[528]

---

519. *Babatunde v. Akinbade* (2006) 6 NWLR (Pt. 975) 44; *Dashi v. Satlong* (2009) 5 NWLR (Pt. 1134) 281.
520. *Okpala v. Okpu* (1996) 8 NWLR (Pt. 468) 589.
521. *Uche v. Eke* (2005) 7 NWLR (Pt. 955) 574; *Akinlagun v. Oshoboja* (2006) NWLR (Pt. 993) 60.
522. *Akintola v. Oyelade supra* n. 518; *Dashi v. Satlong supra* n. 519.
523. *Salami v. Lawal* (2008) 14 NWLR (Pt. 1108) 546.
524. *Lasisi v. Tubi* (1974) 12 SC 71; *Salami v. Lawal supra* n. 523 at 565–566.
525. *Archibong v. Ita* (2004) 2 NWLR (Pt. 858) 590.
526. *Abioye v. Yakubu* (1991) 5 NWLR (Pt. 190) 130.
527. *Lawal v. Adeniyi* (1964) 3 NSCC 231; *Onisiwo v. Fagbenro* (1954) 21 NLA 3.
528. *Evbuomwan v. Elema* (1994) 6 NWLR (Pt. 353) 638.

§6. Easements and Profits

279. An easement has been defined as a right attached to land which allows the owner of that land (the dominant owner) either to use the land of another person (the servient owner) in a particular manner otherwise known as positive easement, or to restrict its user by that other person to a particular extent otherwise known as negative easement, but does not allow him to take any part of its natural produce or its soil.[529] It is a right over the land of another for the benefit or better enjoyment of the dominant property.

280. It is different from a profit a prendre to the extent that it does not involve taking part of the servient's natural produce or its soil. It confers on its owner not proprietary right in the land affected, but merely imposes a definite and limited restriction upon the proprietary rights of the owner.[530] Rights recognised by law as easements include right of way, right to store materials in a shed, right to use a park for recreation (positive easement), and right to air or light through defined channels (negative easements).

I. Characteristics of Easements

281. A right to be enjoyed as an easement must satisfy four conditions as follows:

(1) There must be two separate tenements; a servient tenement over which the easement is exercisable, and a dominant tenement for the benefit of which the right exists. The claimant of an easement (the owner of dominant tenement) must show either that he had an interest in land at the date of grant, or at least that the dominant land is described with sufficient certainty in the agreement of grant.[531] The servient tenement must not only exist at the time of acquiring the dominant tenement, it must be clearly identifiable and its extent certain.[532]
(2) The dominant and servient owners must be different persons. Where ownership of both the dominant and servient tenements belongs to one and the same person, there is practically no easement.
(3) Easement must accommodate the dominant tenement. The use of the servient tenement must be connected with the use, enjoyment, and occupation of the dominant tenement; the servient tenement must make the occupation of the dominant tenement more convenient or enhance the occupation of the tenement.[533]
(4) The right must be capable of forming the subject matter of a grant. There must be the existence of a legally capable grantor with a proprietary interest in the

529. *Manning v. Wasdale* ER vol II 1335; *Okunzua v. Amosu & Anor* (1992) 6 NWLR (Pt. 248) 417.
530. *Okunzua v. Amosu & Anor supra* n. 529.
531. *Bell v. Voice* (1893) 11 Ch.D 59.
532. *London & Blenheim Ltd v. Ladbroke Park Ltd* (1992) 1 WLR 1278.
533. *Re Ellenborough Park* (1956) Ch. 131.

servient tenement,[534] and a grantee legally capable of receiving the grant.[535] The right must not be vague, uncertain or indefinite, e.g., the privilege of wandering at will over every part of another's field or park,[536] and there must be no exclusive or joint user of the servient tenement.[537]

II. Acquisition of Easements

282. An easement must have its origin either in grant[538] or in reservation; or in a statutory provision.[539]

III. Express Grant or Reservation

283. Acquisition of easement by express grant is through express words in a deed of assignment of a legal estate to the owner of the dominant tenement. A deed of assignment of a legal interest in land such as an assignment of a right of occupancy on land or a lease, automatically passes all rights, privileges, and easements.[540] Also, a vendor who sells part of his land may expressly reserve easement over the land sold in a deed of assignment and require the purchaser to execute same by way of a regrant of the easement to him. The grant must be by deed otherwise and in the absence of statutory or prescriptive creation, it takes effect as an equitable easement provided that it is specifically enforceable.[541] It is important that the grantor grants easement for no more than his interest in the land otherwise, the easement will be binding on him only.[542]

IV. Implied Grant or Reservation

284. The law will imply a grant of easement in favour of the grantee on the ground of necessity; or where it is the common intention of the parties that an easement be granted; or where the rule in *Wheeldon v. Burrows* apply.

---

534. *Mulliner v. Midland Railway Co.* (1879) 11 Ch. 611 at 619.
535. *Quicke v. Chapman* (1903) Ch. 659 at 668, 671.
536. *AG v. Antrobus* (1905) 2 Ch.D 188 at 198, 199, and 205. A right to view or a right of uninterrupted access to light or air which does not come through defined channels do not qualify as easement though they may be acquired by way of restrictive covenant preventing the owner of neighbouring land from building on the land in such a way as to obstruct the view or block access to light or flow of air.
537. *Copeland v. Greenhalf* (1952) Ch.D 438.
538. *De Facto Bakeries Ltd v. Ajilore & Anor* (1979) All NLR 385.
539. *See,* for example, s. 5(1) Land Use Act Cap L5 2010 which empowers the governor to make a grant of easements along with a grant of statutory right of occupancy.
540. *See* s. 6 Conveyancing Act 1881; s. 87(1) Property and Conveyancing Law Cap 100 LWN 1959; s. 84(2) Cap 100 Laws of Akwa Ibom State 2000, Cap 122 Laws of Bauchi State 2006; s. 86(2) Cap 23 Laws of Abia State 2005 and corresponding provisions in the laws of other States.
541. Smith, I.O. *supra* n. 244 at 435.
542. *Ibid.*

Necessity

285. Where a property would be inaccessible without the easement, the court will imply a grant.[543] Easement of necessity will be granted only where the property retained cannot be used at all without the easement; mere difficulty or inconvenience is not enough.[544] Easement of necessity may be excluded expressly by agreement.[545]

Common Intention of Parties

286. Where parties intended at the time of assignment that easement should be granted, the court may imply an easement in favour of the grantee,[546] provided that it was intended that the subject of the grant should be used in some definite and particular manner.[547]

The Rule in Wheeldon v. Burrows[548]

287. The rule is that where the grantor who owns two adjoining tenements conveys to another, one of the tenements for the benefit of which he had been in the habit of using in a particular manner (e.g., walking over it from the one conveyed to reach the highway), the law implies an easement of way in favour of the grantee. The rule applies only to those quasi-easements which are capable of being easements. The right must be continuous and apparent and must be necessary for the reasonable enjoyment of the property. Also, the quasi-easement must have been enjoyed by the grantor up to and until the date of the relevant grant.[549] Once the conditions for the application of the rule are satisfied, easement is implied as soon as the assignment of the property is made and even before the actual assignment by deed.[550] Thus, a vendor desirous of excluding the enjoyment of a quasi-easement by the purchaser must expressly exclude the rule in *Wheeldon v. Burrows* in the contract of sale before exchange of contract otherwise, the purchaser becomes entitled to the easement after exchange of contract, and a provision later in the deed of assignment excluding the enjoyment of the right is ineffectual.[551]

288. The law will not, as a general rule, imply reservation of an easement in the absence of express reservation except where an easement is a necessity or when it is the common intention of the parties that an easement should be reserved.

---

543. *Altman v. Boatman* (1963) 186 EG 109.
544. *MRA Engineering Ltd v. Trimster Co. Ltd* (1988) 56 P&CR 1, CA.
545. *Nickson v. Barradough* (1981) 3 All ER 369.
546. *Wong v. Beaumont Property Trust Ltd* (1965) 1 QB 173.
547. *Pirback Colliery Co. Ltd v. Woodman* (1915) AC 634.
548. (1879) 12 Ch.D 31.
549. *Re Clements Leigh on Sea* (1988) 1 WLR 720 at 729.
550. Smith, I.O. *supra* n. 244 at 438.
551. *Ibid.*

V. Presumed Grant

289. A grant of legal easement is presumed in favour of a dominant owner who has used the servient land over a period of time, in the absence of a deed of grant. The right of prescription may be at common law, under the doctrine of lost modern grant or under the Prescription Act 1832. A claimant of a right of prescription in any of these ways must satisfy some basic requirements: The act of user must be without force, secrecy, or permission (i.e., nec vi, nec clam, nec precario);[552] user must be as of right and must be continuous.[553]

Prescription at Common Law

290. At common law, where the right alleged to be an easement has been enjoyed for a long time as to give rise to a prescription at law that the easement has been granted, a grant is presumed. At one stage, it was required for an easement to be established under this head that the right must be shown to have been enjoyed from time immemorial which date became fixed for 1189. However, if the claimant can show that the right has been enjoyed for more than twenty years, there is a rebuttable presumption that right has been enjoyed before 1189.[554]

Prescription under the Lost Modern Grant

291. After the actual enjoyment of an easement has been shown for a reasonable time, the court presumes that an actual grant was made at the time when the enjoyment began but that the conveyance had been lost and so, if user back to 1189 cannot be proved, and no deed is produced but user is shown for twenty years, there is a presumption that a grant of easement has been made by deed after 1189, but that the deed has been misplaced or lost.[555] This presumption is rebuttable by showing that at some time during the twenty years of user, no person was capable of making or receiving the grant.[556]

Prescription Act 1832

292. Section 2 of the Act provides that there is a right of prescription to an easement other than easement of light if it has been enjoyed for twenty years before the action is brought. The easement is indefeasible unless it can be shown that it could not have existed or been enjoyed for the whole of the twenty-year period. If such an easement has been enjoyed for forty years, it is absolute and indefeasible. The period of enjoyment must be uninterrupted in the sense that there must be no act or obstruction showing that the easement is disputed in any way.[557]

552. *Sturges v. Bridgman* 11 Ch.D 582, 863.
553. *Hollins v. Verney* 13 QBD 304, 315.
554. *Angus & Co. v. Dalton* (1877) 3 QB 85 at 105.
555. *Bryant v. Foot* (1867) 2QB 161.
556. *Rochdale Canal v. Raddiffe* (1852) QB 287.
557. *Larr v. Foster* (1842) 3 QB 581.

VI. Statutory Grant of Easement

293. The Governor of the State is empowered by section 5(1) of the Land Use Act[558]to grant a statutory right of occupancy for all purposes including other interests such as easements, appurtenants. This right of easement is conveyed to the holder of the right of occupancy by deed under a certificate of occupancy issued by the Governor and enures for the duration of the contract which may be for ninety-nine years or less,[559] and is extinguished when the right is revoked at any time upon the grounds stated under section 28 of the Act or upon enforcement of planning regulations.

294. Statutory grants may be made also to public utility bodies which supply electricity, water, or dump wastes.[560]

VII. Enforcement of Easements

295. An easement once created, runs with the land, and attaches burden and benefit to the servient and dominant tenement respectively. It is enforceable as between the original servient and dominant owners as a matter of contract, and subsequently as between their successors in title if burden and benefit have passed to them expressly under a deed of assignment, or by operation of statute.[561] In the case of a legal easement, the burden automatically runs with the servient land and the successor in title is bound by it whether he had notice or not, while in the case of an equitable easement, the successor in title is bound by the burden only if he had notice of it.

VIII. Extinguishment of Easements

296. An easement may be extinguished by release, express, or implied. An express release must be by deed,[562] but there is a proper equitable release where there is an informal agreement supported by consideration given by the servient owner, or where it would be inequitable for the dominant owner to deny the extinguishment.[563] There is an implied release where there is clear evidence of abandonment.[564]

---

558. Cap L5 LFN 2010.
559. Section 8 of the Land Use Act which establishes a contract between the governor and the holder of right of occupancy provides that it shall be for a definite term, it does not suggest any specific term.
560. *AG of Southern Nigeria v. John Holt Co.* (1910) 2 NLR 1.
561. *See* Land Use Act Cap L5 LFN 2010, s. 5(1).
562. *Lovell v. Smith* 140 ER 685 at 687.
563. *Davies v. Marshall* (1861) 142 ER 627 at 633.
564. To determine what amounts to an abandonment, the test is 'whether the dominant owner has envinced a clear intention never at any time thereafter to assert the right himself or to attempt to transmit it to anyone else': *Tehidy Minerals Ltd v. Norman* (1971) 2 QB 528 at 553.

297. Easement may be extinguished in the event of a merger of the servient and dominant tenements in the hands of one person. A mere unity of possession without unity of ownership does not extinguish an easement.

298. Where easement ceases to accommodate the dominant tenement, it becomes automatically extinguished. An easement is also extinguished upon revocation of a right of occupancy pursuant to section 28 of the Land Use Act[565] or upon enforcement of planning regulations.

§7. LICENCES

299. A licence has been defined as 'a personal privilege in the form of authority or permission granted a person to enter and use premises to perform some acts therein which would otherwise be wrongful or amount to trespass'.[566]

300. It is different from a leasehold to the extent that it does not create a proprietary right in favour of the licensee, and it lacks the essential of exclusive possession which characterises a leasehold interest.[567] Consequently, unlike a leasehold interest, an unauthorised interference by the licensor in the land occupied by the licensee does not amount to trespass since the licensee, unlike the lessee, has no exclusive possession of the property subject matter of licence.[568] Unlike a lease, parties to a licence can only be bound by express terms contained in the licence; no term or condition may be implied which is not contained in the licence. Unless a licence is coupled with an interest, made by grant or for valuable consideration, a licence, unlike a lease, may be revoked by the licensor giving reasonable notice to the licensee.[569] Since the licence gives a mere personal right to the licensee, it can neither, unlike a lease, be assigned nor can a 'sublicence' be created out of it. A licence, unlike a lease, is determined by the death or change in grantor.

301. The foregoing characteristics of a licence notwithstanding, it is interesting to note that in Nigeria, a licensee holding over upon the expiration or lawful determination of his contractual licence, is treated like a statutory tenant[570] and is therefore protected by statute and cannot be turned out except the licensor complies with

565. Cap L5 LFN 2010.
566. Smith, I.O. *supra* n. 244at 350, relying on the Supreme Court of Nigeria's decision in *Mobil Oil (Nig) Ltd v. Johnson* (1961) All NLR 93.
567. *Ibid.*, at 255.
568. But the licensor may be liable in damages for breach of contract or unlawful ejectment: *Sefga Ltd v. Cotgas Ltd* (1981) OYSTC 49; *Mobil Oil (Nig) Ltd v. Johnson supra* n. 566.
569. *Smith v. West African Pictures Ltd* (1975) 6 CCHCJ 933 at 934; *Okoye v. Dumez supra* n. 354.
570. *See* Hubbard Ag FJ in *Enigbokan v. Akinosho* (1957) SCNLR 9 at 11–12; *African Petroleum Co. Ltd v. Owodunni* (1991) 8 NWLR (Pt. 210) 139.

the provisions of statute by not only serving on the licensee notice of owners' intention to recover possession, but also bringing the appropriate action in court for possession.[571] This anomalous situation has been taken care of by the provisions of the Tenancy Law of Lagos State 2011 which has made specific provisions for the termination of a licence.[572] The law has also excluded service tenancy[573] from its ambit leaving the status of such servient tenants to be determined under the general law relating to licences.

I. When Is a Licence Desirable?

302. A licence is desirable in the following situations:

(1) In circumstances requiring a temporary or transient occupation of premises either gratuitously,[574] or at a fee.[575]
(2) In a situation where an individual, corporate body, or government is contractually entitled to exploit the land or improvements on it.[576]
(3) Where an individual, corporate body, or government desires to extract valuable materials therefrom.[577]

303. In these situations, a lease may be considered unnecessary as a result of the temporary or transient nature of occupation requiring no tenure; or undesirable because exclusive possession of the property is not required to fulfil the essence of the contract; or where the power to extract materials from the land is statutory and creation of a lease thus becomes ultra vires.

II. Types of Licence

304. A licence may be categorised as bare licence, contractual licence, or statutory licence.

Bare Licence

305. A bare licence gives the licensee permission to enter and use premises or reside therein without furnishing any consideration.[578] The licensee has no interest

571. What the law requires to acquire the status of a statutory tenant is lawful occupation which a licensee has: *See Enigbokan v. Akinosho* (1957) SCNLR 9; *African Petroleum Co. Ltd v. Owodunni supra* n. 570.
572. *Lagos State Tenancy Law,* 2011 s. 14.
573. *Ibid.*, s. 1(2)(a).
574. *Anifowoshe v. Siyanbola* (1956) SCNLR 139.
575. *Smith v. West African Pictures Ltd* (1975) 6 CCHCJ 933.
576. An improvement is anything of quality attached to the land directly resulting from the expenditure of capital and labour.
577. *Okoye v. Dumez supra* n. 354.
578. Smith, I.O. *supra* n. 244 at 350.

whatsoever in the land and has to comply strictly with the conditions of grant.[579] For example, in *Anifowoshe v. Siyanbola*,[580] permission to live on the premises by an act of grace was held to be a bare licence.

Contractual Licence

306. This type of licence is given for valuable consideration such as payment of fees for the use of premises as an event centre, or for the enjoyment of right therein e.g., cutting timbers to sell under a contract, or the right to enter cinema or railway station after purchase of ticket.[581] A contractual licence may be coupled with definite interest on land or on things attached to or forming part of the land either naturally or as improvements.[582]

Statutory Licence under the Land Use Act[583]

307. Pursuant to the provision of section 12(1) of the Land Use Act, the Governor may grant licences to any person to enter any land which is not the subject of a statutory right of occupancy, mining lease, mining right, or exclusive prospecting licence granted under the Minerals Act or any other enactment, for the purpose of extracting building materials or other substances meant for manufacturing of building materials. Such licence may be granted for such period and subject to such conditions as the Governor may think proper or as may be prescribed, over an area not exceeding 400 hectares,[584] and it is non-transferable without the consent of the Governor first had and obtained otherwise, such transfer shall be void.[585]

308. The licence is revocable by the Governor upon failure by the licensee to comply with any of the conditions of the licence.[586] Although no notice is prescribed for such revocation but in practice, the nature of such licence as one given for valuable consideration and for a purpose makes it necessary that reasonable notice be given.[587] A breach of any of the conditions of the licence by the licensee makes him liable in damages to the licensor-Governor for the period of the breach, and the Governor may recover such damages in lieu of revocation of licence.[588]

III. Formalities

309. A licence may be created orally or in writing, but not necessarily by deed. Since a licence creates mainly a personal privilege as opposed to an estate in land,

579. *Ibid.*, at 349–350.
580. (1956) SCNLR 139.
581. *Smith v. West African Pictures supra* n. 575; *Umezurike v. George* (1973) CCHCJ 62.
582. *Okoye v. Dumez supra* n. 354.
583. Cap L5 LFN 2010.
584. *Ibid.*, s. 12(2) and (3).
585. *Ibid.*, s. 12(4).
586. *Ibid.*, s. 12(5).
587. *Oyekoya v. G.B Ollivant* (1969) 1 All NLR 80; *Okoye v. Dumez supra* n. 354.
588. Smith, I.O. *supra* n. 244at 490.

there is no statutory requirement of writing, and this is so, notwithstanding that the licence is coupled with a grant of an interest in land.[589] It is however advisable to have a licence created in writing for purposes of not only ascertaining parties intention with regards to the creation of the licence, but also to make agreed terms and conditions certain, as the court will not imply terms and conditions into a licence.[590]

310. An agreement creating a licence will normally carry a 15k adhesive stamp, but where the licence given for valuable consideration is coupled with a grant of interest in land to be enjoyed by the grantee, it attracts an ad valorem stamp duty as a conveyance on sale for the premium so paid or, where rent is paid by the licensee, as a lease at the rent so payable.[591]

IV. Revocation of Licence

311. A licence may be revoked by giving notice of revocation to the licensee. Where the licence is given gratuitously, it is revocable at any time by giving notice, and the licensee must vacate the premises forthwith, otherwise, he becomes a trespasser.[592] A licence given for valuable consideration or coupled with a grant of interest in land requires reasonable notice before revocation and reasonable time to enable the licensee remove his things from the land.[593] What constitutes reasonable notice is a question of fact and depends on the circumstances of each case which include the type of user rights permitted by the licence and the commitments of the licensee at the time of serving the notice of revocation.[594]

312. The power of the licensor to revoke the licence is subject to the contract between the parties the terms of which must be properly construed. Where the licence given for value has a limited purpose and duration, it is irrevocable until the purpose is fulfilled.[595] If the duration of notice is fixed under the agreement, a shorter notice constitutes a breach.[596] Where notice is shorter than that required under the agreement or falls below what the circumstances of the case require to satisfy the test of reasonableness, the licensee is entitled to damages for loss of earning for the remaining period under the agreement or for such period as would be

589. *Chilufya v. City Council* (1967) ZLR 115.
590. Smith, I.O. *supra* n. 244at 351.
591. Stamp Duties Act Cap S8 LFN 2004, s. 64.
592. *Smith v. West African Pictures Ltd supra* n. 575.
593. *Oyekoya v. G.B Ollivant Ltd* (1969) 1 All NLR 80; *Okoye v. Dumez supra* n. 354.
594. *Smith v. West African Pictures Ltd supra* n. 575.
595. *Ibid.*
596. Smith, I.O. *supra* n 244at 353.

reasonable in the circumstances.[597] But the licensee in such cases can neither restrain the licensor from entering into possession by way of an injunction,[598] nor can he sue the licensor for trespass.[599]

§8. Restrictive Covenants

313. Restrictive covenants are common in situations where a landowner is desirous of preserving the saleable value of his property, or keen on maintaining the aesthetics of the environment or restricting certain activities in the interest of the landowner. Positive or negative covenants are imposed on the purchaser under a contract imposing certain obligations on the latter which remain binding between the parties. However, the situation may not be the same as between the original covenantor or covenantee and their successors in title with regards to running of the benefit and burden of such covenants.

I. Running of Benefit

314. As between the original covenantor and successor in title of the original covenantee, common law allows both the benefit and burden of a covenant positive or negative to run so that third parties can enforce same provided that: (i) the covenant touches and concerns the benefited land;[600] (ii) the original covenantee at the time of making the covenant had legal estate in the benefited land[601] with the successor having the same legal estate in the benefited land;[602] and there was an intention that the benefit should run with the benefited land at the date of the covenant.[603] Where the benefit of the covenant does not run at common law for want of fulfilment of the conditions highlighted, it may run in equity provided it touches and concerns the land and the original covenantee has acquired the benefit in any of the following three ways:

(a) *By Annexation:*
This may be expressly manifested in the terms of the deed of assignment, but it is implied in many States of Nigeria with property legislation,[604] so that such

597. *Mobil Oil (Nig) Ltd v. Johnson supra* n. 566.
598. *Adesina v. Oladotun* (1972) UILR 214 at 248–249.
599. *Aina v. Okusedun* (1975) 4 CCHCJ 517.
600. *Smith & Snipes Hall Farm Ltd v. River Douglas Catchment Board* (1949) 2 KB 500.
601. *Webb v. Russell* (1789) 3 TR 393 402.
602. *Westhoughton UDC v. Wigam* (1919) 1 Ch.D 159.
603. *Rogers v. Hosegood* (1900) 2 Ch. 388.
604. Conveyancing Act 1881, s. 58 applicable in Lagos State and some Eastern and Northern States without Property legislation; Property and Conveyancing Law Cap 100 Laws of Western Nigeria 1959, s. 102(1) applicable and adopted in Oyo, Ogun, Ondo, Osun, Ekiti, Edo, and Delta States and Law of Property applicable in various other States of Nigeria: Cap 100 Laws of Akwa Ibom State, 2000 s. 99(1), Cap 122 Laws of Bauchi State 2006, Cap P10 Laws of Kwara State 2007; s. 101(1) Cap 110 Laws of Abia State 2005, Cap 114 Laws of Sokoto State 1996, Cap 114 Laws of Kebbi State 1996.

a covenant, when contained in the deed of assignment, shall be deemed to be made with the covenantee's heirs and assigns, provided the land is ascertainable or capable of being ascertained, and relates to the whole of the covenantee' land or annexed to the particular part conveyed.

(b) *By express assignment:*

There could be an express assignment of the benefit to the covenantee's successors in title contemporaneously with the transfer of the benefited land.

(c) *By a devise of scheme of development:*

This is a devise by which a series of sales indicate an intention that all purchasers should be bound by restrictive covenants and that each should be able to enforce them against others. The conditions for the existence of a building scheme were laid down by the Supreme Court of Nigeria in *Rosanwo v. Sarkis*[605] as follows:

(i) that the title must have been derived from common vendor;
(ii) that the common vendor must have laid out the estate involved in defined plots subject to common restrictions consistent with a general scheme of development;
(iii) that the common vendor must have intended the restriction to be for the benefit of all plots within the scheme;
(iv) that the original purchasers must have acquired their plots on the understanding that the restrictions should be enforced by the owners of the other plots; and
(v) that the area covered must be clearly defined.

Protection of Benefit of Restrictive Covenant by Registration

315. Section 67(1) of the Lagos State Lands Registration Law[606] allows a holder of a right or interest in land entitled to the benefit of a restrictive covenant (not being a covenant made between a sub-lessor and sub-lessee) to apply to the Registrar to enter notice of the benefit in the register, and the Registrar shall enter the notice accordingly by reference to the document containing the covenant and shall file the document in the lands registry.[607]

II. Running of Burden at Common Law

316. At common law, the burden of positive covenants cannot run with the land and no such covenant is enforceable against the successors in title of the original covenantor.[608] This shortcoming has made some conveyancing devises necessary to make such positive covenants enforceable. A lease on land may be created so that positive covenants become enforceable against the assignee of the covenantor under

605. (1970) 2 All NLR 283.
606. Law No. 1 2015.
607. Such restrictive covenant must enure against the title to the land intended to be burdened for it to bind the holder of such land or his successor in title: *See* s. 67(2) of that law.
608. *Austerberry v. Oldham Corporation* (1885) 29 Ch. 750.

the doctrine of privity of estate;[609] the covenantor may protect himself by taking a covenant of indemnity from his purchaser while each successive purchaser gives similar covenant to his vendor resulting in a chain of indemnity covenants being created; or the covenantor may take advantage of the doctrine in *Halsall v. Brizell*[610] which obliges a person who wishes to take advantage of a service facility to undertake the corresponding obligation to contribute to the cost of providing or maintaining it.[611]

III. Running of Burden in Equity

317. Since the decision of the court in *Tulk v. Moxhay*,[612] a covenant negative in substance will, subject to certain conditions, be enforceable by the subsequent owners of the land and the duty to observe it will pass to all persons who take the burdened land except a purchaser of the legal estate for value without notice. The conditions for enforceability of the burden of restrictive covenant in equity are as follows:

(a) The covenant must be negative in substance. A covenant is negative in substance if compliance with it will not involve expenditure of money.[613]
(b) The covenant must touch and concern the dominant land and must affect the land as regards mode of occupation and not merely from the collateral circumstances affect the value of the land.[614]
(c) The beneficial land must be sufficiently close to the burdened land so that the covenant imposed on the burdened land can benefit the benefited land.
(d) It must be the common intention of the parties that the burden of the covenant shall run with the land of the covenantor.
(e) The covenantee must, at the time of creating the covenant and afterwards own land for the protection of which the covenant is made. Where the covenantee retains no adjacent land or owns no land capable of being protected by the covenant, the covenant cannot be enforced against a person other than the covenantor even if he has notice of it.[615]Once the following conditions are satisfied, a restrictive covenant becomes an equitable interest and becomes enforceable against all persons who acquire the burdened land except the purchaser for value of the legal estate without notice of the covenant. Also, the occupier of the burdened land is liable irrespective of the character of his occupation.

---

609. *See Spencer's case* (1583) 5 Co. Rep 16.
610. (1957) Ch. 169.
611. The shortcoming of this doctrine however lies in the fact that it cannot be invoked where the burdened owner does not enjoy any services or facility to which his obligation attach or has no sufficient interest in the continuance of those benefits.
612. 14 ER 1143.
613. Per Lindley LJ in *Haywood v. Brunswock Permanent Building Society* (1881) 8 QBD 403 at 410.
614. *Rogers v. Hosegood* (1900) 2 Ch. 388.
615. *London County Council v. Allen* (1914) 3 KB 642.

IV. Remedies for Breach of Restrictive Covenant

318. A breach of restrictive covenant entitles the plaintiff to damages, provided damages will be adequate compensation.[616] A prohibitive injunction may be granted to prevent a breach of positive covenants, or an order of specific performance may be made where there is a breach. In the case of breach of a negative covenant, a mandatory injunction may be granted by the court directing the performance of a positive act to remedy the breach.[617]

V. Discharge of Restrictive Covenant

319. Restrictive covenant may be discharged where the benefited and burdened land come into common ownership,[618] or where there is mutual agreement in writing that the restrictive covenants be discharged.

616. *Federated Homes Ltd v. Mill Lodge Properties Ltd* (1980) 1 All ER 371 at 381.
617. *Wakeham v. Wood* (1982) 43 P & CR 40.
618. *Re Tiltwood Sussex* (1976) Ch. 269.

Chapter 5. Security Interests

320. Under Nigerian law, various security interests may be created on real property by a holder of a right of occupancy or any person deriving interest therefrom, in favour of the creditor. Such arrangement is known to both customary law and the general law.

321. The popular arrangement which is known to customary law as a pledge is usually created on agricultural land with possession of the land delivered to the lender (the pledgee) who enjoys benefits or profits from the land yields until the loan is liquidated by the borrower (the pledgor).

322. Parties to a loan transaction may agree that the borrower assign a proprietary interest in real property to the lender as security subject to cesser on redemption otherwise known as a mortgage under the general law. It may be agreed that real property be appropriated to the contract of loan with neither title nor possession yielded by the borrower (the chargor) to the lender (the chargee) otherwise known as a charge. Also, statutory charge otherwise known as a charge by deed expressed to be by way of legal mortgage is known to some States within the Nigerian federation.

323. Security interest in the form of conveyancing lien may arise by operation of law in the course of sale transaction on land. For example, the vendor's lien may arise where part of the purchase price remains unpaid after an assignment of the vendor's interest in land; or purchaser's lien where the vendor fails to execute a deed of assignment in favour of the purchaser and convey the land to him after receiving the full purchase price. (Details of security interests in real property are discussed in Part V).

Chapter 6. Joint Ownership

§1. Joint Ownership of Immovable Property

324. The concept of co-ownership or joint ownership at common law involves concurrent enjoyment of land by two or more persons. At common law, concurrent interests exist either as joint tenancy at law or as tenancy in common in equity. The distinction between the two lies in the two principal features namely: the 'four unities' and the right of survivorship (jus accrescendi).

I. At Common Law

325. Joint tenancy is a common law concept which applies where property is transferred to two or more persons jointly.[619] The position is that even in the absence of an express direction that the grantees are to hold the land jointly, the presumption of law is in favour of joint tenancy, unless there are clear words of severance in the instrument of grant or the incidence of severance could be inferred therefrom.[620]

326. Joint tenancy is characterised by unity of possession to the extent that each joint tenant is as much entitled to possession of any part of the land as the others;[621]unity of interest in the sense that the interest of each joint tenant is the same in extent, nature, and duration;[622]unity of title in the sense that each joint tenant claims title to the land under the same act or document;[623] and unity of time to the extent that the interest of each tenant vests at the same time.[624] The absence of any of these four unities means that the intention to create a joint tenancy fails and instead, a tenancy in common is created. Indeed, apart from unity of possession which is common to both joint tenancy and tenancy in common,[625] tenancy in common does not share the existence of other unities which may be absent and is known to hold in undivided shares[626] in the property.

327. Tenancy in common may be created at law where there is absence of any of the unities or where there are words of severance showing that the tenants were each to take a distinct share in the property.[627] It also arises in equity where purchasers of property provided purchase money in unequal shares;[628] or where two or

619. *Agbaje v. Khawam* (1986) 5 NWLR (Pt. 42) 496.
620. *Odunlami v. Odunlami* (1974) 11 CCHCJ 1719; *Shonekan v. Smith* (1964) NMLR 59.
621. *Ipaye v. Aribisala* (1930) 10 NLR 10; *Kuri v. Kuri* (1924) 4 NLR 78.
622. Smith, I.O. *supra* n. 244at 155–156.
623. *Ibid.*
624. *Ibid.*
625. *Ibid.*
626. *Ibid.*
627. *Atinuke v. Oshodi* (1966) NMLR 195.
628. Kodilinye *supra* n. 160 at 22; *Steads v. Steads* (1889) 22 QB 537.

more persons advanced money on mortgage in equal or unequal shares;[629] or where partners acquired land as part of the partnership assets.[630] In all these cases, tenancy in common is presumed in equity.

328. Under the right of survivorship rule, the interest of a joint tenant upon death passes to the other joint tenants,[631] while the interest of a tenant in common upon death passes under his will or intestacy to his successors in title.[632]

329. Joint tenancy and tenancy in common may be brought to an end by partition,[633] or by union in a sole tenant.[634] Joint tenancies may, in addition, be determined by severance[635] thereby converting them into tenancies in common.

II. Under the State Property Legislations

330. The application of the rule of co-ownership has been streamlined in Nigeria under the various State property legislations.[636] For example, 'a legal estate is not capable of subsisting or of being created in undivided shares in land'.[637] In other words, tenancy in common cannot be created at law, and where land is expressed to be transferred to any persons in undivided shares, such transfer shall, where the grantees of not more than four in number are of full age, operate as if the land had been expressed to be transferred to the grantees; and where they are more than four, to the first four named in the transfer as joint tenants upon statutory trust[638] for the other beneficiaries.[639]

629. *Ibid.*
630. *Ibid.*
631. *Shonekan v. Smith* (1964) NMLR 62; *Obasohan v. Omorodion* (2001) 13 NWLR (Pt. 729) 206.
632. *Ayeni v. Sowemimo* (1982) 5 SC 60 at 80; *Obasohan v. Omorodion supra* n. 631.
633. The right of the party seeking partition in court is absolute and not subject to the discretion of the court except where the law disallows it: *See Agbaje v. Khawam supra* n. 619.
634. This happens where other tenants in common sell their interests to one of them.
635. *Ipaye v. Aribisala supra* n. 621.
636. These legislations take after the PCL Cap 100 LWN 1959 with some modifications: *See,* e.g., Cap 132 Laws of Osun State of Nigeria 2002; Cap 120 Laws of Ondo State of Nigeria 2006; Cap 110 Laws of Abia State of Nigeria 2005; Cap 114 Laws of Sokoto State of Nigeria 1996; Cap 100 Laws of Akwa Ibom State of Nigeria 2000; Cap P10 Laws of Kwara State of Nigeria 2007; Cap 114 Laws of Kebbi State of Nigeria, to mention but a few.
637. *See,* for example, s. 1(6) Cap 100 Laws of Akwa Ibom 2000; s. 3(6) Cap P10 Laws of Kwara State 2007, Cap 114 Laws of Sokoto State 1996, Cap 114 Laws of Kebbi State 1996.
638. Land held upon 'statutory trusts' shall be held upon trusts and subject to the provisions following, namely, upon trust to sell the name and to stand possessed of the net proceeds of sale, after payment of costs and of the net rents and profits until sale after payments of rates, taxes, costs of insurance, repairs, and other outgoings, upon such trusts and subject to such powers and provisions as may be requisite for giving effect to the rights of the persons (including an encumbrancer of a former undivided share or whose encumbrance is not secured by a legal mortgage) interested in the land': *See* s. 22 Cap 114 Laws of Sokoto State 1996 and corresponding provision in the Property legislation of other States.
639. *See* s. 19(2) Cap 100 Laws of Akwa Ibom State 2000; s. 21(2) Cap 114 Sokoto State, and corresponding provisions in the laws of other States.

331. Where property is held upon statutory trust as aforesaid, the land must be sold unless all trustees concur in postponing sale, or a sale would defeat the object of the trust or would be in breach of the contractual obligations of the trustees of sale.[640] Upon sale of the property and payment of purchase money to two or more trustees of sale, the legal estate in the trustees passes to the purchaser and the interests of beneficiaries in the property are overreached.

332. The position under the various States property legislation in Nigeria unlike the position at common law is that a joint tenancy cannot be severed so as to create a legal tenancy in common.[641] However, one joint tenant may release his interest to other joint tenants, or sever the joint tenancy in equity by giving other joint tenants a notice in writing of such desire.[642] The effect of the severance in equity is to limit the tenants' interests in equity in the proceeds of sale.

III. Application to Apartment Buildings

333. In the case of apartments, a lease or purchase for work or living by joint owners carries with it a full responsibility for the property in the absence of his or her cohabitants. For example, suppose A and B rent an apartment together to reduce living expenses, both parties as join tenants are each responsible for paying rent and paying for applicable utilities for the apartment. Thus, if B leaves without notice and becomes unreachable, any lapse in payments falls solely on A. Where A and B own the property, this transfer occurs without a probate.

§2. Joint Ownership of Movable Property

334. Goods may be subject of ownership by two or more persons. For example, under the Nigerian Merchant Shipping Act,[643] ship may be held by owners in common in undivided shares.[644] The legal consequences of co-ownership of goods are the same as in real property with the following differences:

(a) Unlike the position under co-ownership of real property, goods may be owned by way of joint tenancy and tenancy in common *at law.*
(b) In the case of a thing in action, it is only possible to have a joint tenancy as opposed to tenancy in common.

640. *Ibid.*, ss 20 and 23(1) respectively.
641. *See* Cap 100 Laws of Akwa Ibom State 2000, s. 21(2); Cap 114 Laws of Sokoto State 1996, and corresponding provisions in other States.
642. *Ibid.*, s. 21(3) and s. 23(3) respectively, and corresponding provisions in the Property Law of other States.
643. No. 17 2007.
644. *Ibid.*, s. 2.

335. Where goods are held in joint tenancy, the four-unity rule, the rule of survivorship, and rules of severance apply as in the case of real property[645] with the following variations:

(a) Livestocks can only be held in tenancy in common and the rule of survivorship does not apply.[646]
(b) There is no right of survivorship in respect of goods forming part of a partnership property.[647]
(c) Where chattels are purchased from a joint account, unless that account has been set up for a specific purpose, there is no presumption that goods or other property are purchased in joint names; rather, goods belong to the party who purchased the property.

645. Blackstone W Bl Comm II 399 cited by Bridge, M., et al., *The Law of Personal Property* 4–6 (Sweet & Maxwell 2013).
646. *Jefferys v. Small* (1680) 23 ER 424.
647. Partnership Act 1890, ss 20–24.

Chapter 7. Neighbourhood and Urban Problems

336. Nigeria has numerous environmental and planning challenges which are being addressed by certain regulatory regimes put in place by both the Federal and State governments. Section 20 of the Constitution of the Federal Republic of Nigeria 1999 as amended provides that 'the State shall protect and improve the environment and safeguard the water, air and land, forest and wild life of Nigeria',[648] while there are Federal and State Laws dealing with environmental and planning challenges.

337. Among the environmental and planning challenges are environmental pollution which encompasses land, water, and air pollution; problem of waste generation and planning issues.

§1. Environmental Pollution

338. Environmental pollution may come about as a result of foul or noxious odour discharged from animal facility or poultry farm[649] or may result from dangerous automobile fumes, burning of refuse, bush burning, gas flaring, and emissions from factories. The various pollutants often result in adverse health conditions ranging from intestinal irritation, serious respiratory discomfort to carcinogenic diseases, and generally lowering the quality of life in the cities.

339. In Nigeria, noise pollution is a common phenomenon in urban centres where urban dwellers are subjected to varying degrees of noise emission from the neighbourhood due to the very high volume of noise emitted by record players in public, power generating plants, construction, transportation, industrial, and religious activities. Noise pollution which affects the comfort, convenience, or well-being in private domestic life may amount to private or public nuisance depending on where it is taking place, and the aggregate number of people affected.

340. Land contamination in peri-urban centres due to increasing use of land for industrial purposes or waste disposal is a challenge which may prevent subsequent redevelopment due to the immediate or long-term hazards to human health, plants, and amenities, and may contaminate underground percolating and pipe borne water (due to broken pipes) thereby polluting water supply. Oil exploration, production, and distribution may also lead to land contamination as a result of spills and leakages.

---

648. This provision comes under Chapter II of the Constitution on Fundamental Objectives and Directive Principles of State Policy with eleven sections (ss 13–24) which although non-justiciable, provides a blueprint for the three arms of government. For example, s. 13 thereof provides that: 'It shall be the duty and responsibility of all authorities and persons, exercising legislative, executive or judicial powers to conform to, observe and apply the provisions of this Chapter of the Constitution'.

649. *See Abiola v. Ijeoma* (1970) All NLR 613.

341. Discharge of domestic and industrial effluents in rivers and streams pollutes the major source of water supply for washing and means of livelihood such as fishing, and destroys aquatic ecosystem with adverse effect on income earnings.

§2. Improper Industrial Waste Generation and Disposal

342. Waste recycling is known to be an efficient way of managing waste generation, and the use of incinerators a potent way of managing waste disposal. These two mechanisms are not in place in many industries in some urban centres in Nigeria, resulting in poor management of waste generation and disposal. The emissions from the dumping of these industrial wastes constitutes serious health hazards to the populace, contaminates the land mass, and pollutes water sources.

343. Flooding of the land space due to non-natural use of land,[650] dumping of domestic wastes in drains,[651] and inefficient environmental planning by government.[652] The problem is critical in urban centres and has been a major nightmare to government.

Legal and Institutional Responses

344. Apart from the common law remedies in the tort of nuisance[653] and the rule in *Rylands v. Fletcher*[654] with respect to the use of land by a person resulting in deleterious or hazardous effect on the enjoyment of land by neighbours for which damages may be awarded or injunction granted by the court, a number of legislations exist to curb or minimise the drastic consequences of environmental pollution as a result of public nuisance. Examples could be found in the Associated Gas Reinjection (continued flaring of Gas) Act[655] and regulations made pursuant to the Act, Bush Burning Law and Regulations,[656] Air quality Standard for specific industry,[657] and Environmental Impact Assessment Act (EIA).[658] Apart from regulating standards in relation to emissions, it is a criminal offence to pollute the environment

650. Non-natural use of land is 'some special use bringing with it increase danger to others and must not merely be the ordinary use of land or such use as is proper for the general benefit of the community': *See Rickards v. Lothian* (1913) UKPC 1.
651. This continues despite government's efforts to discourage this through enlightenment in the media.
652. Failure to carry out Environmental Impact Assessment in respect of certain sensitive projects connected with dredging and sand filling of the River, Lagoon, and the Ocean are factors contributing significantly to flooding in urban centres such as Lagos.
653. Nuisance is an unlawful and unreasonable interference with the enjoyment of the property of another.
654. (1866) LR 1 Exch. 265.
655. *See* Cap A25 Laws of the Federation of Nigeria 2010.
656. *See* National Environmental (Bush burning) Regulation 2011; Prohibition of Bush Burning Law 1986 (Ogun State); Prohibition of Bush Burning Amendment Law, 1990 (Ogun State) and Bush Burning (Control) Law 1985 as amended (Kadune State).
657. *See*, for example, National Environmental (Textile, Wearing Apparel, Leather, and Footwear Industry) Regulations 2009.
658. Cap E12 Laws of the Federation of Nigeria 2010.

through emissions hazardous to the health of persons in general dwellings or carrying on business in the neighbourhood.[659] It is also an offence to carry, deposit, dump, transport, import, sell or offer for sale, purchase or deal in any harmful waste inimical to the atmosphere.[660]

345. Where an act is unwarranted by law or where an omission endangers the life, health, property, morals, or comfort of the public or obstruct the public in the exercise of rights common to the citizens, an action in public nuisance by the victim would lie only where the latter can show that he has suffered damage or loss over and above that suffered by the general public. Majority of public nuisance are now subject to statutory controls.[661]

§3. Building Rights and Planning Controls

346. Building rights are regulated by planning laws and regulations[662] to check indiscriminate utilisation of land in the national interest and prevent individual landowners from using their land in a way detrimental to their immediate environment including threat to lives and limbs. While there appears to be adequate provisions of the law on planning and planning control regulations in place to check abuses, enforcement, and monitoring of compliance with the planning law and planning control regulations are slack. Consequently there have been cases of building collapse in some parts of the country particularly in urban centres including Lagos and its environs, resulting in loss of lives and serious bodily harm to survivors.[663]

347. There is also the problem of imbalances in development resulting in the proliferation of urban slums existing side by side urban development[664] and consequently resulting in lopsided physical development and inequitable distribution of infrastructural facilities.

---

659. *See* s. 247 of the Nigeria Criminal Code.
660. Harmful Waste (Special Criminal Provisions etc.) Act Cap H1 Laws of the Federation of Nigeria 2010.
661. *See* the Public Health Law Cap P25 Laws of the Federation of Nigeria 2010; Environmental Sanitation Laws in the States (e.g., Cap E6 Laws of Lagos State 2003); Environmental Pollution Control Law Cap P25 Laws of Lagos State 2003.
662. *See* the Nigerian Urban and Regional Planning Act (NURPA) No. 88 1992 now Cap N138 Laws of the Federation of Nigeria 2010 and the regulations made thereto, applicable in the Federal Capital Territory of Nigeria; the Lagos State Urban and Regional Planning and Development Law (URPDL) and the regulations made thereto: *see* Cap U2 Laws of Lagos State 2015; and the Town and Country Planning Laws applicable in many other States of the Federation: *See,* for example, Cap 163 Laws of Oyo State 2000; Cap 158 Laws of Osun State 2001; Cap 133 Laws of Akwa Ibom State 2000; Cap 159 Laws of Kwara State 2007; Cap 136 Laws of Adamawa State 1997, to mention a few.
663. For the very many cases of building collapse in Nigeria, *see* generally Fagbenle O.I.& Olawunmi A.O., in *Building Failure and Collapse in Nigeria: The Influence of Informal Sector*' 3 J. Sust. Dev. 268 (December 2010).
664. Examples are the slum of Obalende existing side by side with Ikoyi on the Lagos Island and Ajegunle existing side by side with Apapa GRA on the Lagos Mainland.

Legal and Institutional Responses

348. Sequel to the Supreme Court decision in *Attorney General of Lagos State v. Attorney General of the Federation & 35 Ors,*[665] a major source of planning law consists of the Nigerian Urban and Regional Planning Act (NURPA) absolutely applicable to the Federal Capital Territory, Abuja; the existing Urban and Regional Planning and Development Law in Lagos State (URPDL); and the Town and Country Planning Laws applicable in many other States of the Federation as well as the various regulations made under these laws.

349. These laws make it mandatory for any developer of property to apply for and obtain development permit before embarking on any development.[666] The developer may be required to take out an insurance policy in respect of a development above two floors,[667] and in some cases, the law may require the consent of the Governor for special development.[668] The development control agency is responsible for monitoring compliance with standards and may ask that any contravention be pulled down.

350. Defective building which poses threat or risk to lives may be demolished at the expense of the developer after service of requisite notice and non-compliance with the abatement of same by the developer.[669] Also, where the cost of demolition is not paid by the defaulter three months after the demolition of the defective building, the said property shall be forfeited to the State.[670]

351. To ensure even development and eradicate or reduce the proliferation of urban slums, the Lagos State URPDL makes provisions for improvement or regeneration of new areas by the Urban Renewal Agency which may involve repairs, renovation, or demolition of existing structures.[671]

665. (2003) 12 NWLR (Pt. 833) 1.
666. *See* s. 30 NURPA.
667. *See* s. 48 of URPDL.
668. *Ibid.,* s. 4.
669. *Ibid.,* ss 71, 72.
670. *Ibid.,* s. 72(2).
671. *See* generally Part IV of URPDL.

Chapter 8. Agrarian Problems

352. Agriculture in Nigeria is challenged by many factors ranging from environmental and technological factors to inefficient land use regulation and restriction on access to credit, to boost mechanised agriculture and improve productivity.

§1. Environmental Factors

353. In some parts of Northern Nigeria, desertification has made land deficient in the necessary nutrients sufficient to support the growing of food and cash crops. Migratory locusts and other species of migratory pests destroy food and cash crops as well as other vegetation and stored crops. Bush burning in different parts of the country and oil pollution in the Niger Delta area of Nigeria in particular impoverish the soil and destroy basic soil components.

§2. Technological Factors

354. The unaffordability of mechanised farming by Nigerian farmers coupled with lack of adequate assistance from government to make fertilisers available and provide farmers with modern farming implements and efficient storage facilities are significant drawbacks in attaining optimum productivity. Lack of access to quality seedlings and failure of farmers to appreciate farming methodology dictated by modern technology constitute challenge to the attainment of high yields.

§3. Unsustainable Land Use Regulation and Administration

355. While it is the case that about 80% of the land is suitable for agriculture in Nigeria,[672] its sustainable use is being hampered by inefficient land administration and regulation. It is observed[673] that land use regulation and administration are unsustainable because both undermine security to land use or ownership, deprive land owner's access to land, and restrict access to credit.

356. Certain provisions of the Land Use Act ('the Act') which was enacted in 1978[674] contain pitfalls which are inimical to agricultural development. Access to land under the Act is not guaranteed for, although the Governor or local government has the power to make a grant, there is no duty to make such grant even where conditions for the grant have been fulfilled. Foreign investors are not encouraged to

672. USAID, *USAID Country Profile: Property Rights and Resource Governance in Nigeria* (2010) online <http/landise.landesa.org/record/1326>accessed 19 Mar. 2016.
673. Ihugba, B., *Resolution of Farmland Disputes and Agricultural Development: An Examination of the Judicial System in Settlement of Farm Disputes*, in *Food and Agricultural: Readings on Sustainable Agriculture and the Law in Nigeria* 49 (R.T. Ako & D.S. Olawuyi ed., ABUAD Publications 2015).
674. Cap L5 Laws of the Federation of Nigeria 2010.

access land for agricultural purposes as a result of the discriminatory policy of the Act in restricting use and benefit of the land to Nigerians.[675]

357. There are no known guidelines for the exercise of power of grant by the Governor and nothing stops the Governor from exercising the power to further oil exploration and production to the detriment of agriculture as it has been the case in the Niger Delta region.

358. Customary land rights upon which commercial agricultural investments have taken place may be overridden by the Governor in order to promote mineral development, and where this happens, 'the benefits delivered to generations of communities and families would be displaced by mineral development that hardly delivers any benefits to the communities and families'.[676] This calls for a policy change that gives better recognition to customary land rights.

359. Section 6(2) of the Act which provides that 'no single customary right of occupancy shall be granted in respect of an area of land in excess of 500 hectares if granted for agricultural purposes or 5,000 hectares if granted for grazing purposes, except with the consent of the Governor', shows a lack of concern for equity. In terms of the limited land resources for both agriculture and animal husbandry, allowing individuals to acquire 500 or 5,000 hectares of land could mean denial of the right of occupation to many farmers with negative consequences for improved production and sustainable agriculture.

360. Land titling is a mirage under the extant land tenure regime in Nigeria. The certificate of occupancy does not guarantee title[677] and traditional titles are unreliable and subject of proof through non-documentary evidence which may result in endless litigation. Many farmers are faced with uncertainties in the enjoyment of possessory rights to their land notwithstanding the seeming recognition or protection by certain provisions of the Act. Section 36(2) of the Act provides with regards to agricultural land in non-urban areas:

> Any occupier or holder of such land, whether under customary right or otherwise howsoever shall if the land was on the commencement of this Act being used for agricultural purposes continue to be entitled to possession of the land for use for agricultural purposes as if a customary right of occupancy had been granted to the occupier or holder thereof by the appropriate Local Government and the reference in this section to land being used for agricultural purposes includes land which is, in accordance with the custom of the locality concerned, allowed to lie fallow for purposes of recuperation of the soil.

---

675. The provision of s. 1 of the Act restricts grantees of a right of occupancy to Nigerians. *See Ogunola v. Eiyekole* (1990) 4 NWLR (Pt. 146) 632.
676. Nwapi, C., *Land Ownership, Mineral Development and Agriculture in Nigeria,* in *Readings on Sustainable Agriculture and the Law in Nigeria* at 40 (R.T. Ako & D.S. Olawuyi eds).
677. *See Ogunleye v. Oni* (1990) 2 NWLR (Pt. 135) 745.

361. It has been observed,[678] and rightly too, that the provision leaves owners and occupiers of land everywhere in the country vulnerable to the claims of the intruder who may succeed in getting registered as a holder of a customary right of occupancy under section 36(3)[679] of the Act. Many farmers in the non-urban areas are not able to avail themselves of the opportunity offered by the provision of section 36(3) for lack of information and the cost or fear of bureaucratic hassles likely to be involved.[680]

362. The Act does not recognise the peculiarities of the socio-economic structure of landholding in some parts of the country. It is reported[681] that although the Act recognises grant of a customary right of occupancy for grazing land,[682]it does not recognise the right of farmers to graze their animals in land owned by others, even when not in use. It does not recognise grazing rights while a concurrent right to occupancy still exists on behalf of other persons for other purposes i.e., rights for crop farming purposes to one person, and rights for animal grazing at different times of the year to another.[683] These concurrent rights in land are prominent in the northern part of the country as between the Fulani herdsmen and the Hausa farmers and have been a significant cause of land dispute in that part of the country leading to loss of lives and property especially agricultural properties like crops and livestock.[684] In the other parts of the country, there are regular conflicts between the Fulani herdsmen and farmers from the various localities over destruction of farmlands, crops, and livestock by cattle in the course of grazing, with death toll of about 5,000 recorded in 2017.[685] This ugly situation has resulted in the passing of anti-open grazing laws in Ekiti and Benue States, while the Houses of Assembly in other States such as Ebonyi, Ondo, Abia, Imo, and Ogun are already considering bills to enact laws criminalising open grazing.

363. The provision of section 5(2) of the Act which allows an actual statutory grant made by the Governor to extinguish 'all existing rights to the use and occupation of the land which is the subject of the statutory right of occupancy', is inimical to security of land holding by the farmer under customary law notwithstanding the Supreme Court decisions in *Dantsoho v. Mohammed*[686] and *Ibrahim v. Mohammed*.[687] Several land rights exist at customary law which may confer on the farmer

---

678. Mabogunje, A., 'Land Reform in Nigeria: Progress, Policies and Prospects' in Law Reform Publications Abuja 2009.
679. This provision entitles the deemed grantee of a customary right of occupancy using the land for agricultural purposes at the commencement of the Act, upon proof of the description of the land and possession of the said land, to be registered as the person to whom a customary right of occupancy has been issued.
680. Mabogunje, A. *supra* n. 678.
681. Ihugba, B. *supra* n. 673 at 52.
682. *See* s. 6(2) of the Act.
683. Ihugba, B. *supra* n. 673 at 54.
684. *Ibid.*
685. That was reported as the Research finding of the SBM Intelligence in 2017 by the Saturday Punch of 11 Nov. 2017 at p. 2.
686. (2003) 6 NWLR (Pt. 817) 457.
687. (1983) 6 NWLR (Pt. 817) 615.

mere possessory or usufructuary interest (as opposed to proprietary interest) which a grant of statutory right of occupancy may extinguish automatically without recourse to the provisions on revocation[688] under the Land Use Act.

364. The power of revocation vested in the Governor may pose a threat to security of tenure over agricultural land. In the past, agricultural lands subject of acquisition had been granted to wealthy individuals, politicians, corporate organisations, and public co-operatives for their personal use thereby defeating the purpose of the law.[689] The possibility of dispossessing farmers of their land for public purposes may result in lack of enthusiasm to invest in long-term improvements on their farms.

365. Certain provisions of the Act have diminished the status of land as security for loans to farmers. The provisions on requirements of consent for alienation of a right of occupancy[690] constitute a clog on access to credit facility since the process for obtaining consent is slow, expensive, and generally fraught with corruption.[691] Also, since the bulk of agricultural land is situated in non-urban areas, the provision of section 36(5) of the Act which prohibits alienation of any sort of such land makes access to credit facility illusory. Banks are reluctant to grant credit to farmers who do not have documentary proof of assured access to agricultural land. (For further reading, *see* Smith, I.O. 'Promoting commercial agriculture in Nigeria through a reform of the legal and institutional frameworks' AJICL 26.1 (2018): 64–83).

688. Provisions for revocation are contained in s. 28 of the Act.

689. While it is hoped that judicial authorities such as *Ereku v. Military Governor of Mid western State* (1974) 10 SC 59 may curb the excesses of our land administrators in this regard, lack of awareness of the position of the law and failure to follow up on the execution of the public purpose for which revocation was meant especially after receipt of compensation by the holder of the revoked right of occupancy, paved way to the proliferation of executive lawlessness in this regard.

690. *See* ss 21 and 22 of the Land Use Act.

691. El-Rufai, N., *Why Nigeria Must Revisit Land Reform,* Premium Times (21 Dec. 2012) available at http://www.premiumtimesng.com/opinion/112128-why-nigeria-must-revisit-land-reforms-by-nasir-ahmad-el-rufai.html accessed 12 Mar. 2017.

Part II. Movable Property and Personal Property/Chattels

Chapter 1. General Classification

366. It appears settled that all properties that do not qualify as real properties or immovables are movables or personal properties.[692] Technically, personal property may be classified broadly into chattels real and chattels personal.

§1. Chattels Real and Chattels Personal

367. Chattels real are leasehold interests in land which is now treated in Nigeria, following English law, as an interest in land.[693] Chattels personal which is considered in modern time to be personal property properly so called, are usually classified into things or choses in possession i.e., tangible personal property; and choses in action i.e., intangible personal property.[694]

§2. Choses in Possession

368. Choses in possession comprise of assets that are 'tangible, movable and visible and of which possession can be taken'.[695] They basically cover various forms of goods 'which form a very large subcategory of tangible personal property',[696] and other tangible assets such as ships and aircraft.

692. *See* generally, Bridge, M. et al., *The Law of Personal Property* 4–6 (Sweet & Maxwell 2013).
693. This is consequent upon the reception of English law in Nigeria: *See* Law (Miscellaneous Provision) Act Cap 89 Laws of Nigeria 1958; Interpretation Act Cap 123 LFN 2010.
694. Blackstone expressed the view that 'property in chattels personal may be either in possession; which is where a man hath not only the right to enjoy, but hath the actual enjoyment of the thing; or else it is an action; where a man hath only a bare right without any occupation or enjoyment': Blackstone, W., *Commentaries on the Law of England* 1765–1769 (1st ed. Univ. of Chicago Report ed. 1979) (BL Comm) II 389.
695. *Armstrong DLW GmbH v. Winninton Networks Ltd* (2012) 3 All ER 425.
696. Bridge, M., et al. *supra* n. 692.

§3. Choses in Action

369. A chose in action is every intangible right in property which is not in possession but which may be realised and brought into possession by means of an action in court[697] and covers a wide spectrum of interests in intangibles such as shares, insurance policies, book debts and other receivables, intellectual property.

§4. Funds

370. The categorisation into choses in possession and choses in action is not a neat one. For example, money in the modern world is said to cover not only physical cash which is a chose in possession, but also intangible money as a form of medium of exchange and a repository or store of value.[698] Also, when money in its physical form is paid into a bank account, it becomes the property of the bank while the customer becomes the owner of a chose (thing) in action.[699] Recent development in patent law suggests that neither a patent nor a patent application is a thing in action although both are classified as personal property,[700] and a distinction is now drawn[701] between pure and documentary intangibles making it imperative to recognise other intangible properties.

371. This part deals with the legal principles of both tangible and intangible personal property. For tangibles however, emphasis is placed on goods or personal chattels as opposed to other tangibles such as Ship or Aircraft.

§5. Sources of Nigerian Law of Personal Property

372. Principally, Nigerian law of personal property consist of the general principles of common law and equity as applied by the Nigerian courts and relevant legislations such as the Factors Act 1889, the Sale of Goods Act 1893,[702] the Merchant Shipping Act,[703] the Civil Aviation Act,[704] and relevant Conventions.[705]

697. *Torkington v. Magee* (1902) 2 KB 427 at 430.
698. *BP Exploration (Libya) Co Ltd v. Hunt* (No. 2) (1979) 1 WLR 783.
699. *Lipkin Gorman v. Karpnale Ltd* (1991) 2AC 548 at 574.
700. Bridge, M., et al. *supra* n. 692 at 10 para. 1-021.
701. McKendrick, E., ed. *Goode on Commercial Law* 51–53 (4th ed. Butterworths 2009).
702. States have re-enacted the Act as State Law: *See,* for example, Sale of Goods Law Cap S2 Laws of Lagos State, 2003.
703. No. 17 2007.
704. Cap C13 LFN 2010.
705. *See,* for example, Cape Town Convention on security over roaming objects, 2001.

Chapter 2. Legal Interests

§1. Legal Interests in Tangibles

373. Generally, interests in tangibles or choses in possession may be legal or equitable.[706] Legal interests may exist in the form of ownership and possession which may be indivisible or subject of co-ownership in the form of joint tenancy and tenancy in common. All other interests in goods are capable of subsisting in equity.

I. Ownership

374. Both the common law[707] and statute[708] recognise the right of ownership of goods as a bundle of rights. It may be coupled with possession, but need not be; it suffices that the claimant has a right to possession which may be exercised at any time for a variety of reasons.[709] Ownership here connotes absolute ownership;[710] limited holdings such as life and successive interests only take effect in equity, although it is possible to have concurrent interests in the form of co-ownership of goods, and lesser interests may be created in the form of leases, or passing of possession in the form of a pledge[711] or bailment.[712]

II. Possession

375. Possession covers all proprietary interests in goods short of outright ownership.[713] It may be actual or constructive. Actual physical possession connotes having custody of the goods to the exclusion of others, but possession need not be singular and could be consensually shared such as where bailor and bailee are said to have possession,[714] or where the joint tenants and tenants in common possess in law. Constructive possession connotes possession through an agent of goods or

706. Exceptionally, a bailment is a creation of the common law, and it has been said that there can be no bailment of an equitable as opposed to legal interests in goods: In Re Bond Worth (1980) 1 Ch. 228 at 263.
707. *See* the old English case of *Armory v. Delamierie* 93 ER 664 where the court recognised both the concepts of the 'rightful owner' and 'absolute property or ownership'.
708. The Sale of Goods Act 1893 refers to passing of property in the goods and defines property to mean 'general property' (i.e., ownership) as opposed to special property associated with the interest of the pledgees and all other bailees of goods.
709. Apprehension of damage to goods in the custody of the bailor or disappearance of goods subject matter of proprietary security are good examples.
710. Bridge, M. et al. *supra* n. 692 at 50–51 para. 2-027.
711. *Ibid.*
712. *Ibid.*
713. *Ibid.*, n. 692 para. 2-038.
714. *Ancona v. Rogers* (1876) 1 Exch. D 285 at 292.

documents of title to goods.[715] Possession may coincide with retention but not coterminous with it for, a person may exercise the right to possession without retention.

376. Ownership may follow from possession, and where there is doubt as to who is entitled to possession, possession follows title or right to possession.[716] It is said that 'as against a wrongdoer, possession is as good as title, and as against strangers generally, possession has the incidents of ownership and is a root of title'.[717]

§2. Legal Interest in Intangibles

377. Legal interest in intangibles or choses in action are rights enforceable and recoverable by an action at law such as in the case of a debt or benefit under a contract. Such debt or other chose in action may be assigned at law through a legal assignment under the provisions of statute where there is absolute assignment of the whole debt or other chose in action in writing under the hand of the assignor to the assignee with express notice in writing to the obligor, trustee, or other person from whom the assignor would have been entitled to receive or claim such debt or chose in action. Where an owner of the legal property unintentionally fails to comply with the legal formalities required by statute in effecting an assignment in law, equity gives effect to an informal assignment of the legal property and the assignor is said to hold the property on trust for the assignee. (Details of such assignment are dealt with in Part III under Acquisition of Property rights.)

715. *See* Factor Act 1889, s. 1(2).
716. *Ramsay v. Margaret* (1894) 2 QB 18 CA.
717. Pollock, F. & Wright R, *An Essay in Possession at the Common Law* 22 (1888).

Chapter 3. Equitable Interests

378. All other interests outside the legal interests of ownership and possession in goods discussed in paragraphs 377 are equitable interests and they include beneficiary's interest in a trust dealt with in Part IV, and the interests of an equitable mortgagee, chargee or lienee of goods, dealt with in Part V. Equitable interests in intangibles exist in the form rights and interests of a beneficiary in trust fund, interest under a legacy, right to a relief against forfeiture of a lease for non-payment of rent, beneficial interest in a partnership, and reversionary interest under a Will. Such equitable interests may be assigned either in law or in equity. (Details of such assignment are dealt with in Part III under Acquisition of property rights).

Chapter 4. Security Interests

379. Security interests in personal property or chattels may be proprietary as in the case of a mortgage of personal chattels for a loan. Where this is the case, a bill of sale is contemplated and unless the mortgage instrument complies with the statutory form as prescribed by the Bills of Sale Act[718] or Law,[719] it does not create a valid security. A bill of sale must not only be registered, the security created by it shall not be enforceable unless the mortgagee complies with the provisions of the Bills of Sale Act or Law.

380. A possessory security in the form of a pledge may be created over personal chattels which may be sold by the pledge upon default by the pledgor, and after service of reasonable notice on the latter without liquidation of the loan.

381. A charge of personal chattels in the form of hypothecation whereby neither property in the goods nor the possession of them is given to the lender could be subject matter of security. The personal chattels remain in the possession of the borrower or a third party, while security over them is granted by means of letter of hypothecation. Being an equitable charge, the chargee may enforce the security by way of a judicial sale or by appointment of a receiver.

382. A lien may arise over personal chattels by agreement of the parties or by operation of law. How such lien arises and enforced depends on the nature of lien-.(For a detailed discussion of security interests in personal chattels, *see* Part V).

718. *See* Bills of Sale Act 1923 Cap 27 Laws of Nigeria, 1958 which re-enacted the Bills of Sale Act 1882 (a statute of general application) which has been omitted in the Laws of the Federation of Nigeria since 1990. It comes within the legislative competence of State: *See* Item No. 18 on the concurrent legislative list, Part II, Second Schedule, Constitution of the Federal Republic of Nigeria 1999 and it is therefore deemed to be a State Law which may be repealed or amended by the State.

719. *See* Cap 12 Laws of Oyo State 2000; Cap 11 Laws of Ondo State 2006, Cap 12 Laws of Lagos State 2015.

Part III. Acquisition of Property Rights

Chapter 1. Transfer of Property by Contract *Inter Vivos*

§1. SALE OF LAND

383. Purchase of land under customary or Islamic law or under the general law is one of the most popular methods of acquiring interest in land in Nigeria. When land is sold or interest therein assigned, the purchaser or assignee for value without notice of pre-existing interests in fact or in law, takes free of them.

384. Acquisition by purchase may take effect at customary law, or may be effected under the general law.

I. Sale of Land under Customary Law

385. A sale of land under customary law is validly concluded and the purchaser has a valid title where there is evidence of payment of purchase price and the purchaser is put into possession in the presence of witnesses.[720]

386. Payment of purchase price means payment of the full purchase price as opposed to a part payment as sale is complete only when the full purchase price is paid.[721] Money and delivery of possession to the purchaser must be contemporaneous, and the purchaser must take physical possession and remain in possession thenceforth.[722] The concept of delivery of possession in the presence of witnesses is notional, and the court will hold that delivery had taken place where purchaser can show possession of the land;[723] it is not necessary to adduce evidence of a ceremony

720. *Cole v. Folami* (1956) SCNLR 180; *Egonu v. Egonu* (1978) 11–12 SC 111; *Obi v. Onyemelukwe* (2014) 1 NWLR (Pt. 1228) 400.
721. *Odufuye v. Fatoke* (1977) NSCC vol. ii 141; *Ogundalu v. Mac job* (2006) 7 NWLR (Pt. 978) 170.
722. *Griffin v. Talabi* (1948) 12 WACA 371.
723. *Adebo v. Saki Estates Ltd* (1999) 7 NWLR (Pt. 612) 525; *Basil v. Fajebe* (2001) 11 NWLR (Pt. 725) 592.

of handing over before title under customary law can pass.[724] Where the concurrence of certain persons is required under customary law (e.g., consent of the head of the family and the principal members), the sale is only valid where such consent is sought and obtained.[725]

387. Sale must be concluded in the presence of witnesses who saw the actual handing over of the property to the purchaser.[726] Although multiple witnesses may be desirable, the presence of only one witness is sufficient for a valid sale.[727]

388. Proof that the foregoing requirements for sale of land under customary law were met is conclusive of sale, and it is not necessary to have the transaction reduced into writing.[728] Also a valid sale by a vendor under customary law will defeat a subsequent sale by the vendor to another purchaser even where a deed of conveyance was executed to a bona fide purchaser of a legal title.[729]

389. A sale at customary law may be subject to certain rights of natives of a particular area and where this is so, those rights must be taken cognisance of.[730]

II. Sale of Land under the General Law

The Requirement of Writing

390. A sale under the general law, unlike a sale under customary law, passes no title in law to the purchaser unless it is evidenced by a note or a memorandum in writing signed by the party to be charged (i.e., the vendor). That is the strict requirement of the law as prescribed by section 4 of the Statute of Frauds 1677 (a statute of general application in Nigeria)[731]and section 77 of the Property and Conveyancing Law applicable in the old western and mid-western states of Nigeria.[732] There is no special form prescribed for a note or memorandum of contract for sale of land. The note or memorandum may be in one document, or may consist of several documents, at least one of which is expressly or impliedly referable to another or others in a way to justify the reading of the documents together.[733] From the chain of

---

724. *Ayinla v. Sijuwola* (1984) 5 SC 44 at 68.
725. *Ekpendu v. Erika* (1959) 4 FSC 79; *Solomon & Ors v. Mogaji* (1982) 11 SC 1.
726. *Folarin v. Durojaiye* (1988) 1 NWLR (Pt. 70) 351; *Nwafor v. Obiefuna* (2011) 1 NWLR (Pt. 1229) 205.
727. *Adeniji v. Onagoruwa* (2000) 1 NWLR (Pt. 639) 1; *Kopek Construction Ltd v. Ekisola* (2010) 3 NWLR (Pt. 1182) 61.
728. *Ogunbambi v. Abowaba supra* n. 356; *Mustapha v. Abubakar* (2011) 3 NWLR (Pt. 1233) 123.
729. *Ogunbambi v. Abowaba supra* n. 356; *Soremekun v. Sodipo* (1959) LLR 30; *Etajata v. Ologbo* (2007) 16 NWLR (Pt. 1061) 554.
730. *Kubuyi v. Odunjo* (1926) 7 NLR 51.
731. *See* Law (Miscellaneous Provisions) Act 1964.
732. Cap 100 LWN 1959.
733. *Timmins v. Moreland Street Property Co Ltd* (1958) Ch. 110.

judicial authorities,[734] a document satisfies the description of a note or memorandum within the meaning of statutory provisions when it contains accurate description of the parties, the property to be assigned, the price to be paid, signature of person to be charged or that of his agent or representative.

Acts of Part Performance

391. However, the statutory requirement that a contract of sale of land or of an interest in land must be in writing to be enforceable is not inviolable. A court may, in certain circumstances, enforce an agreement caught by the statutory provision notwithstanding that there is no note or memorandum in support of such agreement. Such agreement, though unenforceable in law, may be enforced in equity where a party seeking to rely on it can show sufficient acts of part performance.[735] The basis of the application of the doctrine of part performance is that when one of two contracting parties has been induced or allowed by the other party to alter his position on the facts of the contract as for instance, by taking possession of land, and has expended money in building or other similar acts, it would be unconscionable of the other party to turn round and say that the contract was illegal.[736] The rationale behind the doctrine of part performance is that a party, having altered his position on the faith of the contract, acquires an equity against the defendant.

392. For a plea of acts of part performance to succeed thereby entitling the party to a court order of specific performance, there must be proper oral evidence to prove or establish the terms of the contract; the contract must be specifically enforceable, in other words, it must not be a contract of personal service or the like; the contract must be unequivocally referable to an agreement as that alleged;[737] and the claimant must have wholly or in part, executed his part of the parol agreement in the confidence that the defendant would do same.[738]

393. The doctrine of part performance will apply upon the fulfilment of the conditions that such acts of part performance must be definite and refer exclusively to and denote the existence of the alleged contract; the act must be such as to render it a fraud on the part of the defendant to take advantage of the contract not being in writing; the contract to which the acts of part performance denote must be capable of being enforced by a decree of specific performance; the parol evidence which is

734. *See* among a host of others, *Hamilton v. Kofi Mensah* (1937) 3 WACA 224; *Ogundalu v. Macjob* (2006) 7 NWLR (Pt. 978) 148.

735. *Onayemi v. Idowu* (2008) 9 NWLR (Pt. 1092) 306.

736. *International Textile Industries (Nig) Ltd v. Aderemi* (1999) 8 NWLR (Pt. 614) 268 at 297.

737. It is however enough if the act is such as to prove the existence of some contract and is consistent with the contract alleged.

738. *Mba-Ede v. Okufo* (1990) 2 NWLR (Pt. 135) 787, *Obijiako v. Offiah* (1995) 7 NWLR (Pt. 409) 510, *Biyo v. Aku* (1996) 1 NWLR (Pt. 422) 1 at 33–34, *Paye v. Gaji* (1996) 5 NWLR (Pt. 450) 589, *Adeniran v. Olagunju* (2001) 17 NWLR (Pt. 741) 169, *Onayemi v. Idowu* (2008) 9 NWLR (Pt. 1092) 306.

let in by the act of part performance must establish a finally concluded contract; and the act of part performance relied upon must have been done by the claimant and not by the defendant.[739]

394. A successful plea of acts of part performance entitles the party to the equitable remedy of specific performance. An order of specific performance made by the court would direct that the vendor execute a deed of assignment transferring title over the land to the purchaser.

The Contract of Sale

395. Sale of land is usually preceded by an agreement by the vendor to sell and the purchaser to buy. It details, apart from the essential particulars of sale, other terms and conditions of sale such as issues relating to the capacity in which the vendor is selling;[740] deposit and/or part payment payable;[741] whether vacant possession would be delivered and when; details of fixtures and fittings to be sold along;[742] issues pertaining to insurance; date of completion.

396. It is expected that the contract of sale be prepared by a solicitor (usually the vendor's solicitor) who prepares it in duplicate for the purpose of exchange. However both parties may be represented by the same solicitor. The contract of sale shall be executed by the vendor usually, and in some cases also by the purchaser where there are some terms and/or conditions to be fulfilled by the purchaser.

397. Where parties to the contract are represented by different solicitors, the contract of sale is not complete and there is no valid contract until there is an exchange of the same between the vendor's solicitor and the purchaser's solicitor.[743] But where both parties are represented by the same solicitor, no exchange is required.[744] Such contract attracts a stamp duty[745] and in the old eastern and western regions of Nigeria, it is registrable as an estate contract.[746] A contract of sale being an agreement to assign, it does not require consent under section 21 or 22 of the Land Use Act.[747]

739. *Ohiwerei v. Okosun* (2003) 11 NWLR (Pt. 832) 463.
740. For example, as a 'beneficial owner', 'mortgagee', 'trustee', 'personal representatives', etc.
741. Deposit is given as security for completion of the sale and unlike a part payment, may be forfeited.
742. It is advisable that the fixtures and fittings be conveyed together with the real property to obviate mandatory compliance with the provisions of the Bills of Sale Law: *See* Bills of Sale Act 1923 which incorporated the English Bills of Sale Act 1878 and 1882. Also, for purposes of stamping, it may not be advisable to include the cost of fixtures in the body of the contract; a separate receipt issued as acknowledgement of payment suffices.
743. *Eccles v. Bryant* (1948) Ch. 93.
744. *Smith v. Mansi* (1962) 2 All ER 857.
745. Schedule to the Stamp Duties Act Cap S8 LFN 2010.
746. *See* s. 2 Land Instruments Registration Law Cap 72 LEN 1963, and the Land Instruments Registration Law Cap 56 LWN 1959. In Lagos State, an agreement to sell may be protected by caution under the Lagos State Lands Registration Law No. 1 2015, s. 69(1).
747. *I.T.I v. Aderemi* (1999) 6 SC 1.

398. After exchange of contract, the vendor becomes a trustee of the legal estate for the purchaser.[748] The vendor has a duty to maintain the property as long as he retains possession of it,[749] and he will be liable to the purchaser for any wilful damage or neglect. In the case of leases, the vendor must perform the covenants in the lease before completion failure which the whole lease is rendered voidable, entitling the purchaser to rescission of the contract. Pending completion, the vendor may, subject to contract, retain possession of the property until payment of the purchase money. Consequently, he is entitled to a lien on the property as security for the unpaid purchase price or balance and, upon purchaser's default to complete, the vendor may charge interest on the balance of the purchase money. The vendor is entitled to rents and profits pending completion,[750] although he has a duty upon completion to account not only for the rents and profits realised, but also for what he should have received had he not allowed the property to lie fallow.

399. The purchaser, on the contrary, is a holder of an equitable interest which may be charged, assigned, or devised by Will, and may form the basis of an action in court for specific performance mandating the vendor to execute a deed of assignment in his favour. In the event of a sub-sale, the purchaser's contract becomes a vital document of title.

400. Except otherwise agreed by the parties to the contract, risk passes to the purchaser after exchange of contract subject to the vendor's duty of maintenance, and it is up to the purchaser to insure against risk of damage or destruction to the property. The death of either of the parties to the contract does not affect the rights and obligations of parties as these would pass to the personal representatives.

Investigation of Title

401. Investigation of title by the purchaser is germane to the acquisition of good title. Thus, the vendor is usually required to send to the purchaser's solicitor after exchange of contract, an abstract of vendor's title along with relevant documents not only to show an unbroken chain of the title deduced, but also to know how the vendor came about his title. The purchaser peruses the abstract against the backdrop of the accompanying documents and raises queries on any missing links or ambiguities in the abstract. The purchaser's solicitor then raises requisitions to be addressed by the vendor's solicitor usually within a specific period. In deducing title, the purchaser may rely on certain presumptions of law as to the existence of good title.[751] The vendor is expected to furnish answers to the requisitions within the time stipulated in the contract or within a reasonable time failing which the purchaser may rescind the contract.

748. *Wall v. Bright* 37 ER 456.

749. *Phillips v. Lamdin* (1949) 2 KB 33.

750. *Re Hamilton Snowball Conveyance* (1959) Ch. 308 at 312.

751. There is presumption of good title where vendor's root of title goes back to thirty years in the old western and mid-western Nigeria as well as other States with Property legislation: *See,* e.g., Property and Conveyancing Law Cap 100 LWN, s. 71(1) and forty years in other States: *See* Vendors and Purchasers Act 1874, s. 1.

402. A purchaser may, upon discovery of a defect in the vendor's title, rescind the contract before the completion date and collect his deposit or part payment back from the vendor with interest and other expenses incurred in investigating the title.[752]

The Assignment

403. Acquisition of interest in land by the purchaser in a sale requires that there must have been a valid sale in the sense that parties must have capacity[753] and must have agreed under a contract of sale to sell and to purchase respectively; the purchaser must have paid a purchase price with the vendor acknowledging receipt of same; there must be an execution of a deed of assignment[754] with the requisite consent,[755] and such deed of assignment must be duly stamped and registered.

404. A Power of Attorney is not a title document as it is not one that confers, transfers, limits, charges, or alienates any title to the donee, but a mere instrument of delegation.[756] Thus, the execution of a Power of Attorney by the vendor in favour of the purchaser does not assign title to the latter.[757]

405. Payment of purchase price accompanied by a valid deed of assignment executed in favour of the purchaser gives the latter a legal title, while receipt of payment coupled with possession by the purchaser gives the latter an equitable title.[758] However, a receipt simpliciter may be evidence of sale of property; it is not a document of title and cannot pass title from the assignor to the assignee.

406. Where under a sale agreement, only part payment is made by a purchaser who has been led into possession and the time fixed for payment of the balance has lapsed, or where time is not of essence but the vendor has demanded for the balance and the purchaser has refused to pay, the vendor may rescind the contract of sale and resell the property.

---

752. *Re Stone and Savile's contract* (1963) 1 All ER 353.
753. Capacity here means both legal capacity and capacity to convey. For legal capacity, natural persons must have attained age of majority which is twenty-one years in Nigeria; corporate bodies must have derived power from the objects as contained in the Memorandum of Association otherwise, transaction would be ultra vires; in the case of partnership, Trustees are expected to act; and in the case of administrators, power must be derived from the Administration of Estates Law or Administration of Real Estates Law as the case may be. Also vendor must have capacity to transfer.
754. A deed of assignment has replaced the old deed of Conveyance of freehold estates in Nigeria by virtue of the Land Use Act regime which allows holder of a right of occupancy a limited interest in the form of a term of years: *See* Cap L5 LFN 2010, s. 8.
755. *See* Cap L5 LFN 2010, ss 21 and 22.
756. *Ude v. Nwara supra* n. 279 and *Amadi v. Nsirim* (2004) 17 NWLR (Pt. 901) 111.
757. *Ibid.*
758. Such equitable title is good against third parties except a bona fide purchaser of the legal estate for value without notice of the equitable interest: *See Ogunbambi v. Abowaba supra* n. 356; *Okoye v. Dumez supra* n. 354.

Deed of Assignment

407. A deed of assignment is a document in writing signed by the grantor whereby a right of occupancy in land is assigned to another. A duly executed deed of assignment is sufficient evidence to support a transfer of title to the beneficiary of the deed of assignment.[759] It is a prima facie evidence of title to land.[760]

408. It is important that the assignor has a good title to the land sought to be sold[761] and must describe accurately in what capacity the assignment is done. However, where the assignor did not have title to the land at the time of the deed of assignment but subsequently obtains title, the title of the assignee will not be affected. This point was made by Ayoola, JCA (as he then was) in *Chinwuba v. Alade*,[762] that:

> Recitals in a deed are representations on the facts of which a stranger to the deed is entitled to act without enquiry. The concept of 'feeding the estoppel' may come into operation as a result of the recital, so that where the vendor purports to convey an estate which he does not have at the time, but he afterwards acquires it, that estate will immediately pass in effect to the purchaser without any further consequence.

409. Recitals in a deed of assignment twenty years old at the date of a contract are sufficient evidence of the truth of the facts stated therein, unless proved to be inadequate.[763] Facts clearly stated in recitals operate by way of estoppel against the party making it and his successors in title in favour of the other party and his successors.[764] A recital in a deed of assignment may assist in resolving the ambiguity in the operative part or in the covenants contained therein,[765] and may function to meet the end of statutory provisions.[766]

410. Where the assignor conveys as a beneficial owner, it is implied that he has the right to convey, the right of quiet enjoyment and freedom from encumbrances.[767] In an assignment of a leasehold interest, there is implied, in addition, a further covenant that the lease is valid and subsisting and that the rent and lessee's

---

759. *Idundun v. Okumagba* (1976) 1 NMLR 200, *Aliyu v. Sodipo* (1994) 5 NWLR (Pt. 340) 1 and *Olumide v. Ajayi* (1997) 8 NWLR (Pt. 517) 433.
760. *Fayemi v. Awe* (2009) 15 NWLR (Pt. 1164) 315.
761. Where the vendor has no title at the time of the assignment, the assignment conveys no title on the assignee as the rule is 'Nemo dat quod non habet'—no title can pass where there is none: *See Yusuf v. Eboda* (1994) 3 NWLR (Pt. 334) 568; *Olowo Ake v. Salawu* (2000) 11 NWLR (Pt. 677) 127.
762. (1997) 6 NWLR (Pt. 507) 85 at 97 C–D.
763. Evidence Act 2011, s. 162; *Johnson v. Lawanson* (1971) 1 All NLR 56.
764. *Poulton v. Moore* (1915) 1 KB 400.
765. *Jenner v. Jenner* (1864) LR 1 Eq. 361.
766. *See,* for example, s. 40(6) Administration of Estate Law LNN 1959, and Cap A3 Laws of Lagos State 2003.
767. *See* s. 100 Property and Conveyancing Law Cap 100 LWN 1959 (2nd Schedule); s. 74(2) Cap 100 Laws of Akwa Ibom State 2000, Cap 122 Laws of Bauchi State 2006, Cap P10 Laws of Kwara

covenants have been performed to date. In an assignment as a trustee, personal representative or mortgagee, the only covenant implied is that the assignor has not himself encumbered the land.[768]

411. Where the area of land conveyed in a conveyance is shown in a survey plan attached to the deed of assignment, it cannot be said that the land is not defined.[769] Where there is a defect in a survey plan attached to a deed of conveyance, this does not affect the authenticity of the deed of conveyance.[770] Also, an error in date on which a deed of conveyance was executed is not necessarily material.[771]

412. The signature of the purchaser of a grant by deed under seal is superfluous. The execution by the vendor in the presence of a witness is sufficient in law.[772] However, a document that is not signed, stamped, or registered cannot operate as a valid deed of assignment.[773]

Delivery of a Deed of Assignment

413. A deed is effective only when it is delivered as the act and deed of the party expressed to be bound by it, as well as sealed. No special form of observance is necessary for the delivery of a deed. It may be either by words or by conduct. What is essential to the delivery of the document as a deed is that the party whose deed the document is expressed to be shall by words or conduct expressly or impliedly acknowledge his intention to be immediately and unconditionally bound by the provisions contained in it.[774] In *Anambra State Housing Development Corp v. Emekwue*,[775] Ogundare JSC explained the law thus:[776]

> It is the law that to be effective a deed must be delivered as the act and deed of the party expressed to be bound by it and the deed takes effect from the date of delivery which may, or may not be the date expressed on the instrument … Delivery does not take a special form or observance; what is essential is the intention of the parties, particularly the party whose deed the document is expressed to be which intention may be expressed in words or by conduct.

State 2007; s. 76(2) Cap 110 Laws of Abia State 2005, Cap 114 Laws of Sokoto State 1996 and corresponding provisions in the laws of other States.

768. *Ibid.*
769. *Famuroti v. Agbeke* (1991) 5 NWLR (Pt. 189) 1.
770. *Lanlehin v. James* (1986) 2 NWLR (Pt. 6) 262, *Obaro v. Rivers State Housing and Property Development Authority* (1997) 9 NWLR (Pt. 521) 425, and *Ejimele v. Opara* (1998) 9 NWLR (Pt. 567) 587.
771. *Jegede v. Citicon Nigeria Ltd* (2001) 4 NWLR (Pt. 702) 112.
772. *Nnadi v. Okoro* (1998) 1 NWLR (Pt. 535) 573.
773. *Arin v. Chaka* (2001) 14 NWLR (Pt. 734) 612.
774. *Awojugbagbe Light Industries Ltd v. Chinukwe supra* n. 382, *Jegede v. Citicon Nigeria Ltd supra* n. 771; *First Bank of Nigeria Plc v. Sangonuga* (2007) 3 NWLR (Pt. 1021) 230; *Brossette Manufacturing Nig. Ltd v. Messrs Ola Ilemobola Ltd* (2007) 14 NWLR (Pt. 1053) 109.
775. (1996) 1 NWLR (Pt. 426) 505.
776. *Ibid.*, at 539–540 H-C.

414. There are two kinds of delivery recognised by law: absolute and conditional. If a document is delivered either to a party to it or to a stranger with an intimation, express or implied, that it is not to become effective until some condition has been performed, it is called an escrow. In such a case, the deed is inoperative until the condition is performed, but upon performance it takes effect as a deed without further delivery, and relates back to the time when it was delivered as an escrow. A delivery of a deed as an escrow is a final delivery in the sense that it cannot be withdrawn by the grantor before the grantee has had an opportunity to decide whether to fulfil the condition or not. A deed delivered subject to such a right of withdrawal is not an escrow, but merely an undelivered deed.[777]

Perfection

415. The law requires that consent of the Governor be sought and obtained to a deed of assignment[778] otherwise, the instrument is void and the transfer to the purchaser, ineffectual.[779] It must also be stamped[780] and registered.[781] An unregistered document loses priority to a subsequent registered instrument on the same land[782] and is inadmissible in evidence in court as a title document[783] although, it may be evidence of payment of purchase price in a sale transaction and where purchaser takes possession, an equitable interest accrues in favour of the purchaser.[784]

Setting Aside a Deed of Assignment or Declaring It Void

416. A court can set aside a voidable sale of land or a deed of assignment[785]and generally, only a party to a deed of conveyance or deed of lease can apply to the court to have it set aside or cancelled; a stranger to a deed cannot do so,[786] except

777. A common example of delivery as an escrow occurs when a vendor executes a deed of conveyance and gives it to his solicitor for transference to the purchaser upon payment by the latter of the purchase money.
778. Land Use Act 1978 Cap L5 LFN 2010, s. 22.
779. *Ibid.*, s. 26.
780. *See* the Stamp Duties Act Cap S8 LFN 2010, s. 23(3).
781. A deed of assignment is a registrable instrument as it is an instrument 'affecting land whereby one party confers, transfers, limits or charges in favour of another party any right or title to or interest in land': *See,* for example, s. 2 Land Registration Act No. 36 1924 applicable in the Federal Capital Territory Abuja, with corresponding provisions in the Registration Laws of other States. Section 2 of the Lagos State Lands Registration Law No. 1 2015 makes 'every document of interest or title to land in Lagos State' a registrable instrument which shall be registered. Registration must be done within six months, otherwise it is void.
782. *See* s. 16(1) Land Registration Act Cap 515 LFN 2004; s. 29(1) Law No. 1 of Lagos State 2015 and corresponding provisions in the Registration Laws of other States. *See also Amankra v. Zankley* (1963) 1 All NLR 304.
783. *See* s. 15 Land Registration Act No. 36 1924; s. 30 Law No. 1 of Lagos State 2015. *See also Ojugbele v. Olasoji* (1982) 4 SC. 310. Such unregistered instrument cannot be pleaded and where it is, the court shall strike out the affected paragraph(s) in the Pleadings.
784. *Okoye v. Dumez supra* n. 354; *Onagoruwa v. Akinremi* (2001) 12 NWLR (721) 38 at 56, 63.
785. *Sanusi v. s Daniel* (1956) SCNLR 288, *Ekpendu v. Erika* (1959) SCNLR 186 and *Salako v. Dosunmu* (1997) 8 NWLR (Pt. 517) 371.
786. *Foko v. Foko* (1968) NMLR 441 at 445–446, *Ordor v. Nwosu* (1974) 1 All NLR (Pt. 2) 478, *Omoyinmi v. Olaniyan* (2000) 4 NWLR (Pt. 651) 38, *Savannah Bank Plc v. Ibrahim* (2000) 6 NWLR (Pt. 662) 585, *Onwuchekwa v. Nigeria Deposit Insurance Corporation* (2002) 5 NWLR (Pt. 760) 371

where a member of a family applies to set aside a deed relating to sale of family land made without the consent of the principal members, or where a person has acquired some legal interest such as an assignment of any right under the deed.[787]

417. Where a deed is a nullity, it can be challenged in court by any person affected by it, even a stranger to the deed, asking for a declaration that the deed is a nullity. In such cases, the court will declare it as such but not set it aside as there is nothing to set aside. In *Shobajo v. Ikotun*,[788] Aderemi, JCA (as he then was) said:[789]

> The law is now well settled that where a plaintiff seeks that transaction or an instrument be declared void, and that it should be set aside, it will only be declared void, if it is found to be void and it will not be set aside because there is nothing to set aside. Indeed it is inappropriate to set aside what is void for ex nihilo nihil venit – if at the end of trial it is found that the transaction complained of is void, a declaration to that effect might issue but it is absolutely wrong thereafter to make an order setting it aside.

Rectification of a Deed of Assignment

418. The courts have jurisdiction to rectify instruments including a deed of assignments where it is established that there was a mutual mistake in reducing the agreement of parties on the sale of land into the deed of assignment. Rectification of written documents is about correcting mistakes in recording what the maker or makers of the document had recorded.

419. The object of rectification is to bring a document, which was intended to give effect to a prior agreement into harmony with that prior agreement. For rectification to receive consideration, the antecedent agreement must be clear and unequivocal and must have continued unchanged until the execution of the final document. Thus, where a relief of rectification is sought in court, it must be proved that the final document did not carry out the parties earlier and unchanged agreement[790] in the sense that a mistake, whether of fact or law, had been made in recording the parties' intention, and that the alleged intention to which it is desired to make the agreement conformable continued concurrently in the parties' minds down to the time of execution of the instrument.[791]

---

at 391, *Adegbaye v. sIshola* (2003) 11 NWLR (Pt. 831) 343, *Nangibo v. Okafor* (2003) 14 NWLR (Pt. 839) 78, *Shobajo v. Ikotun* (2003) 14 NWLR (Pt. 840) 237.

787. *Alfotrin Ltd v. Attorney General of the Federation* (1996) 9 NWLR (Pt. 475) 634 and *Cooperative and Commerce Bank Ltd v. Nwokocha* (1998) 9 NWLR (Pt. 564) 98.
788. (2003) 14 NWLR (Pt. 840) 237.
789. *Ibid.*, at 258 paras E–F.
790. *The Vessel 'Leona II' v. First Fuels Ltd* (2002) 18 NWLR (Pt. 799) 439.
791. *Basil v. Fajebe* (2001) 11 NWLR (Pt. 725) 592, *Irawo v. Adedokun* (2005) 1 NWLR (Pt. 906) 199.

420. Since the objective of the party seeking rectification is to make the document accurately define the rights and obligations of person who claims rights or are subject to obligations under it, a person who can neither claim rights under a written document nor be subjected to an obligation under it is a stranger and cannot therefore seek to rectify the document.

421. The competence of a party to seek rectification of a deed of assignment must be determined within the privity rule and not on the basis of a benefit that a stranger may derive from the contract. This is because as a general rule, a contract cannot confer rights or impose obligations on any person except the parties to it or, as an exception to the general rule, a person on whom such parties confer a benefit who is to be distinguished from a person who may benefit from a contract. That a person may benefit from the performance of a contract does not alone give him a right to enforce the contract.[792]

422. Since equity rectifies instruments and not contracts, a document which accurately records a prior agreement or the intention of the maker cannot be rectified merely because the intention was formed in error or because the maker had no authority to enter into the agreement in the first place.[793]

Cancellation of a Deed of Assignment

423. A party who alleges that the deed of assignment is tainted with fraud, mistake, misrepresentation, or undue influence may ask the court for cancellation of the instrument. A deed of assignment may be lawfully cancelled either by the person who has it in his possession as being solely entitled under it, or by anyone to whom the person has delivered it up to be cancelled, or by mutual consent, or under the terms of agreement between the parties or by an order of court. The cancellation of a deed is accomplished by obliterating or removing the seal or otherwise altering or defacing it with intent that it shall become void.

424. When a deed is cancelled it becomes void and no action can thereafter be maintained on any covenant or promise contained in it. However, the cancellation has no retrospective operation, as it does not make the deed void ab initio and if the deed operated as an assignment of any property, its cancellation does not have the effect of revesting or reconveying the estate or interest which was so assured.[794]

425. Cancellation of a deed of assignment can only be at the instance of the parties to the deed or of persons claiming through or under them but not at the instance of third parties.[795] Thus, the appropriate relief in the case of a third party in relation

792. *Ibid.*
793. *The Vessel 'Leona II' v. First Fuels Ltd* (2002) 18 NWLR (Pt. 799) 439.
794. *Nnubia v. Attorney General, Rivers State* (1999) 3 NWLR (Pt. 593) 82 and *Ajagungbade III v. Adeyelu II* (2001) 16 NWLR (Pt. 738) 126 at 192–193.
795. *Foko v. Foko* (1968) NMLR 441, *Agbo v. Nwokolo* (1975) 5 ESCLR 300, *Adegbayi v. Ishola* (2003) 11 NWLR (Pt. 831) 343, *Nangibo v. Okafor* (2003) 14 NWLR (Pt. 839) 78, *Shobajo v. Ikotun supra* n. 786, *Ironbar v. Federal Mortgage Finance* (2009) 15 NWLR (Pt. 1165) 506.

to the execution of deed of assignment by which one party purported to convey claimant's land to a second party is not by way of equitable relief of cancellation of the deed but by a declaration of title or where there had been trespass, an action for damages.[796]

§2. SALE OF GOODS

I. Contract of Sale of Goods

426. A contract of sale of goods is a contract whereby the seller transfers or agrees to transfer the property in the goods to the buyer for a price.[797] It may be absolute or conditional.[798] A transfer of property in the goods from the seller to the buyer is a sale; but where the property in the goods is to take place at a future date or subject to some condition thereafter to be fulfilled, the contract is an agreement to sell.[799] An agreement to sell becomes a sale when time elapses or the conditions are fulfilled subject to which the property in the goods is to be transferred.[800]

II. Transfer of Property in the Goods

427. The purpose of a contract for sale of goods is to transfer the property in those goods from the seller to the buyer.[801] 'Property' in this context means an absolute interest in the goods and an interest is absolute when the seller agrees to divest himself of all the interest in the goods.[802] But this is not without some qualifications: first, it is possible to sell a part ownership interest in goods, that is, an undivided share.[803] Second, it is possible to specify in a contract of sale of goods that the seller will transfer only that title which he has. Further, a seller may sell goods to a buyer and pass property when someone else has the immediate right to possession. However, the seller must purport to transfer an ownership interest rather than a lesser interest. Thus, the transfer of the interest of a lessee is not a sale.

428. Property in the Sale of Goods Act means legal ownership as opposed to equitable ownership. It follows therefore that where there is a contract for the sale of goods but legal ownership has not passed, the doctrine that equitable ownership

796. *Chief Sam Esi v. Itsekiri Communal Land Trustees* (1961) WNLR 15, *Adegbayi v. Ishola supra* n. 795, *Shobajo v. Ikotun supra* n. 786.
797. *See* s. 1(1) Sale of Goods Act 1893 replicated in the various State Laws in Nigeria as Sale of Goods Law. There may be a contract of sale.
798. *Ibid.*, s. 1(2).
799. *Ibid.*, s. 1(3).
800. *Ibid.*, s. 1(4).
801. *See Rowland v. Divall* (1923) 2 KB 500. An exception to this provision is where parties agreed expressly or impliedly in the contract of sale that the seller shall only transfer such rights as he or a third person may have: *See* s. 12(3) of the Act.
802. Bridge, M. et al., citing Battersby, G., *A Consideration of 'Property' and 'Title' in the Sale of Goods Act* 1 JBL (2001).
803. *Ibid.*, s. 2(2).

passes when the contract is made if the contract is one which is specifically enforceable, will not apply. Also, there are clear judicial statements that the doctrine of equitable lien does not apply to contracts for the sale of goods.[804]

III. Time at Which Property Passes

429. In the case of sale of specific or ascertained goods, property in the goods passes at the time intended by the parties.[805] In the absence of parties' intention in this regard, regard is to be had to the terms of the contract, the conduct of the parties, and the circumstances of the case.[806]

430. Section 18 of the Sale of Goods Act contains presumptions of law for the passing of property in goods in the absence of any express term to the contrary. Where there is a contract for the sale of specific goods in a deliverable state, property passes when the contract is made; it is immaterial whether the time of payment or delivery is postponed.[807] In the case of contract for the sale of specific goods and the seller is bound to do something to the goods for the purpose of putting them in a deliverable state, property does not pass until the thing is done and the buyer has notice that it has been done.[808]Where there is a contract for the sale of goods in a deliverable state, but the seller has to weigh, measure, test or do some other act or thing with reference to the goods for the purpose of ascertaining the price, property does not pass until the act or thing is done and the buyer has notice that it has been done.[809] Property in the goods delivered to the buyer on approval or on sale or return or other similar terms will pass to the buyer when he signifies his approval or acceptance to the seller, or does any other act adopting the transaction; if he does not signify his approval or acceptance to the seller, but retains the goods without giving notice of rejection, then, if a time has been fixed for the return of the goods, on the expiration of that time, and if no time is fixed, on the expiration of a reasonable time.[810] In the case of contract for the sale of unascertained or future goods by description and in a deliverable state unconditionally appropriated to the contract either by the seller with the assent of the buyer or by the buyer with the assent of the seller, the property in the goods passes to the buyer; and the assent may be express or implied, and may be given either before or after the appropriation is made.[811]

431. In all these cases, the presumption may be rebutted by a contrary intention of the parties who may intend that property passes either before or after the time stipulated by the rules.

---

804. *Re Stapylton Fletcher Ltd* (1994) 1 WLR 1181.
805. Sale of Goods Act 1893; s. 17(1).
806. *Ibid.*, s. 17(2).
807. *Ibid.*, Rule 1.
808. *Ibid.*, Rule 2.
809. *Ibid.*, Rule 3.
810. *Ibid.*, Rule 4.
811. *Ibid.*, Rule 5.

IV. Effects of Passing of Property

In Insolvency Proceedings

432. Where property passes to the non-insolvent party before commencement of insolvency proceedings, those goods do not form part of the insolvent party's assets and are not available for distribution to unsecured creditors.[812] Where a non-performing party becomes insolvent, the performing party who does not have property in the goods only has the right to prove in the non-performing party's liquidation for the entire loss of performance.[813] An unpaid seller is protected against the insolvency of the buyer by the unpaid seller's lien and the right of stoppage in transit.[814] If neither party has performed under the contract, then the potential loss on the insolvency of one party is merely the loss of potential profit.[815]

Transfer of Title by the Buyer

433. If property has not passed to a buyer, he cannot transfer good title to another person in any other transaction, whether that transaction is a sale, a gift, or a security interest unless one of the exceptions to the nemo dat rule applies.[816]

Remedies Between Buyer and Seller

434. If property in the goods has passed to the buyer, this may give him an immediate right of possession to them and enable him to bring an action against the seller for delivery up on the grounds of wrongful interference with the goods or for damages for conversion.[817] If property has not passed to the buyer, the seller may, in addition to any contractual right to retake possession, be able to obtain possession of the goods either by retaking or by bringing an action for wrongful interference with the goods.[818]

Other Contractual Implications

435. Risk passes with property,[819] and whoever owns the goods bears the risk of any damage to them as a natural incidence of ownership. Also, a seller cannot sue for the price of the goods unless property has passed. Once the property passes, the seller has fulfilled his obligation and contract cannot therefore be frustrated.

---

812. Bridge, M. et al. *supra* n. 692 at 265 para. 10-017.
813. *Ibid.*, at 266 para. 10-017.
814. *Ibid.*
815. *Ibid.*
816. Bridge, M. et al. *supra* n. 692 at 266 para. 10-018.
817. *Ibid.*
818. *Ibid.*, 266–267 paras 10-019–10-020.
819. *See* Sale of Goods Act, s. 20.

V. Retention of Title

436. The protection afforded the unpaid seller by law where the goods have not been delivered even though property has passed to the buyer is non-existent where the goods have been delivered in which case, the seller should, if he wants protection, bargain for it. The incorporation of the retention of title clause in the contract of sale gives the seller the opportunity of retaining title in the goods until the buyer pays for them. The effect of this is that if the buyer becomes insolvent before payment and/or defaults in payment, the contract is terminated and the seller, as owner, may repossess the goods. Because the retention of title survives the buyer's insolvency, the seller is in a vantage position since he has an ownership right that cannot lose priority to any other secured creditor or the buyer. Since property in the goods remains in the seller or lessor, the seller or lessor gets priority over all equitable interests created, or purported to be created over the goods by the buyer or lessee.

§3. Assignment of Choses in Action

I. Transfer of Proprietary Interest in Choses in Action

437. Perfection of transfer of proprietary interest in choses in action, unlike choses in possession, is by assignment of the legal or equitable chose in action rather than by transfer of property coupled with delivery. The assignment may be by way of legal or equitable assignment. A chose may be legal or equitable. It is a legal one if right to its enforcement is by an action in law prior to the Judicature Act 1873, for example, debts[820]and benefit under a contract.[821] It is equitable if it is a right which owe its existence to a matter which before the Judicature Act 1873 would only be recognised and enforced by the court of Chancery, for example, the interest and rights of a beneficiary in a trust fund, interest under a legacy, partner's beneficial rights, and reversionary interest under a Will. It is a future chose in action where the right it confers would only be acquired at a future date, for example, the beneficial interest and rights under a Will during the lifetime of a testator.

Legal Assignment

438. Any debt or legal thing in action may be assigned at law. This is provided for by statute in Nigeria.[822] The legal assignment has been judicially construed as extending to equitable as well as legal choses. A statutory assignment of legal or equitable chose in action takes effect as a valid assignment in law when it is an absolute assignment in writing with a written notice given to the debtor or trustee.[823] Any assignment which fails to comply with these requirements takes effect only as an equitable assignment.

820. *SeeWestern Finance Corporation v. West Coast Builders* (1971) 1 UILR 93.
821. *Lawal v. Union Bank Ltd* (1995) 2 NWLR (Pt. 378) 407.
822. Judicature Act 1873; s. 25(6); Property and Conveyancing Law Cap 100 LWN. 1959; s. 150.
823. *Ibid.*

439. An absolute assignment is that which assigns the totality of the interest of the assignor to the assignee; an assignment of a part, even if definite, is insufficient.[824] The format of the agreement in writing is irrelevant provided that the content show clearly that all the interests of the assignor are being assigned.[825] The law does not require any particular form of notice of assignment; a simple express notice in writing will suffice.[826]

440. An effective legal assignment in compliance with statutory requirements constitutes the assignee owner of the chose at law, and he may sue the debtor without making the assignor a party to the action and without furnishing consideration for the assignment.

Equitable Assignment

441. An assignment which does not comply with one or more statutory requirements takes effect as an equitable assignment. An equitable assignment does not require any particular form, and, except where the interest assigned is a beneficial interest in a trust,[827] it need not be in writing. It may be addressed to the assignee or to the debtor and where it is made to the latter, it suffices that it is made in a plain language to show 'that the debt has been made over by the creditor to some third person'.[828] The assignment must identify the chose which is being assigned[829] and must be communicated to the assignee. As a general rule, consideration is not required for a valid equitable assignment of a legal or an equitable chose, provided the assignor has done everything required by him to be done to transfer the chose. However, consideration is required in the case of an assignment of an expectancy such as a legacy hoped for under a Will of a living person, or where the assignment is not absolute, but by way of charge only. Notice to the debtor or trustee may not be necessary provided there is a complete and binding equitable assignment between the assignor and assignee. But notice to the debtor or trustee may be desirable to prevent the debtor or trustee from paying the original creditor or beneficiary (i.e., the assignor);[830] or to prevent the trustee from setting up against the assignee any new and independent equities which may arise between the debtor and the assignor; or to preserve priority over subsequent assignees.[831]

824. *Western Nigeria Finance Corporation v. West Coast Builders* (1971) 1 UILR, 93; *Accra Perfumery Co. Ltd v. Thomas* (1947). 12 WACA 160.
825. *Udakason Enterprises Ltd v. Olisa* (1972) ECSLR 71.
826. *Ibid.*
827. This is an equitable interest within s. 9 of the Statute of Frauds 1677 or s. 78(1) of the Property and Conveyancing Law, to which the requirement of writing applies.
828. *Thomas v. Harris* (1947) 1 All ER 444.
829. *Brice v. Bannister* (1878) 3 QBD 569.
830. *Stocks v. Dobson* 43 ER 411.
831. If the chose assigned is equitable, it is governed by the rule in *Dearle v. Hall* 38 ER 475, and same applies to an equitable assignment of a legal chose: *See Marchant v. Morton Down & Co.* (1901) 2 KB 829.

442. An equitable assignee of an equitable chose, may sue the debtor in his own name without joining the assignor, provided the assignment is of the whole interest.[832] Where the chose assigned is legal (e.g., a debt), the assignor should be joined whether the assignment is of full or part of the debt.[833]

II. Rules of Priority in Successive Equitable Assignments

443. Successive equitable assignments of an existing equitable interest in choses in action rank, as between the assignees, according to the order in which the notice of the assignments is given to the trustees or other persons responsible for the distribution of the property, and not according to the order in which the assignments were made. This is the rule in *Dearle v. Hall.*[834] However, an assignee who had notice (actual, constructive, or imputed) of a previous assignment when his own was made, cannot obtain priority over the previous assignment by being the first to give notice.[835] The notice need not be formal, but must be clear and unambiguous, and should be given to all the trustees.

III. Assignment and Equities

444. A legal or equitable assignment of choses in action is subject to equities such as right of set-off and other defences such as fraud, that the debtor or trustee could have raised against the assignor, since the assignee cannot be in a better position than the assignor was.[836] But equities arising after notice of assignment have been given to the debtor or trustee do not affect the assignee.[837]

IV. Unassignable Choses

445. Certain choses such as salary of a public officer or public servant, alimony or maintenance granted to a spouse by the court, and assignments savouring of maintenance or champerty, cannot be assigned on grounds of public policy.[838] So also, is the right to sue on a contract of a personal or fiduciary nature,[839] except it

832. In the case of an assignment of a part of the interest of the assignor or by way of charge on the trust fund, the assignor still has some interest in him, and will have to be joined.
833. *Accra Perfumery Co. Ltd v. Thomas* (1947) 12 WACA 160; *Laibru Ltd v. B & C.E Contractors* (1962) 1 ALL NLR 387.
834. 38 ER 475.
835. *Re Holmes* (1885) 29 Ch.D 786. Where he acquires notice after his own assignment was made, his knowledge will not bar him from gaining priority by giving notice first.
836. Kodilinye *supra* n. 160 at 175, 53–54 citing *Roxburghe v. Cox* (1881) 17 Ch.D 520.
837. *Ibid.*
838. *Ibid.*, at 55.
839. *Ibid.*, at 55.

would make no difference to a third party in which of two persons he is to discharge his obligations.[840]

840. *Ibid.*, at 56.

Chapter 2. Transfer of Property by Death: Acquisition of Land by Inheritance

446. Acquisition of land by inheritance is very prominent in Nigeria where preservation of property for the enjoyment of generations yet unborn is a way of life. Persons entitled to inheritance and the quantum of such inheritance depends on the law applicable to the estate of the praepositus, subject to the Land Use Act 1978,[841] the provisions of the Constitution of the Federal Republic of Nigeria, 1999 as amended and the applicable international instruments as domesticated.

§1. Intestate Inheritance

I. Inheritance under Customary Law

447. The position under Nigerian customary law is that the property of an intestate devolves upon his heirs who acquire title thereto. This position is supported by the provision of section 24(b) of the Land Use Act which provides that the devolution of a right of occupancy upon the death shall, in the case of statutory right of occupancy, be regulated by the customary law of the deceased occupier at the time of his death relating to the distribution unless non-customary law or other customary law applied.[842] Succession to the property of a person who died intestate is determined neither by the place of burial of the deceased intestate, nor by a life policy made inter vivos,[843] but by the customary law of the deceased. The principles that determine who constitute heir of a deceased's intestate and what they inherit from his property vary under a different customary law.

Yoruba Customary Law

448. Under Yoruba customary law, the property of a deceased Yoruba person who died intestate devolves on all his children both male and female in equal shares to the exclusion of other relations.[844] But where the deceased died without an issue but with surviving parents, the property devolves on them, and in the absence of the parents, to the brothers and sisters.[845]

449. Where a man died without an issue leaving inherited property behind, the property will devolve on the members of the family from which he came.[846] The grandchildren of a deceased succeed to such rights as their immediate parents had in the family property.[847] There are two methods of distributing the estate of a man who died intestate under Yoruba customary law namely: the Idi-Igi (per stripes)

841. Cap L5 LFN 2010.
842. *Umaru v. Pam* (2010) 2 NWLR (Pt. 1178) 404.
843. *Obusez v. Obusez* (2007) 10 NWLR (Pt. 1043) 430 at 451 paras F–H.
844. *Dawodu v. Danmole* (1958) 3 FSC 46.
845. *Amusan v. Olawunmi* (2002) 12 NWLR (Pt. 780) 30.
846. *Idowu v. Hausa* 13 NLR 96; *Suberu v. Sunmonu* (1957) SCNLR 45.
847. *Lewis v. Bankole* (1909) 1 NLR 82; *Falomo v. Onakanmi* (2005) 11 NWLR (Pt. 935) 126.

method i.e., distributing the estate according to the number of wives the deceased had; and the Ori Ojori (per capita) method i.e., sharing the property equally among the children.[848]

Benin Customary Law

450. Benin customary law recognises the right of the eldest son to the house where the deceased lived and died, which he inherits as the 'Igiogbe' to the exclusion of the other children. The right of the eldest son to inherit the 'Igiogbe' is subject to the performance of the final burial rights by the eldest son.[849] A Bini man can have only one 'Igiogbe' which must be situated in the Benin Kingdom and must have legally belonged to the deceased.[850] If the deceased is a Benin woman, the house in which she lived and died cannot constitute an 'Igiogbe' and such property will be shared among others, among her children in order of seniority. Upon the death of the eldest son, his own eldest son inherits the 'Igiogbe' after performing the final burial rights of his father. However, where the eldest son failed to perform the final burial rights, he does not inherit the 'Igiogbe' but holds it along with other properties in trust for the other beneficiaries. Where the deceased has other properties, they are distributed according to the number of wives in order of seniority with the male child taking precedence in each stripe.

Ibo Customary Law

451. In many Ibo communities where the family grouping is patrilineal, an intestate's heir is his paternal next of kin. In consonance with the rule of premogeniture, on the death of the father, the eldest son inherits his residence to the exclusion of other children. The residence of a wife is inherited by her eldest son to the exclusion of all other children, subject to the wife's right of residence during her widowhood. While the right of the eldest son to the residence of the deceased intestate is sacrosanct, he cannot deal in the property in a way prejudicial to possessory rights of other family members in occupation.

452. Other properties are held in trust by the eldest son for himself and other sons of the deceased. The custom of Ibo communities generally do not allow female members of the family to inherit property, and where a landowner dies leaving no male issue, the property passes to his brothers or other male paternal next of kin. Also, a widow cannot inherit the property of the husband though both the widow and the daughter have their right of residence with the consent of the family. This rule of custom was endorsed by the Supreme Court in *Nezianya v. Okagbue*.[851]

848. *Obidairo v. Bakare* (2005) All FWLR (Pt. 256) 1382; *Vincent v. Vincent* (2008) 11 NWLR (Pt. 1097) 35.
849. *Ogiamen v. Ogiamen* (1967) NSCC 189; *Oke v. Oke* (1974) NMLR 356; *Arase v. Arase* (1981) 5SC 33; *Idehen v. Idehen* (1991) 6 NWLR (Pt. 198) 382.
850. *Ibrahim v. Osunde* (2009) 6 NWLR (Pt. 1137) 382.
851. (1963) 1 All NLR 352.

However, a number of Court of Appeal decisions[852] frown on this custom and considered same unenforceable on the grounds of repugnancy to natural justice, equity, and good conscience; violation of section 42(1) and (2) of the Constitution of the Federal Republic of Nigeria, 1999 as amended which prohibits discriminatory practices against citizens of Nigeria by reason of his place of origin, sex, religion, or political opinion; violation of section 43 of the Constitution which guarantee the right of every citizen to acquire and own immovable property; and non-conformity with the provisions of the African Charter on Human and Peoples' Rights. This position of the Court of Appeal has recently been endorsed by the Supreme Court[853] which has now put to rest many years of controversy on the validity of the Ibo custom which prohibits female children from inheriting property. Such custom has now been proclaimed invalid.

II. Islamic Law of Inheritance

453. The question whether Islamic law applies to the determination of the rights of succession to and inheritance of a deceased estate as opposed to customary law is not merely whether the deceased praepositus was a Muslim or not; in addition to the acceptance of Islamic faith, the deceased must have lived his life and conducted his affairs in accordance with Islamic injunctions.[854] The intestate must also have evinced the intention to be bound by Islamic law otherwise, customary law applies.[855]

454. Although there exists different schools of thought on the content of Islamic law relating to inheritance,[856] the Maliki School of Islamic law applies in Nigeria.[857]

455. There are three categories of heirs recognised by the Maliki School[858] namely, sharers at law, residuaries, and distant kindred; each category is entitled to succeed as heir to the estate of the deceased in order of priority.[859] Where a person dies, his heirs are permitted by law to appoint a person learned in Islamic law to share his estate among them according to Islamic law in accordance with the prescribed sharing formula, and where a court is called upon to determine the appropriate sharing formula, the judge is expected to take cognisance of the opinion of learned expert. Details of the order of sharing are beyond the scope of this monograph and may be sought elsewhere.[860]

---

852. *Udensi v. Mogbo* (1976) 6 ECSLR 354; *Mojekwu v. Mojekwu* (1997) 7 NWLR (Pt. 512) 283; *Muojekwu v. Ejikeme* (2000) 5 NWLR (Pt. 657) 402 at 423–424.
853. *See Ukeje v. Ukeje* (2014) All FWLR (Pt. 730) 1323.
854. *Mariyama v. Sadiku Ejo* (1961) NLR 81; *Asiata v. Goncallo* (1900) 1 NLR 41.
855. *Re Alayo* (1946) 18 NLR 88.
856. They include the Hanafis, the Malikis, the Shafis, the Zahiris, and the Shias.
857. *Zaidhan v. Mohssen* (1973) NSCC 516.
858. Nasir J., *The Islamic Law of Personal Status* 205 (Graham and Totnam 1986).
859. *Supra* n. 855.
860. *See* Smith, I.O. *supra* n. 244at 590–594.

III. Inheritance Consequent upon Marriage under the Marriage Act

456. Where the deceased intestate contracted a marriage under the Marriage Act, any property which the intestate might have disposed by Will shall be distributed in accordance with the provisions of the Administration of Estates Law in the States where the law exists,[861] or otherwise, in accordance with the provisions of the Marriage Act,[862] notwithstanding any customary law or Islamic law to the contrary.[863]

457. Both the Administration of Estates Law and the Marriage Act recognise as heirs, the widow or husband of the deceased along with all the children of the deceased irrespective of their sex. However, while the Administration of Estates Law recognises children born within and outside wedlock so long as the deceased acknowledge their paternity in his lifetime,[864] the Marriage Act recognises only children born within wedlock and excludes children born out of wedlock from inheritance.[865]

§2. Inheritance under a Will

458. A Will may devise real (or personal) property to a named beneficiary which may vest in the said beneficiary using a deed of assent. There are however limitations to the testator's freedom of disposition under a Will in Nigeria. First, the freedom of disposition does not apply to any property which the testator had no power to dispose of by Will[866] or otherwise, under customary[867] or Islamic law[868] to which he was subject. Second, where a testator is survived by a wife or husband, a child, parent, brother or sister who, immediately before the death of the deceased was being maintained either wholly or partly by the deceased, that person may apply to court within six months from the grant of probate, for an order that reasonable provision be made for the applicant.[869]

---

861. The main objective of the Administration of Estates Law is to vest real and personal properties of a deceased intestate in his personal representatives for management and administration under the authority of the letters of administration and where necessary, transfer by way of assignment or deed of assent to the person entitled to inherit it.
862. Cap M6 LFN 2010.
863. *Agbogu v. Agbogu* (1995) 1 NWLR (Pt. 372) 411.
864. *Salubi v. Nwariaku* (2003) 7 NWLR (Pt. 819) 426.
865. It would however appear that the exclusion is unconstitutional in view of the provision of s. 42(1)(2) of the Constitution of the Federal Republic of Nigeria 1999 as amended.
866. An example is family property allocated to a member: *See Akeju v. Suenu* (1956) 6 NLR 87.
867. For example, the provision of a Will on disposition of the house in which the testator lived and died—the 'Igiogbe', cannot supersede the Benin customary law which makes the first son entitled to it: *See Idehen v. Idehen* (1991) 6 NWLR (Pt. 198) 382 at 411 paras E–F. *See also* proviso to s. 1(1) of the Wills Law Cap W2 Laws of Lagos State 2003 and corresponding provisions in the Wills Law of many Southern States of Nigeria.
868. *See* s. 3(2)(b) Cap 144 Laws of Taraba State of Nigeria and corresponding provision in the laws of other Northern States of Nigeria.
869. *See,* e.g., s. 4(1) of the Wills Law Cap 170 Laws of Oyo State 2000, Cap 168 Laws of Bauchi State 1991; s. 2(1) Cap 141 Laws of Rivers State 2002 and corresponding provisions of the Wills Law of other States. For what amounts to 'reasonable financial provision', *see* subs. (2) of the Laws referred to.

459. A beneficiary under a Will cannot benefit there from unless the Will complies with the requirements of formal validity as prescribed by the various Wills Law of the various States in Nigeria.[870] In effect, the Will has to be in writing; signed by the testator (or in his name, or by another person in his presence); in the presence of at least two witnesses present at the same time attesting and subscribing the Will in the presence of the testator. Also, the beneficiary should not attest the Will, otherwise the legacy is lost.[871] The testator must have testamentary capacity for the Will to be valid. For example, he must not be under the age of 18;[872] must have a sound disposable mind at the time of making the Will;[873] and the Will must not be vitiated by duress or undue influence.[874]

§3. Vesting Legal Estate in Land on Intestacy or under a Will

460. Neither a Will nor letters of administration is a document of title and ipso facto, vests no title in the beneficiary. To properly vest interest in the beneficiary, a deed of assent is required. The Administration of Estates Law[875] empowers a personal representative to assent to the vesting of a legal estate which devolved upon the representative, in the beneficiary or any person who may be entitled by devise, bequest, devolution, appropriation, or otherwise. Also the executor under a Will is empowered to assent to a vesting of legal estate in the beneficiary under the Will.

461. For an assent affecting a legal estate to be effective, it must be in writing, signed by the personal representatives or the executors and contain the name of the person in whose favour it is given; but an assent need not be by deed to convey a legal estate in land. While an assent is an effective way of vesting legal estate in a person entitled to it under a Will or rules of intestacy, it cannot pass title to the purchaser; title can only be vested in the purchaser by another deed. An assent attracts no stamp duty in so far as it merely gives effect to the right under a Will or intestacy,[876] and it is not a registrable instrument[877] even where it is made by deed.

---

870. *See* s. 4(1) Cap 37 Laws of Abia State of Nigeria vol. II 1999, Cap 143 Laws of Akwa Ibom State of Nigeria 2000; s. 6(1) Cap 152 Kebbi State of Nigeria 1996; s. 7(1) Cap 168 Laws of Kwara State of Nigeria 1994 and corresponding provisions in the Wills Law of other States of Nigeria.
871. *See* s. 8 Wills Law Cap W2 Laws of Lagos State of Nigeria 2003, Cap 141 Laws of River State of Nigeria; s. 11 Wills Law Cap 163 Laws of Kaduna State of Nigeria 1991; s. 10 Wills Law Cap 155 Laws of Jigawa State of Nigeria 1998 and corresponding provision in the Wills Law of other States. The Will is however saved where there are at least two other non-beneficiary witnesses: *See* proviso to the provisions of the Wills Law of the States cited.
872. Wills Law of Lagos State Cap W2 Laws of Lagos State 2003, s. 3, Cap 141 Laws of Rivers State of Nigeria 2002; Wills Law of Kaduna State, s. 6, Cap 163 Laws of Kaduna State of Nigeria 1991; Wills Law of Jigawa State Cap 155 Laws of Jigawa State of Nigeria 1998, s. 5 and corresponding provisions in the Wills Law of the various States of Nigeria.
873. *Bankes v. Goodfellow* (1870) LR 5QB 549; *Adebajo v. Adebajo* (1973) 4SC 25.
874. *Johnson v. Maja supra* n. 142.
875. *See,* for example, s. 40(1) Administration of Estates Law of Lagos State Cap 3 Laws of Lagos State 2003.
876. *Ibid.,* s. 40(11).
877. For the definition of instrument, *see* s. 2 Land Registration Act 1924 and corresponding provision in the State Laws.

Chapter 3. Acquisition by Possession: Long and Adverse Possession

462. Consequent upon the provisions of the Statute of Limitation which bar a right of action for recovery of land after twelve years in the case of the individual owner and thirty years in the case of the State after the cause of action accrued,[878] title can be acquired to land by adverse possession.[879] To establish title by adverse possession, there must be proof of non-permissible use which is actual, open, notorious, exclusive, and adverse for the prescribed statutory period.[880] In *Adedeji v. Oloso*,[881] the Supreme Court said that adverse possession by a defendant is one which derogates from and is inconsistent with the ownership title of a person who claims to be the true owner of the land.

463. A person acquires title to land by adverse possession by showing not only that he has been in possession for the requisite number of years, but also that the title holder has been dispossessed or has discontinued his possession. In the words of Uwaifo, JSC in *Majekodunmi v. Abina*:[882]

> The fact of dispossession or discontinuance of possession must be beyond dispute before the limitation period can begin to run. It has been held that mere non-user does not amount to discontinuance of possession: *see* Littledale Vs Liverpool College (1900) 1 Ch. 19 at 22. It is also said that there must be an abandonment of the actual and legal possession of the land: *see* Norton Vs London and North Western Railway Co. (1879–80) 13 Ch. D. 268 at 273. In the case of dispossession by an adverse possessor, Lord Denning M. R. has said 'There must be something in the nature of an ouster of the true owner by the wrongful possessor': *see* Wallis's Ltd Vs Shell-Mex and BP (1974) 3 All ER 575 at 580. …
> From the above, it seems to me that it is not enough that a claimant is able to show that he has been in possession of land for the requisite number of years. The burden on him is higher than that. He has to show something more. He is the one claiming that land owned by the title holder has now become his. It has become his because the owner has either been dispossessed or has discontinued possession. Therefore the claimant has the clear onus to prove that the title holder has been dispossessed or has discontinued his possession. …
> I think I ought to say here that the fact of legal estate in fee being obtained through possession is subject to the adverse possessor proving that the title

878. *See,* for example, s. 15(1)(2)(a) Limitation Law of Lagos State Cap L67 Laws of Lagos State 2003.
879. In Lagos State, adverse possession 'includes the receipt of rent by a person wrongfully claiming the land in reversion': *See* s. 2 Lagos State Lands Registration Law No. 1 2015.
880. *See* Black's Law Dictionary 5th ed. 49. In *Adejumo v. Olawaiye* (1996) 1 NWLR (Pt. 425) 436, the Court of Appeal held that for an action based on adverse possession to succeed, such possession must be adequate in continuity, in publicity, and in extent to show that the possession was adverse to the competitors.
881. (2007) 5 NWLR (Pt. 1026) 133.
882. (2002) 3 NWLR (Pt. 755) 720.

holder has been dispossessed, or has discontinued possession and that he has extinguished the right of every other person to challenge his having become the absolute owner in fee.

464. While ordinarily, an adverse possessor including a trustee of a trust property acquires title to the land after the period of limitation as against the actual title holder, in the case of trustees, they cannot ordinarily obtain title by adverse possession against the beneficiaries, and adverse title may be established only where the trustees exhibit actions inconsistent with the title of the person who bestowed on them the trust property, or, as the case may be, the beneficiaries.[883]

465. It is important to note that knowledge by the true owner of the land subject of adverse possession is not required for the commencement of the running of the period of limitation, and unlike the equitable defences of latches and acquiescence, the fact that the true owner was not aware of acts of adverse possession is inconsequential.[884]It is said that 'under the Limitation Law, the right to land is extinguished, in the absence of fraud, after discontinuance of possession for the period enacted in the law, although the owner so discontinuing possession was unaware that adverse possession had been taken … ',[885] and 'to enter the land without the knowledge of the owner does not constitute concealed fraud'.[886]

466. An effective adverse possession not only bars any right of action for recovery of land, it extinguishes the title of the true owner in favour of the adverse possessor. Title to land obtained by adverse possession is registrable under the Lagos State Lands Registration Law.[887]

467. Acquisition of title by adverse possession is unknown to customary law,[888] and the Statutes of Limitation contains provisions specifically making the law inapplicable under customary law.[889] The only situation in which stale claim may be upheld under customary law is where the rule of 'standing by' as enshrined in *Awo v. Cookey Gam*[890] applies. The rule in *Awo v. Cookey Gam* is that acquisition of title by prescription will apply in equity where injustice will be done to an innocent party who has been in continuous and undisturbed possession for many years to the knowledge of the owner and in the belief that he has a valid title thereto, has been led to expend money or otherwise alter his position.

---

883. *Ogbah v. Bende Divisional Union, Jos Branch & 17 Ors* (2001) 3 NWLR (Pt. 701) 579.
884. *Ajibona v. Kolawole* (1996) 10 NWLR (Pt. 476) 22; *Duzu v. Yunusa* (2010) 10 NWLR (Pt. 1201) 80.
885. *Ibid.*
886. *Ibid.*, per Ogwuegbu JSC.
887. This is done pursuant to an order of court sought and obtained by a claimant: *See* 112(2) Lagos State Lands Registration Law No. 1 2015. *See also Rihawi v. Aromashodun* (1952) 14 WACA 204; *Majekodunmi v. Abina* (2002) 3 NWLR (Pt. 755) 720.
888. *Mora v. Nwalusi* (1962) 1 All NLR 681; *Olohunku v. Teniola* (1991) 5 NWLR (Pt. 192) 501 at 513.
889. *See,* for example, s. 67(1) Cap L67 Laws of Lagos State 2003.
890. (1913) 2 NLR 100.

468. Islamic law recognises acquisition of title through laches and acquiescence known as *Hauzi*. The rule is that where a person has been in peaceful possession of land without a challenge for ten years and he is not related by blood to the true owner, he acquires title by prescription.[891] Where the party in possession and enjoyment of land is related by blood to the claimant, the period of prescription is forty years,[892]although where there is enmity between the party in possession and the claimant who are blood relations, the period of prescription is ten years.[893] A person may sustain a defence of Hauzi only where he has been in exclusive possession of the property in dispute for the period prescribed by law.[894] Thus where the property is on loan, pledge, or meant for safekeeping, the defence of *Hauzi* would fail.[895]

469. The claimant or true owner may be able to claim his property back if he can come within established exceptions to the *Hauzi* principle. Some of these exceptions are: (a) where claimant advances cogent reasons for not complaining in time such as blood relationship or fear of harm from authority; or (b) where claimant is a minor; or (c) where the person is put in possession as a tenant, licensee, or trustee; or (d) where claimant is a relative, partner, or co-proprietor of the person in possession.[896]

891. *Yaro Ningi v. Dan Katsina* (1991) 3 NWLR (Pt. 177) 76.
892. *Tumburkai v. Tumburkai* (1996) 2 NWLR (Pt. 433) 745.
893. *Saya-Saya v. Saya-Saya* (1990) 7 NWLR (Pt. 164) 652.
894. *Kankia v. Magemu* (2003) 6 NWLR (Pt. 817) 496.
895. *Gulma v. Bahago* (1993) 1 NWLR (Pt. 272) 766; *Dauda v. Asabe* (1998) 1 NWLR (Pt. 532) 102.
896. *Garba v. Dongo Yaro* (1991) 1 NWLR (Pt. 165) 102; *Dandume v. Adamu* (1997) 10 NWLR (Pt. 525) 452.

Chapter 4. Accession

470. Accession is a principle derived from the civil law system. It is the right to all that a property (whether movable or immovable) produces, and the right to that which is united to it by accession either naturally or artificially.

471. The common law equivalent of it applies to ownership of land to the extent that whatever is attached to land naturally or due to the expenditure of capital or labour, belongs to the land and the owner of the land is the owner of the attachments. The Latin maxim is: *Quicquid plantatur solo solo cedit.*

472. That common law principle applies under Nigerian law and has been discussed under classification of real property in Part I, Chapter 1 of this monograph.

Chapter 5. Appropriation

473. Appropriation is a process whereby property, especially land, is earmarked for certain specific purposes. Under the Nigerian land tenure system, land may be earmarked as stool land, communal land, family land, ceremonial land, etc.

474. Detailed discussion of the various methods of appropriation of land in Nigeria is contained under the subhead, 'Land as the Earth Surface' in Part I, Chapter 1 of this monograph.

Chapter 6. Expropriation

§1. Introduction

475. The Land Use Act regime does not guarantee enjoyment of a right of occupancy[897] in perpetuity. Apart from the limited term for which it enured,[898] a right of occupancy can be revoked on the various grounds stipulated therein. But upon revocation, the holder is entitled to payment of compensation both as a fundamental right under the Constitution,[899] and as a legal right to compensation for deprivation of proprietary interest in real property. This chapter discusses the powers of the Governor and the local government to revoke a right of occupancy, the grounds for revocation and procedure for valid revocation, right to compensation and the quantum payable.

§2. Revocation of a Right of Occupancy

I. Power to Revoke a Right of Occupancy

476. Both the Governor of a State and the local government have the right to revoke a right of occupancy under the Land Use Act. The Governor is empowered to revoke a statutory right of occupancy over land whether or not in an urban area, or customary right of occupancy over land in non-urban area for overriding public interest.[900] The power of the local government to revoke a customary right of occupancy is restricted to public purpose and with respect to land not within an area declared to be an urban area pursuant to section 3 of the Act; or not subject to a statutory right of occupancy; or not within an area compulsorily acquired by the Federal or State government concerned; or not the subject of any law relating to minerals or mineral oils.[901]

477. It is important to draw a line of distinction between the power of the Governor of a State and that of the local government to revoke a right of occupancy: while a Governor may revoke a statutory or a customary right of occupancy in respect of land in an urban or a non-urban area respectively, a local government may revoke a customary right of occupancy mainly in respect of land in a non-urban area.[902] Whereas a Governor may revoke a right of occupancy for overriding public

897. A right of occupancy is the highest interest existing on land in Nigeria sequel to the enactment of the Land Use Act 1978, Cap L5 LFN 2010.
898. Land Use Act 1978, Cap L5 LFN 2014; s. 8.
899. The Constitution of the Federal Republic of Nigeria, 1999 as amended, s. 44(1).
900. Land Use Act 1978 Cap L5 LFN 2014, s. 28(1).
901. *Ibid.*, s. 6(3).
902. *Ibid.*

interest[903] which includes public purpose[904] with regards to customary rights of occupancy, a local government may revoke a customary right of occupancy for public purpose[905] only.

478. The power of revocation with regards to land in the Federal Capital Territory Abuja shall be exercised by the President of the Federal Republic of Nigeria through the Minister of the Federal Capital Territory.[906] However, where the Federal Government requires land for public purpose in any State, it shall issue a notice to the State government to that effect, and the Governor of that State owes an obligation to revoke the right of occupancy on the land in question. The Governor's obligation in this regard follows from the mandatory provision of section 28(4) of the Land Use Act, and the Governor cannot refuse to perform the duty of revoking a right of occupancy on behalf of the president. Also, being a public duty, an order of Mandamus may be issued by the court to compel the performance of the duty accordingly.

II. Grounds for Revocation

479. The grounds for revocation of a right of occupancy depend on whether the Governor of a State or the local government is exercising the power of revocation.

Revocation by the Governor

480. A Governor may exercise his power of revocation for overriding public interest. Section 28(2) of the Land Use Act defines overriding public interest in the case of a statutory right of occupancy to mean unlawful alienation, requirement of land by the local, State or Federal Government for public purpose, or the requirement of the land for mining purpose or oil pipelines or any purpose connected therewith. In the case of a customary right of occupancy, overriding public interest is defined in section 28(3) of the Act almost in the same way as in the case of a statutory right of occupancy, the only difference being the addition of 'requirement of the land for the extraction of building materials'.[907]

481. Where the purpose of revocation is requirement of land by the local, State or Federal Government for public purpose, any of the purposes stated in section 51 of the Act as amended is implied namely:

(a) for exclusive government use or for general public use;
(b) for use by any body corporate directly established by law or by any body corporate registered under the CAMA 1990 as respects which the government owns shares, stocks, or debentures;

903. *Ibid.*, s. 28(1).
904. *Ibid.*, s. 28(3)(a).
905. *Ibid.*, s. 6(3).
906. *Ibid.*, s. 51(2).
907. *Ibid.*, s. 28(3)(c).

(c) for or in connection with sanitary improvements of any kind;
(d) for obtaining control over land contiguous to any part or over land the value of which will be enhanced by the construction of any railway, road or other public work or convenience about to be undertaken or provided by the government;
(e) for obtaining control over land required for or in connection with the development of telecommunications or provision of electricity;
(f) for obtaining control over land required for or in connection with mining purposes;
(g) for obtaining control over land required for or in connection with planned urban or rural development or settlement;
(h) for obtaining control over land required for or in connection with economic, industrial, or agricultural development;
(i) for educational and other social services.

In construing the definition of public purpose, the Supreme Court held in *Osho v. Foreign Finance Corporation*[908] that any other public purpose for revocation of a right of occupancy not specified as public purpose cannot be lawful purpose under the Act. The attitude of the court was informed by the reasoning that: 'to revoke a statutory right of occupancy for public purposes, the letter and spirit of the laws must be adhered to. Since revocation of a grant deprives the holder of his proprietary right, the terms must be strictly complied with and strict construction of the provisions made'.[909]

482. The Governor may also revoke a statutory right of occupancy on the ground of a breach of any of the implied conditions which a certificate of occupancy is by section 10 deemed to contain; or for breach of terms contained in the certificate of occupancy or in any special contract made under section 8; or for refusal to accept and pay for a certificate issued in evidence of a right of occupancy but cancelled by the Governor under section 10(3) of the Act.[910]

Revocation by the Local Government

483. The main ground for revocation of a customary right of occupancy is public purpose as defined in section 51(1) of the Act and no other. For example, the local government cannot, unlike the Governor, lay claim to 'overriding public interest' such as extraction of building materials as a ground for revocation of a customary right of occupancy.[911]

III. Procedure for Valid Revocation by the Governor

484. Section 28(6) and (7) of the Land Use Act laid down conditions for valid revocation of a right of occupancy as follows:

---

908. (1991) 4 NWLR (Pt. 184) 157.
909. *Ibid.*, at 195.
910. Land Use Act 1978, Cap L5 LFN 2010, s. 28(5).
911. This is the sole prerogative of the governor under s. 28(3).

(a) *Revocation must be by a person who has the power to revoke.* This is usually a public officer duly authorised by the Governor or the local government as the case may be.[912] It is also important that the designation of powers for purposes of specific revocation be adhered to for revocation to be valid.
(b) *Notice shall be issued stating the purpose of revocation as prescribed by the Act.* Any revocation for a purpose outside those prescribed by the Act cannot be for a lawful purpose and shall be declared invalid and void by a court of competent jurisdiction. Where the revocation is for a public purpose, the specific public purpose as listed in section 51 of the Act must be stated, otherwise, the notice will not be valid.[913]
(c) *Notice of revocation shall be served on the holder.* Section 44 of the Act stipulates what constitutes good notice as follows:
    (i) delivery of notice to the person to whom it is to be served; or
    (ii) by leaving it at the usual or last known place of abode of that person;
    (iii) by sending it in a prepared registered letter addressed to the person at his usual or last known place of abode;
    (iv) in the case of an incorporated company, or body, by delivering it to the secretary or clerk of the company or body at its registered or principal office or sending it in a prepaid letter addressed to the secretary or clerk of the company or body at that office;
    (v) if it is not practicable after reasonable enquiry to ascertain the name or address of a holder or occupier of land on whom it should be served, by addressing it to him by the description of 'holder' or 'occupie' of the premises, or if there is no person on the premises to whom it can be delivered, by affixing it, or a copy of it, to some conspicuous part of the premises.
(d) *Notice must be proved to have come to the knowledge of the person* concerned i.e., there must be receipt of such notice.[914]

485. Upon the receipt of notice of revocation by the holder of a right of occupancy, his title shall be extinguished forthwith or on such later date as may be stated in the Notice.[915] But an aggrieved person is entitled to be accorded fair hearing by the Governor as provided by section 36(1) of the 1999 Constitution especially where revocation is for breaches of terms of the certificate of occupancy[916] to ensure that the holder is not deprived of his proprietary right without a valid notice or penalised for a breach occurring without his neglect or wilful default.

486. A revocation done by the Governor without compliance with the procedure prescribed under the Land Use Act is void and of no effect. However, a revocation in compliance with the prescribed procedure though valid, may be declared void by

912. *See* s. 28(6) of the Act.
913. *Osho v. Foreign Finance supra* n. 908 at 195.
914. *AG Lagos State v. Sowande* (1992) 8 NWLR (Pt. 261) 589 at 601–602.
915. Land Use Act 1978, Cap L5 LFN 2010, s. 28(7).
916. *Osho v. Foreign Finance supra* n. 908 at 188.

a court of competent jurisdiction if the acquisition was not made to fulfil the legitimate ends of government as contained in the notice of revocation, but meant to transfer the acquired land to an individual or group of persons. In *Osho v. Foreign Finance Corporation*,[917] the plaintiff's right of occupancy was revoked on the pretext of overriding public interest but in reality, the land was thereafter granted to a private individual for his private business. The court held that the revocation was invalid and remarked that: 'with the exception of revocation on ground of alienation under section 28(2)(c), the Governor has no right to revoke the statutory right of an occupier and grant same to a private person for any other purpose than those specified by section 28(2) of the Act'.[918] While the law frowns at a mere reallocation of acquired land to private individuals or corporate bodies and may render such illegitimate transfer void,[919] the court will be ready to hold as valid a transfer of an acquired land to a private company for the purpose of carrying out some 'economic, industrial or agricultural development'.[920]

487. Since the plea of revocation implies an acknowledgement of the existence of a right of occupancy prior to the act of revocation, the burden to plead and prove valid revocation of the right of occupancy rests on the party alleging such revocation.[921] Where revocation is not properly done for reason of public purpose, the revocation is invalid notwithstanding that there was lapse of time between the date of acquisition and the transfer of land to a third party, or that the parcel of land was only a small portion of a larger parcel of land also acquired.[922] Revocation of a statutory right of occupancy notwithstanding, a holder is still liable to government for any debt owed under, or in respect of such right of occupancy.[923]

488. An invalid revocation dates back to the date of revocation so that all transactions carried out on or regarding the purported acquired land shall be void and the position of the holder is as if there was no revocation of his right of occupancy.

489. Where the purpose of revocation is met by government any residue of parcels of land reverts back to the former holder and this is so, notwithstanding that compensation had been paid.[924]

IV. Form and Procedure for Revocation by the Local Government

490. While section 28 of the Land Use Act 1978 is clear as to the form and procedure for revocation of a right of occupancy by the Governor of a State, same cannot be said of revocation of a customary right of occupancy by the local

917. *Supra* n. 908.
918. *Ibid.*, at 201.
919. *Ereku v. Military Governor of Mid western State* (1974) 10 SC 59.
920. *Lawson & Ors v. Ajibulu* (1991) 6 NWLR (Pt. 195) 44.
921. *Osho v. Foreign Finance supra* n. 908 at 189.
922. *Lawson & Ors v. Ajibulu supra* n. 920.
923. Land Use Act 1978 Cap L5 LFN 2010, s. 32.
924. *Onikoyi & Ors v. A.G Federation & Ors.* Suit No. LD/172/93 178.

government. The provision of section 6(3) of the Act makes it 'lawful for a local government to enter upon, use and occupy for public purposes, any land within the area of its jurisdiction ... and for the purpose, to revoke any customary right of occupancy on any such land'. The provision has not detailed the procedure to follow in revoking a customary right of occupancy although, it appears to have made revocation a condition precedent to 'entering upon', 'using', and 'occupying' the land sought to be acquired within its jurisdiction, for public purposes. This omission notwithstanding, the letters, and spirit of the provisions of the Act on revocation of rights of occupancy suggest that the same due process expected in respect of revocation by the Governor should apply. Thus, it is expected that a valid notice in writing stating the grounds of revocation in line with the provisions of the Act will be served on the holder and/or occupier with proof of receipt by the latter.

V. Effect of the Supposed Implied Revocation under Section 5(2) of the Act

491. Section 5(2) of the Land Use Act provides:

> Upon the grant of a statutory right of occupancy under the provisions of subsection 1 of the section, all existing rights to the use and occupation of the land which is the subject of the statutory right of occupancy shall be extinguished.

492. A literal interpretation of the above provision would suggest an automatic destruction or implied revocation of all existing rights on land upon an inconsistent grant made by the Governor on the same land. This literal rule of interpretation actually informed earlier judicial view that a subsequent grant of a statutory right of occupancy made by the Governor extinguishes an earlier statutory right of occupancy granted by him by virtue of section 5(2). However, in the two Supreme Court decisions in *Dantsoho v. Mohammed*[925] and *Ibrahim v. Mohammed*,[926] the court explained the true import of the provision of section 5(2) against the background of its general intendment and in particular, in the light of sections 28 and 29 of the Act on revocation of rights of occupancy and right to compensation respectively. The court held in both cases that reference in the provision to 'existing rights to the use and occupation of land, the subject of a statutory right of occupancy by the Governor under section 5(1)' shall exclude legally vested rights in land either before the Act or by virtue of its provisions. The court considered the provision of section 5(2) against the background of other provisions of the Act particularly sections 28 and 29, and section 44(1) of the Constitution of the Federal Republic of Nigeria, 1999 and held that no vested right could be extinguished except properly revoked in accordance with the requirements laid down in section 28, and compensation paid pursuant to the provision of section 29 and as required by section 44(1) of the Constitution.

925. (2005) 6 NWLR (Pt. 817) 457.
926. (2005) 6 NWLR (Pt. 817) 615.

§3. Right to Compensation

493. The right to compensation in the event of revocation of a right of occupancy is a fundamental right guaranteed under the Constitution of the Federal Republic of Nigeria, 1999.[927] Section 29 of the Land Use Act also contains provisions on the right and quantum of compensation payable to the holder and/or occupier whose right had been revoked under the Act. It is important to note however, that compensation is payable under the provisions of section 29 only where revocation is not penal. For example, compensation is not payable for revocation of a right of occupancy on the ground of unlawful alienation or for engaging in other transactions in breach of express or implied covenants in a certificate of occupancy.

I. Compensation for Unexhausted Improvements

494. Compensation is payable exclusively for unexhausted improvements[928] on land and not on vacant land on which there exist no physical improvements resulting from the expenditure of capital or labour. Where a right of occupancy is revoked on the ground either that the land is required by the local, State or Federal Government for public purpose, or that it is entitled to compensation for the value at the date of revocation, of their unexhausted improvements on the land. The word 'and' between 'the holder and the occupier' may be conjunctive or disjunctive. Where the holder is also the occupier who made the improvements, he shall be entitled to compensation, but where one is different from the other, the right to compensation hinges on the interest of the claimant in such improvements either as the holder or the occupier.

II. Compensation under the Minerals Act

495. Upon revocation of a right of occupancy on the ground that the land is required for mining purposes, or for the laying of oil pipelines or for any purpose connected therewith,[929] the holder and the occupier shall be entitled to compensation under the appropriate provisions of the Minerals Act or the Mineral Oils Act or any legislation replacing same.[930] The phrase 'holder and occupier' shall be construed in the same way suggested in the case of unexhausted improvements.

496. Where the holder or occupier is a community, payment shall be made to the community or the head of the community to hold same in trust for the benefit of the community, or into some fund specified by the Governor for the purpose of being utilised or applied for the benefit of the community.[931] In *Onwuka v.*

927. Cap C23 LFN 2010.
928. Land Use Act 1978, Cap L5 LFN 2010, s. 29(1).
929. *Ibid.*, s. 28(2).
930. *Ibid.*, s. 29(2).
931. *Ibid.*, s. 29(3).

Ediala,[932] the Supreme Court construed the words 'holder' and 'occupier' to mean the customary landowner as opposed to the customary tenant in occupation for purposes of compensation.

III. Resettlement in Lieu of Compensation

497. Section 33(1) of the Land Use Act empowers the Governor to offer in lieu of compensation payable, resettlement in any other place in the event of revocation of a right of occupancy in respect of any developed land on which a residential building has been erected. Where the value of the alternative accommodation provided is higher than the compensation payable, the excess shall constitute a loan payable to the government in the prescribed manner.[933] An acceptance of a resettlement forecloses any right to further compensation by the person concerned.[934]

IV. Allocation of Alternative Agricultural Land

498. Where the land subject of revocation by the local government was used for agricultural purposes, the local government shall allocate an alternative land for use by the holder of the customary right of occupancy for the same purpose.[935]

V. Quantum of Compensation

499. Where a right of occupancy is revoked for public purposes within the State, or on the ground of requirement of the land for the extraction of building materials, the quantum of compensation shall be as follows:[936]

(a) In respect of the land, an amount equal to rent, if any, paid by the occupier during the year in which the right of occupancy was revoked. Where the right of occupancy revoked is in respect of a part of a larger portion of land, compensation shall be computed in respect of the whole land for an amount equal in rent, if any, paid by the occupier during the year in which the right of occupancy was revoked less a proportionate amount calculated in relation to the area not affected by the revocation, and any interest payable shall be assessed and computed in the like manner.[937]
(b) In respect of building, installation[938] or improvements therein, compensation shall be paid for the amount of the replacement cost of the building, installation

932. (1989) 1 NWLR (Pt. 96) 182.
933. Land Use Act 1978 Cap L5 LFN 2010, s. 33(2).
934. *Ibid.*, s. 33(3).
935. *Ibid.*, s. 6(6).
936. *Ibid.*, s. 29(4).
937. *Ibid.*, s. 29(5).
938. 'Installation' means any mechanical apparatus set up or put in position for use or materials set up in or on land or other equipment, but excludes any fixture in or on any building.

or improvements therein as determined by the appropriate officer (less any depreciation) together with interest at the bank rate for delayed payment of compensation. The same assessment follows in the case of such building, installation or improvements thereon standing on the revoked part of a larger portion of land.[939] With regards to reclamation works, the quantum of compensation is such cost as may be substantiated by documentary evidence and proof to the satisfaction of the appropriate officer.

(c) In respect of crops on land, the quantum of compensation is an amount equal to the value as prescribed and determined by the appropriate officer.[940]

500. Disputes arising from the amount of compensation payable shall be referred to the appropriate Land Use and Allocation Committee.[941]

VI. Failure of Local Government to Pay Compensation

501. Where a local government refuses or neglects to pay compensation within a reasonable time to the holder of a customary right of occupancy, the Governor may proceed to the assessment of compensation under section 29 and direct the local government to pay the amount of such compensation to the holder and occupier according to their respective interests.[942]

939. *Supra* n. 9 37, 29(6).
940. 'Appropriate officer' under the Act means the Chief Lands Officer of a State and in the case of the Federal Capital Territory means the Chief Federal Landa Officer: *See* s. 50(1) of the Act.
941. Land Use Act 1978 Cap L5 LFN 2010, s. 6(7).
942. *Ibid.*

Chapter 7. Insolvency

502. Insolvency is a situation where natural or legal entity is unable to pay debt. Although there are pockets of legislations with features of insolvency as there is no exclusive single body of law or code for insolvency practice in Nigeria, insolvency law in Nigeria is based on the common law, precedents, and local statutes such as the CAMA[943]and, to some extent, the Assets Management Corporation of Nigeria (AMCON) Act 2010 as amended[944]

503. Section 868(1) of CAMA defines an insolvent person as:

> Any person in Nigeria who in respect of any Judgment, Decree or Court Order against him, is unable to satisfy execution or other process issued thereon in favour of a creditor and the execution or other process remain unsatisfied for not less than six weeks.

This definition is restrictive and shall be seen shortly, it does not put into consideration other processes that come to play before the order of court.

504. Insolvency may involve an individual or a corporate body. An individual insolvency is the inability of the individual or natural persons to pay a debt, while corporate insolvency is the inability of a corporation or a company to pay its debt. It could also take the form of cash flow insolvency or balance sheet insolvency. While the former is a situation where the corporate body can no longer meet its debt obligations as they fall due, the latter arises where the company's liability exceeds its assets; a clear-cut case of liquidation.

505. While insolvency proceedings is usually associated with unsecured debts as opposed to enforcement procedure of security created as collateral for loan, it is axiomatic that there is an important connect between the law of secured credit and insolvency law since the issue of enforcement of securities and the rating of these securities would arise only when the borrower is unable to meet its contractual obligations.

506. A winding up petition filed on the ground of a company's insolvency cannot succeed where there is substantial dispute as to the amount owed by the company.[945] This is crucial since a company whose amount of indebtedness is in dispute cannot be described as 'unable to pay its debt'.

507. Section 572 of CAMA describes 'inability of the company to pay its debt (that is, insolvency)'. A company shall be deemed to be unable to pay its debt if:

---

943. Act No. 3 2020.
944. No. 4 Laws of the Federation of Nigeria 2010 as amended: See AMCON (Amendment) Act 2015, 2019, 2021.
945. *Stonegate Securities Ltd v. Gregory* (1980) Ch. 576.

(a) a creditor by assignment or otherwise to whom the company is indebted in a sum exceeding N2,000 then due has served on the company by leaving it at its registered office or head office, a demand under his hand requiring the company to pay the sum so due and the company has for three weeks thereafter neglected to pay the sum or to secure or compound for it to the reasonable satisfaction of the creditor; or
(b) execution or other process issued on a judgment, decree or order of any court in favour of a creditor of the company is returned unsatisfied in whole or in part; or
(c) the court after taking into account any contingent or prospective liability of the company is satisfied that the company is unable to pay its debt.

508. The bulk of principles governing corporate insolvency in Nigeria are contained in the various provisions of CAMA subsumed under Chapter 19 on receivership and manager, Chapters 20–24 on winding up of companies, and Chapter 27 on arrangement and compromise.

§1. Receivership

509. Although winding up is one of the consequences of insolvency, it does not follow that an insolvent company shall be wound up automatically. The CAMA makes provisions for the appointment and powers and duties of the receiver and the receiver-manager upon a company becoming insolvent. Certain categories of persons cannot be appointed receivers.[946] When appointed, the receiver shall be entitled to take possession of and protect the property of the company, receive the rents and profits therefrom, discharge all outgoings and manage same with a view to the beneficial realisation of the security.[947] In the case of a receiver-manager, the latter shall manage the same with a view to the beneficial realisation of the security of those on whose behalf he is appointed.[948] In discharging those duties, the receiver or the receiver-manager shall exercise the powers conferred on him by the debenture as well as the powers listed in the eleventh schedule of CAMA.[949]

§2. Winding Up of the Company

510. Chapters 20–24 of CAMA generally deal with winding up. Section 401(1) of CAMA provides that winding up can be by the court; it may be voluntary[950] or subject to supervision of the court.[951]

946. These are infant, person of unsound mind, corporate body, undischarged bankrupt. A director or auditor of the company or any person convicted of offences involving fraud: *See* s. 550 of CAMA. Unfortunately, CAMA contains no provisions on the specific qualification of a receiver or a receiver-manager thereby leaving room for the appointment of incompetent persons as receivers.
947. *See* s. 556(1) of CAMA. But except appointed as a manager, a receiver shall not have the power to carry on any business or undertaking.
948. *See* s. 556(2) of CAMA.
949. *See* s. 556(3) of CAMA.
950. *See* s. 564(1)(a)(b) of CAMA.
951. *See* s. 564(1(c) of CAMA.

Winding Up by the court

511. Section 571(d) provides that a company may be wound up by the court for inability to pay its debt. Petition for winding up may be brought by the company, a creditor either contingent or prospective, official receiver provided the power to do so is contained in the instrument of appointment, a contributory, trustee in bankruptcy, the Commission, or by all or any of those parties together or separately.[952] A court before whom a petition for winding up is brought may dismiss it, adjourn the hearing on a condition or unconditionally or make an interim order or any orders that it deems fit.[953] But the court will not refuse to make a winding up order on the ground only that the assets of the company have been mortgaged to an amount equal to or in excess of those assets, or that the company has no assets.[954] An order for winding up shall operate in favour of all the creditors and of all the contributories of the company as if made on a joint petition of a creditor and of a contributory.[955]

512. In a winding up by the court, any disposition of the property of the company, including things in action and any transfer of shares, or alteration in the status of the members of the company made after commencement of the winding up shall, unless the court otherwise orders, be void.[956] Where a company is being wound up by the court, any attachment, sequestration, distress, or execution put in force against the estate or effects of the company after the commencement of the winding up shall be void.[957]

Voluntary Winding Up

513. A company may be wound up voluntarily if the company resolves by special resolution that the company be wound up voluntarily.[958] Within fourteen days of passing such resolution, the company shall give notice of such resolution by advertisement in the gazette or two daily newspapers and to the Corporate Affairs Commission (CAC).[959] From the date of commencement of the voluntary winding up, the company shall cease to carry on business except so far as may be required for the beneficial winding up.[960] Any transfer of shares, not being a transfer made to or with the sanction of the liquidator, and any alteration in the status of the members of the company made after the commencement of a voluntary winding up shall be void.[961]

952. Section 573(1) of CAMA.
953. Section 574 of CAMA.
954. *Ibid.*
955. Section 581 of CAMA.
956. Section 576 of CAMA.
957. Section 577 of CAMA.
958. *Ibid.*, s. 620.
959. *Ibid.*, s. 621.
960. *Ibid.*, s. 623.
961. *Ibid.*, s. 624.

514. A statutory declaration of the company's solvency may be made by the directors or majority of directors upon a proposal to wind up the company voluntarily but within five weeks immediately preceding the date of the passing of the resolution for winding up by the company, suggesting that the company will be able to pay its debts in full within such period not exceeding twelve months from the commencement of the winding up.[962] Such statutory declaration shall be accompanied by a statement of the company's assets and liabilities as at the latest practicable date before the making of the declaration.[963]

515. A liquidator is appointed either by the shareholders of a company and its creditors in the case of a creditors' voluntary liquidation, or by the court in the case of a compulsory liquidation. Liquidation is irreversible and the company's existence is in due course, ended by dissolution. The powers of the liquidator are extensive and are provided for in CAMA.[964]

516. Subject to the provisions of CAMA as to preferential payments, in every voluntary winding up, the property of a company, shall on its winding up, be applied in satisfaction of its liabilities *pari passu* and, subject to such application shall, unless the articles otherwise provide, be distributed among the members according to their rights and interests in the company.[965] All costs, charges, and expenses properly incurred in the winding up including the remuneration of the liquidator, shall be payable out of the assets of the company in priority to all other claims.[966]

Winding Up Subject to Court's Supervision

517. A resolution for voluntary winding up may, upon petition, order that the voluntary winding up shall continue subject to court's supervision with such liberty for creditors, contributories, or others to apply to court and generally on such terms and conditions as the court thinks just. A voluntary winding up subject to court's supervision shall be deemed to be a petition for winding up by the court.

518. The court may, upon making an order for supervision, appoint additional liquidator with powers and subject to the same obligations akin to that of an appointed liquidator under a voluntary winding up.

519. In a winding up there shall be paid in priority to all other debts, all costs, charges, and expenses properly incurred in the winding up, including the remuneration of the liquidator,[967] all local rates and charges becoming due and payable within twelve months next before that date and all taxes payable; deductions under the Nigeria Social Insurance Trust Fund; all wages or salary of any clerk or servant in respect of services rendered to the company; all wages of any workman or labourer

---

962. *Ibid.*, s. 625.
963. *Ibid.*
964. *Ibid.*, s. 644.
965. *Ibid.*, s. 643.
966. *Ibid.*, s. 647.
967. Section 647 of CAMA.

in respect of services rendered to the company; all accrued holiday remuneration becoming payable to any clerk, servant, workman, or labourer on the termination of his employment before or by the effect of a winding up order or resolution.[968] Until the holders of fixed and floating charges, the preferential creditors, and all the expenses of liquidation have been paid in full, unsecured creditors do not receive any dividend.

520. Following from the foregoing priority rules in the general insolvency law in Nigeria, usually where the assets of the insolvent company are insufficient to meet its liabilities, general creditors are greatly at risk. Both the account holders or direct holders of securities will mostly be treated as trade creditors with their interests being jeopardised where the insolvent company is not asset-rich. Consequently, measures were taken by different legal regimes to protect the interests of investors, depositors, and creditors. For example, the new regime introduced by the Investments and Securities Act 1999[969] regulate priority rules for securities. Also, the Nigerian Deposit Insurance Corporation Act 2006[970] provides for immediate payment of the sum of N 200,000 to account holders upon failure of banks.

§3. Resolving the Non-performing Loan Assets of Banks

521. Powers of the Assets Management Corporation of Nigeria ('the Corporation') under the AMCON Act 2010 as amended[971]

522. One of the various efforts of the Federal Government of Nigeria through the Central Bank of Nigeria in efficiently resolving the non-performing loan assets of banks and thereby minimising losses incurred by financial institutions as a result of non-performing loans, is the establishment of the AMCON .[972] Its main objective is the valuable purchase, effective take over, and efficient management, preservation and disposal of eligible bank assets held by financial institutions with regards to non-performing loans.[973] Section 30 of the principal Act empowers the Corporation to 'acquire an interest in an eligible bank asset of an eligible financial institutions if the Corporation considers it necessary or desirable to do so', or if it is so 'requested by the Nigerian Deposit Insurance Corporation (NDIC) acting in consultation with the Central Bank of Nigeria pursuant to section 38(2) (d) of the NDIC Act. In this either case, the Corporation shall bring a recovery action against the debtor before the Federal High Court within the jurisdiction where the assets are situated.

523. The Corporation shall have power to appoint a receiver for a debtor company whose assets have been charged as security, 'to realise the assets of the debtor

968. Section 657 of CAMA.
969. Section 263(1)(d) of No. 45 1999 now Cap 124 Laws of the Federation of Nigeria 2010.
970. Section 20 of Cap N102 Laws of the Federation of Nigeria 2010.
971. The AMCON Act has been amended in 2015, 2019, and 2021.
972. See Asset Management Corporation of Nigeria (AMCON) Act No. 4 2010 as amended.
973. *Ibid.*, Part IV thereof.

company; enforce the individual liability of the shareholders and directors of the debtor company; and manage the affairs of the debtor company.'[974]

524. To forestall any move by the debtor or debtor company to dissipate the assets, the Corporation may apply to court by motion ex-parte for an order granting possession of the property to the Corporation. Such interim order shall have the effect of an interlocutory order which subsists pending the final determination of the recovery action before the court.

525. Where judgment is entered for the Corporation against an individual debtor for any sum, and the sum is not liquidated within thirty days from the date of the order for payment thereof, the Corporation may apply to the court to issue a receiving order against the debtor[975] and where such order is made, the court may adjudge the debtor bankrupt.[976] A debtor adjudged bankrupt shall be deemed adjudged a bankrupt under the Bankruptcy Act which shall have effect with such modification as are contained in the AMCON Act and a trustee appointed under the Act may seek the directive of the court in respect of any act or thing to be done by anyone under the Bankruptcy Act.[977]

526. Where judgment is entered in favour of the Corporation against a debtor company for any sum and the sum is not liquidated within ninety days from the date of the order for payment, the Corporation may apply to court for a winding up order against the debtor company.[978] In addition to making a winding up order, the court may, on the application of the Corporation, appoint an official receiver to assume the office of a liquidator to wind up the affairs of the debtor company.[979] Any liquidator so appointed, shall have all the powers of a liquidator under the CAMA 2020, and shall perform his duties in accordance with that Act.[980]

974. *Ibid.*, s. 48.
975. *Ibid.*, s. 51(1)
976. *Ibid.*, s. 51(3).
977. *Ibid.*, s 51(7).
978. *Ibid.*, s. 52(1).
979. *Ibid.*, s. 52(2).
980. *Ibid.*, s. 52(3) (4) and (5).

Part IV. Trust and Fiduciary Mechanisms

Chapter 1. Administration of Property

527. Administration of Estate deals with the mechanism for acquiring the possession, control, and management of a deceased's estate in order to distribute it among the beneficiaries and creditors.[981]When a person dies, the administration of his estate is dependent upon whether he died testate or intestate. If he has a valid Will by which he disposes of his property he is said to have died testate, where there is no Will, he died intestate.

528. Although the duties of personal representatives are in relation to the estate of a deceased person while those of trustees are in respect of both the trust inter vivos and testamentary trusts, it must be noted however, that a person may at the same time be a trustee and a personal representative. This will happen in a situation where a Will establishes a person as both executor and trustee.[982] However, if the personal representative has no duties to perform beyond the collection of assets, payment of debts, and distribution of the estate, they are simply personal representatives and not trustees. But where the personal representative is directed to hold any part of the estate upon certain trust for a person in succession, he will resume into the office of trustees as soon as the administration of the deceased's estate is completed.

529. The powers, duties, and appointment of trustees and personal representatives are similar. Personal representatives are made up of executors, administrators, and trustees as the case may be depending on the power of appointment. It is not out of place to state that the position of personal representatives is very similar to that of a trustee except a contrary intention appears from the provisions of the Will or trust instrument. The provisions of the Trustees Act 1893 (a statute of general application) and Trustees Law apply to both.

530. Like trustees, personal representatives from the date the deceased's properties are placed in their care, hold both the legal and equitable interest thereof.[983]

---

981. Itse Sagay., *Nigerian Law of Succession* 331 (Malthouse 2006).
982. This is very common in Wills made in Nigeria.
983. *Ibrahim v. Osunde & Ors* (2009) 1–2 SC (Pt. 11) 109.

531. Where a person tampers with money belonging to another, the law raises a trust by implication and clothes that person with fiduciary duty for the purpose of making the person accountable.[984]Thus, both trustees and personal representatives are under fiduciary duties, and they should not allow their personal interests to conflict with their duties.[985]

532. Also, like trustees who must act in accordance with the trust instrument and limited by the same instrument, personal representatives are also limited by Will or grant by letters of administration.[986] Personal representatives can be sued and have his authority revoked just like trustees can be removed for breach of trust.

§1. Appointment of a Trustee and Administration of Estate

533. Appointment of trustees is governed in Nigeria by the Trustees Act, 1893 a statute of general application excluding States comprising the former western and mid-western region of Nigeria,[987] the Trustee Law[988] applicable in the States comprising the former western and mid-western region of Nigeria,[989] the Public Trustees Act,[990] and the Public Trustees Law.[991]

534. As earlier noted in this chapter, the same categories of persons that may be appointed as trustees may also be appointed to administer the estate of a deceased person. They may be appointed as trustees or personal representatives.

I. Who May Be a Trustee/Personal Representative?

Person of Full Age

535. Persons of full age may be appointed trustees or personal representatives,[992] and they can also create trusts.

---

984. *Udensi v. Ogbo* (1976) 7 SC 1; *Anuruba v. E.C.B Ltd* (2005) 10 NWLR (Pt. 933) 321.
985. *A.G Bendel State v. AG Federation* (2005) 6 SC (Pt. II) 1033.
986. *Amobi v. Nzegwu* (2014) All FWLR (Pt. 730) 1284 at 1303. A personal representative may be a trustee whether under a Will or letters of administration or by operation of law: *See* Trustees Law of Western Nigeria, s. 26(1); *Adeniji v. Probate Registrar of Western Nigeria* (1966) NMLR 125.
987. These are Ogun, Oyo, Osun, Ondo, Ekiti, Edo, and Delta States of Nigeria.
988. Cap 125 LWN 1959.
989. *Ibid.*.
990. Cap 98 LFN 1958. The Public Trustees Act was omitted from the Laws of the Federation of Nigeria (LFN) 1990 and 2004, but applies in Lagos State and the former Western Region as Public Trustees Law with identical provisions.
991. Applicable in Lagos State and the States comprising the former western and mid-western region of Nigeria: *See*, e.g., Public Trustees Law of Western Region of Nigeria 1959; Public Trustees Law of Oyo State 1978.
992. Section 3 of the Wills Law of Lagos State Cap W2 Laws of Lagos State of Nigeria 2003 put the age of qualification at 18: *See Apatira v. Akanke* (1944) 17 NLR 149; (1962) 1 All NLR 130.

Trust Corporation

536. A trust corporation including any corporate body empowered by the court or statute to conduct trustee business (e.g., the trustee department of a bank) may be trustees.

Public Trustees

537. Public trustees are also qualified to administer the estates of the deceased person. The Administrator General as a law officer in the judicial service appointed by the Governor of a State to that office may assume the duty of the administrator of the estate of the deceased person under certain circumstances and hold an estate in dispute in trust for the beneficiaries.[993]

II. Number of Trustees

538. A maximum number of four trustees is required in the case of trust for sale of land,[994] and minimum of one, although it is not advisable to appoint a sole trustee to obviate possibility of fraud and prevent maladministration. Also by virtue of section 6(2) of the Trustees Law, a sole trustee (not being a trust corporation) cannot give a valid receipt for the proceeds of sale arising out of a trust for sale.

III. Appointment of Trustees

Appointment by the Settlor or Testator

539. Normally, original trustees are appointed by the settlor or testator. In the event that the trustees disclaim, the settlor holds as trustee,[995]and in the event of death of all the trustees, the personal representatives of the last survivor holds as trustees.[996] Once a trust is duly constituted, the settlor has no power to appoint additional trustees unless the power to do so is reserved in the Will or settlement otherwise, the relevant provisions of the Trustees Act or Law apply.[997]

Appointment under the Trustees Act 1893 and Trustees Law

540. By virtue of section 10 of the Trustees Act 1893 and section 24(1) of the Trustees Law,[998] a new trustee[999] may be appointed in place of a former trustee where a trustee is dead; remains outside Nigeria for an uninterrupted period of more

993. *Ogbe v. Ogbe* Unreported Suit No. 8/31/09/HC of Mid-Western State, Benin.
994. Trustees Law, s. 22.
995. This principle is premised on the rule that 'Equity never wants for a trustee'.
996. Kodilinye *supra* n. 160 *at* 112.
997. *See* Trustees Act 1893, s. 10 and Trustees Law of the old Western Nigeria, s. 24.
998. Cap 125 Laws of Western Nigeria, 1959.
999. A 'new trustee' means a trustee newly appointed as opposed to a reappointed trustee: *See Olowu v. Renner* (1968) M.N.A.L.R 11.

than twelve months; desires to be discharged or refuses to act; or incapable of acting as a result of minor age, mental disorder, etc. In addition, section 24(6) of the Trustees Law allows new trustees to be appointed even where none of the enumerated events occurred, where none of the existing trustees is a trust corporation, and the appointment will not bring the total number of trustees above four. But whereas, the person exercising the power of appointment may appoint himself when an appointment is being made under section 10 of the Trustees Act and section 24(1) of the Trustees Law, he cannot do so when an additional trustee is being appointed under section 24(6) of the Trustees Law.

541. Such appointment must be in writing and not necessarily by deed, but is advantageous to have the appointment made by deed as that would obviate the need for a separate vesting instrument.

Appointment by the Court

542. The powers of court to appoint new trustees are contained in section 25 of the Trustees Act and section 28 of the Trustees Law, and may be exercised when it is 'expedient to appoint them, and inexpedient, difficult or impracticable to do so without the court's assistance'. Such appointment may be in addition to, or in substitution for the existing one.

543. It is a precondition for the exercise of power by the court that the powers conferred by section 10(1) of the Trustees Act and section 24 of the Trustees Law must be exhausted before an application is made to court for the appointment of new trustees, and this is so notwithstanding that the application has been brought to court by a majority of the beneficiaries.

544. In appointing new trustees, courts normally consider the interest of the settlor and the beneficiaries.[1000] A court also has extensive discretionary powers in matters relating to the administration of estate, and may appoint an administrator pendete lite where it is expedient to do so, and to avoid dissipation where the estate is unmanaged or where there is dispute in court over the estate.[1001]

545. Also, the court reserves the power under sections 8 and 9 of the Public Trustees Act and Law upon application by any trustee or beneficiary to appoint a Public Trustee either as ordinary or custodian trustee.

IV. Acceptance and Disclaimer of Trusteeship

546. An appointed trustee may accept the trust or disclaim the trust at any time before acceptance.

1000. Trustees Act, s. 10, Trustees Law, s. 24.
1001. *Ladejobi & Others v. Odutola Holdings Ltd & Others* (2002) I W.R.N 99 at 1067.

547. Acceptance of the trust may be express or implied; by words or by conduct. Generally, any interference with the subject matter of the trust in the absence of satisfactory explanation amounts to an acceptance,[1002] but a passive conduct will not do.[1003] Also, where a person appointed as executor and trustee under a Will takes out probate, he is deemed to have accepted the trust contained therein.[1004]

548. A trustee may disclaim the trust before doing anything which may be tantamount to an acceptance of it.[1005] Such disclaimer must be in writing or by deed; it may be oral or may be inferred from conduct; and must be a disclaimer of the whole trust.[1006]

549. Where the disclaimer-trustee is a sole trustee, the legal title to the property reverts to the settlor; otherwise, it vests in the remaining trustees.

V. Vesting Trust Property in the Trustees

550. To enable the Trustee Act effectively in law, it is necessary to vest the trust property in him upon appointment. In the case of original trustees appointed under an instrument inter vivos, the vesting is done, for example, in the case of land, by a deed of assignment, and in the case of chattels, by delivery or deed of gift.[1007] Where the trust is a testamentary one, the Will operates to vest the property in the named trustees. In the case of new trustees, trust property could be vested by a vesting declaration by the appointor contained in the deed of appointment;[1008] or by a transfer to the new by the previous trustee in whom the property was vested; or by a vesting order of the court in cases where it is impossible or difficult to procure the transfer of the trust property to the new trustee.[1009]

§2. Duties of Trustees/Personal Representatives under Trust and Administration of Estate

551. Both the trustee and personal representative must ascertain the terms of the trust and testamentary document respectively. The duties of a trustee and that of a personal representative in the administration of estate are essentially the same and in most cases, a trustee performs dual duties once he is an executor and a trustee in the same instrument.

1002. *Urch v. Walker* (1838) 3 My. & Cr. 702.
1003. *Evans v. John* (1841) 4 Beav. 35.
1004. *Mucklow v. Fuller* (1821) Jac. 198.
1005. *Nylander v. Thomas* (1968) 1 All NLR 80.
1006. *Re Lord and Fullerton's contract* (1896) 1 Ch. 228.
1007. In the case of shares in a private company, by entry in the company's register pursuant to a proper instrument of transfer, and in the case of a public company, registration of the shares with the CSCS.
1008. Trustees Act 1893, s. 12; Trustees Law, s. 27.
1009. Trustees Act 1893, s. 25; Trustees Law, ss 28, 31.

552. Having accepted the trusteeship, a trustee or personal representative must observe the duties placed upon him. The duties which are onerous are as follows.

I. Duty to Collect and Safeguard the Trust Properties

553. Both the trustee and personal representative must gather the assets and keep them properly. Gathering of assets of the trust or estate of the deceased is one of the salient duties available to trustee and personal representative. A trustee like a personal representative must reduce the trust property into possession.[1010]

II. Duty to Act Timeously to Collect and Secure the Property of the Trust

554. Where a trustee doubles as an executor in a Will, aside from gathering the estate of the deceased, he must ensure that the properties are protected before the grant of probate. In other words, an executor assumes office where the nature of the properties is such that can be destroyed before the grant of probate.[1011]

A. Duty to Invest

555. The Nigerian legislations namely, the Trustee Investments Act 1957 and 1962[1012] and the Administration of Estates Law govern trustee investment. Section 3(1) of the Trustees Investment Act 1957, authorises trustees to invest in any of the securities mentioned or specified in section 2 thereof.

556. Section 2 of the Act specifically identifies the following investments for trustee:

(i) All securities created or issued by or on behalf of the Federal Government.
(ii) Securities created or issued by or on behalf of a State government, which are declared by the president in a Federal gazette as authorised investments.
(iii) Securities which are declared by the president by notice in the Federal gazette as authorised, being securities created or issued by companies or corporations directly by legislations and which companies or corporations are specified in the schedule i.e., the Nigeria Coal Corporation, the National Electric Power Authority, the Nigerian Port Authority, and the Nigerian Railway Corporation.[1013]

1010. *Nestle v. National Westminster Bank* (1993) 1 WLR 1260.
1011. *Ogbe v. Ogbe supra* n. 993.
1012. These Laws have been consolidated under the Trustees Investment Act Cap T22 LFN 2010.
1013. Trustees Investment Act Cap T22 LFN 2010, s. 2(1)(a)(b) and (c).

557. This power of investment is subject to any consent or direction required by the trust instrument.[1014]

558. Also, section 1(1) of the Trustees Investment Act 1962 extends the power of investment of trustees to include power to invest in debentures and fully paid-up shares of any public company incorporated under the CAMA.[1015] Such company must however satisfy the following conditions:[1016]

(a) the paid-up capital of the company to be invested must be at least one million naira;
(b) the company's securities must be quoted under the stock exchange;
(c) the company must be the one who have paid dividends in the three calendar years immediately preceding the current year, and the aggregate amount of the dividends paid during each of those years in respect of each share ranking for dividend throughout that year was not less than 5% of the nominal value of the share.

559. The investment must not exceed certain percentage of the trust fund. For example, the total investment in shares of companies must not exceed one third of the total value of the trust fund; investment in shares and debentures of a company must not exceed one tenth of the total value of the trust fund; and investment in shares of a particular company must not exceed one twentieth of the total value of the trust fund.[1017]

560. The power to invest can also be derived by the trustee from the trust investment. Under the administration of estate, where a trustee doubles as an executor and trustee this power is also available but must be exercised in accordance with the statutory provision or trust instrument.

III. Duty to Distribute

561. A trustee like a personal representative is under an obligation to distribute trust property or legacies as contained in the Will to those entitled. The trustee will be liable and will have to make good any loss occasioned by his breach. There are liabilities for wrongful payment and underpayment of a particular beneficiary. The main duty of a personal representative is to distribute if he has nothing to hold except he doubles as a trustee.

1014. *Ibid.*, s. 3(3).
1015. *Ibid.*, s. 2(1)(d).
1016. *Ibid.*, s. 2(2)(a)–(c).
1017. *Ibid.*, s. 2(3)(a)–(c).

IV. Fiduciary Duties of Trustees/Personal Representatives

562. It is an inflexible rule of a court of equity that a person in a fiduciary position is not, unless otherwise expressly provided, entitled to make profit in the management of the trust properties or administration of estate. Trustee must know that:

(a) He cannot profit from the trust.
(b) Except where the trust instrument so provide, a trustee generally may not charge for services.[1018]
(c) He cannot purchase the trust property or estate as the case may be. This is because a trustee should not place himself in a position where his duty will conflict with his own interest.

Kolawole J.C.A put it succinctly in *Okesuji v. Lawal*[1019] as follows:

> It is a settled rule of equity that no one having duties of a fiduciary nature to discharge shall be allowed to go into engagements in which he has or can have personal interests conflicting, or which possibly may conflict with the interest of those whom he is bound to protect. One consequence of the rule is that a trustee for sale may not purchase the trust property for himself ... it has been held that however honest and fair the sale may be even if made at public auction, or for a price higher than that obtainable on open market, a beneficiary has an absolute right to have the conveyance set aside.

563. A trustee who sells or leases a trust property to himself is in breach of the fiduciary duty and is liable to have the transaction set aside.

564. The fiduciary mechanism of trustees expects him to keep proper account of the trust he administers.[1020]

V. Duty to Keep Account and to Provide Information

565. This is a duty that relates to fiduciary mechanism of a trustee either under private trust or trust created under a Will. A trustee must keep proper account and provide useful information about the estate. It is the requirement of the law that a trustee renders account of the trust properties in his care to the beneficiaries. The same is the position with an executor or a trustee under the Administration of Estate

---

1018. The rules that trustees are prohibited from remuneration are subject to the following exceptions: (i) authority by court and (ii) statute.
1019. (1986) 2 NWLR (Pt. 22) 417 at 437.
1020. *AG Bendel State v. AG Federation* (2005) 6 SC (Pt. II) 103; *Augustine Lindensi v. Mogbo* (1976) 7 SC; *Anamba v. E.C.B Ltd* (2005) 10 NWLR (Pt. 933) 321.

Law. Where proper account is not kept, the trustee or administrator will be accountable for inconsistency.[1021] Every sum not accounted for by the trustee or an administrator must be refunded except where they are authorised to do so.

VI. Duty to Maintain Equality Between Beneficiaries

566. Equality is equity; equity expects a trustee to maintain a balance between beneficiaries. He must be impartial in the execution of the trust and must not favour the interest of one beneficiary at the expense of another.[1022]

§3. POWERS OF TRUSTEES

567. Trust instrument usually gives certain express powers to the trustee whether under trust or administration of estate. While the duties are compulsory, power is discretionary in most cases. The powers are as follows.

I. Power of Sale

568. Trustees have the power to sell trust property. This power may be available expressly or impliedly in the trust instrument. The trustee must however ensure that the sale is to the maximum advantage of the beneficiaries. The beneficiaries' right to stop any sale either by seeking for an injunction or to impeach the sale is not ruled out under section 5(2) of the Trustee Law and section 14(2) of the Trustee Act.

II. Power to Insure

569. Trustees are under an obligation to take all that are necessary to protect the trust property. He may have to go to the extent of insuring the trust property in order to safeguard the property. This power however is subject to the trust instrument. Section 11 of the Trustees Law empowers trustees to insure against loss or damage by fire, any building or other insurable property up to any amount not exceeding three-fourth, part of the full value of the building or property.

570. Section 1(2) of the Trustees Law empowers the trustee to pay premium without obtaining the consent of anybody entitled to the beneficial interest at that time.

1021. *Okunowo v. Okunowo* (2001) 2 LLR (Pt. 9) 56.
1022. *Llyod's Bank v. Duker* (1987) 1 WLR 1324.

III. Power to Delegate

571. The office of a trustee is confidential. The law therefore requires a trustee to perform his duty in person and as a matter of general rule, trustees are not allowed to delegate their duties, and a trustee who delegated his duty is liable for his agent's default or damage incurred personally, not from the trust money but from his own personal money.

572. However, there are certain statutory provisions which empower trustees to employ agents:

(a) Section 2(4)(c) of the Trustee Investment Act for example, empowers a trustee to employ a person whom he reasonably believes to be competent. Trustees can also appoint a solicitor, banker, stock broker, or any other person relevant to transact any business including the receipt and payment of money. The trustee by virtue of section 14(1) shall be paid all charges in this regard and shall not be responsible for default of any such agent if employed in good faith.
(b) By virtue of section 16(1) of the Trustee Law, a trustee who is outside Nigeria for more than one month may, by Power of Attorney, delegate to any person or trust corporation. Trustee is responsible for the acts and defaults of the donee as if they were his own.[1023]

IV. Power to Pay Money into Court

573. Section 46 of the Trustee Law empowers trustee to pay trust fund into court. The power becomes exercisable in case of difficulties especially where a debtor is being challenged by the trustee and the case is in court.

V. Power to Sue

574. Trustee and personal representative of a deceased person are entitled to take proceedings which are preservatory in nature. They could sue when gathering the assets of the trust especially when the property is in the hands of a third party, or take action of any kind to protect the integrity of the trust.

VI. Power to Advertise for Claimant

575. Section 18 of the Trustee Law empowers the trustee for sale of personal representatives to place an advertisement in the State Gazette and in a newspaper

---

1023. Trustee Law, ss 16(5) and 16(6).

circulating in the area in which the property of the deceased or trust property is. They must therefore wait until the date for distribution specified in the notice or advertisement.

§4. Control by the Beneficiaries and the Court

576. In administering the trust, the trustees are basically guided by the trust instrument and the rules of equity. While they owe a number of duties to the beneficiaries, they owe them no duty of consultation and the beneficiaries have no right to interfere in the performance and exercise by the trustees of their duties and discretions.[1024] However, the beneficiaries are entitled, when they are all sui juris, to unanimously put an end to the trust and compel the trustees to hand over the trust property to them.[1025]

577. The court will not normally interfere with the exercise of discretion of the trustees, and where there is no unanimity in the exercise of such discretion by the trustees, the court will not compel the minority to go along with the majority.[1026] However, where a duty lies in law the court will interfere to compel performance of that duty.[1027]

578. The terms of the trust cannot be varied by the court even if it would be advantageous to the beneficiaries. The only rider is contained in section 40 of the Trustee Law of the old western and mid-western regions of Nigeria which allows departure from the terms of a trust 'where in the management or administration of any property vested in the trustees', the trustees have no power in the trust instrument to effect a transaction that is expedient for the trust. This is more of giving efficacy to the terms of the trust rather than varying the same.

§5. Breach of Trust

579. A breach occurs when a trustee fails to do what he has been appointed to do based on the duties imposed on him in the administration of the trust. Breaches can be wilful and criminal wrongdoing, such as the fraudulent misappropriation of trust fund which is a criminal offence by virtue of section 434 of the Criminal code of Nigeria, or where he has invested in wrong business, contrary to either the trust instrument or the Trustee Investment Act.

1024. Kodilinye *supra* n. 160 at 133. In the case of personalty, one of a number of beneficiaries who is sui juris can demand his own share: *See Re Marshall* (1914) 1 Ch. 192.
1025. This is known as the rule in *Saunders v. Vautier* (1841) Beav. 115.
1026. Kodilinye *supra* n. 160 at 134.
1027. *Ibid.*

580. In the course of administration of estate, trustee or personal representative may also be guilty of breach of trust, and a personal representative may have his grant revoked or terminated like a trustee.

581. The liability in a breach of trust is personal; a trustee is only liable for his own breach and not for the breach of trust in which he did not take part. Examples of possible conduct which may lead to breach of trust are as follows:

(a) making an unauthorised profit out of the trust or estate of the deceased;
(b) purchase of trust property without authority;
(c) investing trust money in unauthorised investments;
(d) favouring a beneficiary at the expense of another;
(e) negligently refusing to act as trustee, thus allowing trust property to waste or left in the hand of a single trustee;
(f) wrong distribution of trust or estate property to the wrong person;
(g) conversion of the trust/estate money for personal use;
(h) wrongful intermeddling with the trust assets.[1028]

582. The Supreme Court in *Adekeye v. Akin Olugbade*[1029] held that where the trustee acted fraudulently, the defence of an action being caught under the Limitation Law cannot be a defence and the length of time has no relevance. Similar decision was reached in *Williams v. CBN.*[1030]

§6. Remedies for Breach of Trust

583. Beneficiaries have the following remedies where there has been a breach of trust by the trustee:

I. Personal Remedy Against the Guilty Trustee

584. A trustee is personally liable for a breach of trust committed or arising from his wilful default in the discharge of his obligations to the beneficiaries or towards the maintenance and protection of the trust property.[1031] The measure of liability is the loss caused to the trust estate as a result of the breach.[1032] In awarding damages for breach of trust, the court may, among other remedies, make an order that the beneficial interest of the trustee in the trust property be impounded so as to make good the loss suffered by other beneficiaries.[1033]

1028. *Williams v. CBN* (2014) UKSC 10; *Michael UzoAgba & Anor v. COP* posted on 23 Nov. 2012 by Easy Law online. The case is on criminal breach of trust, and the Supreme Court confirmed the criminal sentence of the accused for criminal breach of trust.
1029. (1987) 3 NWLR (Pt. 60) 214.
1030. *Supra* n. 1028.
1031. Trustees Act 1893, s. 24.
1032. *Knott v. Cottee* (1852) 16 Beav. 77.
1033. *Doering v. Doering* (1889) 42 Ch.D 203.

II. Tracing of the Trust Property

585. The beneficiary's remedy of tracing is a potent way of recovering trust property or funds. In equity, the beneficiary can follow trust property into the hands of the trustees or any third party, and this includes the right to trace assets in their converted form.[1034] Any property bought with the trust money belongs to the beneficiary and if the proceeds are mixed with trustee's own money to purchase other property, the beneficiary has the first charge on that other property.[1035] However, tracing may be impossible where the trust property has been dissipated such as when it is spent on consumables, or used to pay off a secured or unsecured loan;[1036] or where it would produce an inequitable result;[1037] or where the property has come into the hands of a bona fide purchaser for value without notice of the trust.

III. Personal Action Against Wrongful Recipients

586. In certain cases,[1038] equity will give the beneficiary a personal remedy against the person or persons who have wrongly received the trust property irrespective of whether what has been received has been spent, and notwithstanding that the wrongful payment was made under a mistake of fact or law.[1039]

IV. Injunction

587. A beneficiary may bring an application for injunction to restrain the trustees from committing breach of trust or to prevent anticipatory breach of trust.[1040]

V. Revocation of Grant

588. This is usually a remedy against personal representatives who are not trustees.

1034. *Re Diplock Estate* (1948) Ch. 465.
1035. *Re Oatway* (1903) 2 Ch. 356.
1036. *Re Diplock Estate supra* n. 1034 at 521, 543, 548–550.
1037. Kodilinye *supra* n. 160 at 146.
1038. For example, where the trust property has been dissipated.
1039. *Re Diplock supra* n. 1034 at 517, 557.
1040. *Milligan v. Mitchell* (1833) 1 My & K 446.

Chapter 2. Security: Fiducia Cum Creditore (*See Also* Parts I, II, and V)

589. Insolvency is one of the greatest challenges to creditors in trade and commerce. Upon the insolvency of the individual or corporate body, creditors' claims are made subject not only to a number of preferential payments and securities in existence, but also, unsecured creditors are meant to queue for purposes of payment. However, the ingenuity of the trust mechanism has made it possible for a claimant who has an interest in property or goods or any enrichment in the hands and control of an insolvent which is impress with a trust, to call for return of the trust property to which the general creditors have no right to.[1041] By so doing, the claimant is upgraded from the 'owly position' of an unsecured creditor to the status of a beneficiary of a trust with rights superseding those of other creditors. A number of trust devises have been developed as defences against the priorities accorded the holders of floating charges.

§1. The Kayford Trust

590. This trust distilled from the court's decision in *Re Kayford*[1042] arises from circumstances where a consumer makes prepayment for goods or services which are not supplied immediately. Where, in such circumstances, the consumer creates a trust by using the appropriate words when he makes the prepayment, or the supplier takes suitable steps on or before receiving the money such as opening a separate customers' trust account in which the money paid is held, the money is held on trust for the consumer and would not therefore constitute part of the seller's general assets for distribution on insolvency. In Re Kayford where the rule was formulated, the court stated that the payment of the money into a separate bank account was an indication of an intention to create a trust by the seller on behalf of its depositors. While this trust mechanism provides useful protection to a helpless class of persons, the rule has been criticised as unfair to other creditors being a preference in contravention of insolvency policy, and jeopardises the reasonable expectations of creditors in insolvency proceedings.[1043]

§2. The Quist Close Trust

591. Invented by Lord Wilberforce in *Barclays Bank Ltd v. Quist Close Investment Ltd,*[1044] the essence of the trust is that a plaintiff who advances money to a defendant on the basis that it should hold it for a certain purpose can impress the funds with a trust if the purpose fails to materialise. Failure of the primary purpose

1041. Emiri, F. et al., *Equity and Trust in Nigeria* 63 (Malthouse Press Ltd. 2012).
1042. (1975) 1 WLR 279.
1043. Goodhart, W. & James, G., *The Infiltration of Equitable Doctrine into English Commercial Law* 42 MLR 489 at 496–498 (1980).
1044. (1970) AC 567.

of the trust would automatically impose a resulting trust on the money thereby establishing the relationship of cestui que trust and trustee.

592. The essence of the trust is to give those who provide finance, security interest until their money is applied for the purpose specified. Where the trust is established, the queue of insolvency is completely avoided since the money subject to it is impressed with trust and are therefore not available for the general creditors because they are not company's assets.

§3. Romalpa Trust

593. This trust otherwise known as retention of title clause in commercial agreements has its root in the English Court of Appeal decision in *Aluminium Industrie Vassen BV v. Romalpa Aluminium*.[1045] It gives the unpaid supplier of goods security for payment for his goods by the use of reservation of title clause stipulating that title in the goods would not pass until payment is made by the buyer. Thus title in the goods supplied may remain in the seller until the purchase price is paid in full and, consequently, where the buyer becomes insolvent before payment, the goods would not form part of the buyer's distributable assets but would be impressed on trust for the supplier. It is said that 'since the Sale of Goods Act allows the seller to make reservation of title in contract for sale of goods, and the clause has the attraction of assisting an otherwise unsecured creditor to avoid insolvency queue, suppliers of goods have striven to bring themselves within the Romalpa equation by adopting reservation of title clauses'.[1046]

594. The application of the Romalpa clauses ranges from the simple situation of retention of title over unpaid goods to more complex cases such as where the goods would only be paid for after the buyer has resold same, or what is received is put into a manufacturing process or the proceeds of sale of such manufactured products, as the case may be.[1047]

595. A seller who sells under a reservation of title clause and authorises the buyer to resell on condition that the buyer will account for the proceed of sale may, if the buyer becomes insolvent, enjoy an equitable right to trace to the proceeds, and by so doing, prevent the funds from being treated as assets of the buyer available for distribution. The seller not only enjoys a personal right against the buyer, but he also has a proprietary right to have a charge imposed on the proceeds of the resale and claim back whatever goods the buyer still has in possession.[1048]

1045. (1976) 1 WLR 676.
1046. Emiri, F. et al.*supra* n. 1041 at 643.
1047. Moffat, G., *Trusts Law (Text and Materials)* 531 (2nd ed. Butterworths).
1048. *Ibid.*

Part V. Security over Property

§1. Introduction

596. One of the most significant sources of capital generation for investment and business activities is bank lending, which may be in the form of an overdraft or loan. Some forms of overdraft[1049] may not require formal security[1050] platform as the positive credit history of borrowers generally, and the huge turnover of large business concerns in particular could be sufficient incentive for such advances. However, smaller business concerns with low turnover may not enjoy overdrafts without provision of some forms of security. Negotiation for long, medium, and short-term loans usually attracts a requirement of security which must be met before the release of funds.

I. The Importance of Security

597. Although, in practical terms, the primary consideration in making decisions on provision of credit facility in the form of overdrafts or loans is the credit worthiness of the borrower, and the provision of security is taken as an additional safeguard,[1051] this is not to suggest that the requirement of security is of less importance. From the legal and economic perspectives, the requirement of security for advances is paramount for many reasons: First, a bank may run afoul of the law for making advances without adequate security.[1052] Second, security is a concrete assurance that the borrower would fulfil his repayment obligations towards the lender and

1049. For example, the limited reserve of funds by the banker on a customer's account to meet unforeseen emergencies and which is approved based on the good credit history of the customer.
1050. Usually, the turnover of the customer is relied on as an assurance for meeting credit obligations.
1051. *See* generally, Holden, J.M., *Law and Practice of Banking* Vol. II, Securities for Bankers' Advances, (5th ed. 1971).
1052. This is so where a particular legislation prohibits lending without security. *See* s. 20 of the Banks and Other Financial Institutions Decree No. 25, 1991 which provides credit limit beyond which banks cannot go without security; and the Failed Banks (Recovery of Debts) and Financial Malpractices in Banks Decree No. 18 1994 (as amended). By virtue of s. 15(1)(a) of that Law, any director, manager, officer or employee of a bank who knowingly, recklessly, negligently, wilfully or otherwise grants, approves or otherwise connected with the grant or approval of any credit facility without adequate security or with no security as normally required, or with a defective security, or without perfecting a security is guilty of an offence punishable with five years imprisonment without an option of fine pursuant to s. 16(1)(a).

hence make funds available for further lending.[1053] Third, an unsecured creditor faces the danger of losing money in the event of the debtor's bankruptcy or insolvency, and may not have priority in law in the event of a company's liquidation.[1054] Fourth, valuable assets of the debtor (sometimes acquired with the advance) may no longer be available for attachment after judgment is entered in favour of the lender by the court,[1055] and where available, may be insufficient to meet the debtor's indebtedness. Fifth, the costs of credit tend to be higher and the incentive to grant credit may be hampered greatly where the credit facility is unsecured.[1056]

598. A secured creditor has an overall advantage that assets are 'charged' against repayment from the inception and may be resorted to in the event of default by the debtor, to recoup the loan advanced. It enables the creditor to stay afloat and consequently, makes funds available for economic activities towards economic growth. A secured creditor minimises the risk of debtor's default and boosts confidence in the banker-customer relationship.

II. Types of Security

599. There are broadly two types of security namely: security created by agreement between parties which is the common type of security for most bankers' advances; and security evolving by operation of law in many circumstances not involving parties' consensus, such as a lien.

600. Security by agreement otherwise known as consensual security, are basically of two types; real and personal. Real security which may be created by way of mortgage, pledge, or charge (depending on the type of property) involves holding interest in some tangible assets (such as land and all things attached thereto, goods or chattels of different kinds) or in intangible property (such as choses in action) as security for credit. Personal security are personal 'undertakings' by persons[1057] either to be primarily liable for the debtor's indebtedness in the event of default without the creditor proceeding first against the debtor as in the case of an indemnity, or liable under a collateral contract for the indebtedness only upon the inability of the principal debtor or insufficiency of his assets to meet his obligations, as in the case of a guarantee.

601. While the distinction between real and personal security may be helpful in understanding the rudiments and basic legal principles applicable in the law of

1053. *See* Smith, I.O., *Nigerian Law of Secured Credit* 3 (Ecowatch Publications Nigeria Ltd 2001).
1054. Payment of debts in company's liquidation ranks according to the date of the debt.
1055. Since no specific assets are attached in this case, the debtor might, after court judgment, move valuable things away from attachment.
1056. It has been said that the benefit of secured credit 'will be shared by the borrower in the form of lower interest, a longer term loans or other more favourable conditions'. *See* Pedrazzini, F. & Simpson, W., *The Legal Framework for Secured Credit: A Suitable Case for Treatment* BLI 127 at 129 (1999).
1057. Such persons are called 'Guarantors' or 'Sureties'.

secured credit, a combination of both types of security is often employed by bankers. Lending to corporate bodies on the strength of tangible assets as security is usually complemented by directors' guarantee or indemnity, while a guarantor of personal loans may be required to furnish some form of real security in tangible or intangible assets.[1058]

602. This part deals mainly with Real security over immovable properties and movable personal chattels. A discourse of Real security over choses in action, other chattels such as ship and aircraft, and personal security generally, are beyond the scope of this monograph.

III. Classification of Rights in Real Security

603. Traditionally, real security may be classified into three namely:

(1) *Proprietary security* which involves transfer of title in tangible assets from the borrower to the lender as security, and which title is reconveyed back to the borrower upon liquidation of indebtedness, or divested of the borrower upon default. A legal or equitable mortgage of land and chattels are examples of proprietary security. In a proprietary security, possession of the subject matter of security is not necessary or required by law and may even be disadvantageous to the lender.[1059] The remedies open to the creditor upon default by the debtor includes sale of the property, appointment of a receiver, and foreclosure.[1060]
(2) *Possessory Security*: A possessory security requires that the lender takes actual[1061] or constructive[1062] possession of the subject matter of security for it to be validly created, or presumed by law. Examples of possessory security are the *common law pledge* or *possessory lien.* Such possession must be certain, unequivocal and continuous,[1063] and transfer of title is not required. Upon default by the debtor, the creditor may exercise the right of retention until the loan is liquidated in the case of a possessory lien,[1064] or may sell the subject matter of security in the case of a pledge.[1065]
(3) *Charge or hypothecation:* This form of security gives the creditor neither proprietary nor possessory right in the subject matter of security, but involves a simple appropriation of specific property to the satisfaction of the debt. This is

1058. *See,* for example, *Edu v. National Bank of Nigeria Plc* (1971) (1) NCLR 340.
1059. A mortgagee in possession for example, is liable to account to the mortgagee in equity not only for what he received as rents and profits, but also for what he ought to have made but for his negligence or wilful default: *See White v. City of London Brewery* (1889) 42 Ch.D 237.
1060. *See* generally, 646–663 *infra.*
1061. Actual possession involves direct physical possession by the mortgagee.
1062. This involves possession through agents or being in custody of the means of reaching the subject matter of security such as having the key to a warehouse or possession of the documents to goods.
1063. *Official Assignee of Madras v. Mercantile Bank of India* (1935) AC 53.
1064. *See* Smith, I.O. *supra* n. 1053 at 201.
1065. *Carter v. Wake* (1877) 4 Ch.D 605.

done by a simple agreement which gives the creditor the power to appropriate the subject matter of security through judicial sale or by appointment of a receiver where the debtor defaults.[1066]

604. The creditor should be aware that the type of security to be created in any instance would depend on two major considerations: The first consideration should be the subject matter intended as security. For example, the nature of land as an immovable property would suggest that a mortgage or a charge may be appropriate since the mortgagee need not go into possession to have a valid and potent security. In the case of chattels, a pledge may be appropriate since 'physical control or dominium of the property is necessary not only for its protection, but essentially to forestall disposition of same by the debtor without the creditor's knowledge, bearing in mind that creditors are usually not warned in this regard'.[1067] The second consideration which the creditor may wish to consider is the most profitable and convenient mode of enforcement in the event of default by the debtor, depending on whether title or possession was originally conveyed as security, and whether the security is legal or equitable.

IV. Preliminary Matters

605. Lenders' decision to take security for a loan or an overdraft cannot be actualised without taking care of some preliminary issues which may negative an intention to create a valid security. These preliminary issues are outlined below, while detailed discussion may be sought elsewhere:[1068]

(a) Parties to the contract of loan as well as the secured credit arrangement must be natural or juristic persons.[1069]
(b) Parties must have legal capacity to give or take security.[1070]
(c) Genuine intentions of the parties as free agents must be put in writing[1071] and must not be vitiated by mistake,[1072] misrepresentation,[1073] duress,[1074] or undue influence.[1075] The credit arrangement for which the security is obtained must be meant only for a lawful purpose for the security to be enforceable.[1076]
(d) Party giving security should have title over the subject matter of security.[1077]

1066. *Ogundiani v. Araba* (1978) 1 LRN 280 at 289.
1067. *See* Smith, I.O. *supra* n. 1053 at 11.
1068. *See* Smith, I.O. *supra* Ch. 2.
1069. *Iyke Medical Merchandise v. Pfizer Inc* (2001) 5SC (Pt. 1) 58 at 68.
1070. *See* generally, Smith, I.O. *supra* n. 1053 at 18–23.
1071. *Olanlege v. Afro Continental (Nig) Ltd* (1996) 7 NWLR (Pt. 458) 29.
1072. *Bell v. Lever Brothers Ltd* (1932) AC 161.
1073. On what constitutes misrepresentation, *see Udogwu v. Oki* (1990) 5 NWLR (Pt. 153) 721 at 734 paras C–G.
1074. *Nnadozie v. Dizengoff* (1967) 1 ALR 255 at 256 on what constitutes duress.
1075. On what constitutes undue influence, *see All Card v. Skinner* (1887) 36 Ch.D 145 at 181.
1076. *Alao v. ACB Ltd* (1998) 3 NWLR (Pt. 542) 339.
1077. It is trite law that a person cannot give what he does not have: *Nemodat quod non habet.*

(e) Title over the subject matter of security must be secured.[1078]
(f) The value of the subject matter of security must be commensurate to the indebtedness leaving a comfortable margin between it and the amount of loan or overdraft.[1079]

1078. Security over subject matter of security involves an assurance that the creditor would fall back on indefeasible title in the event of enforcement.
1079. This is necessary to make allowance for depreciation and inflation.

Chapter 1. Security in Immovable Property

§1. Introduction

606. Land as an immovable property provides a reliable and invaluable security for loans and advances in modern times. Unlike movable properties, land titles are usually represented on title deeds, register of titles or instruments. Physical control of the property is hardly necessary and its characteristic feature of immovability affords the creditor a reassuring grip on the security. In time of inflation with the attendant fall in the value of money, land appreciates in value to compensate a creditor who decides to enforce the security upon debtor's default. In an agrarian economy of the developing world, land has always been the subject matter of security from time immemorial. Its availability and value as source of raw materials and cash crops give it a pride of place among other subject matter of security. It offers a convenient way of creating effective encumbrances in favour of the creditor while the debtor remains in possession without hindrance.

607. Land may be taken as security by way of a mortgage (legal or equitable)[1080] or an equitable charge[1081] under the general law. Pledge of land is known only to customary law[1082] and portends a weak security for bankers in terms of its utility[1083] and lack of mechanism for its realisation.[1084]

608. The subject matter of land as security involves not only the ground, but also all things attached to it in the form of structures erected thereon either before or after the execution of instrument of security on the strength of the legal maxim quicquid plantatur solo solo cedit.[1085]

609. All titles to land have been reduced to rights of occupancy under the Land Use Act[1086] which is the main legal title available as subject matter of a mortgage, pledge or charge. The holder of a right of occupancy also has title to all unexhausted improvements on land[1087] which may form the subject matter of security. Mortgage of unexhausted improvements on land as opposed to vacant land is

---

1080. On mortgage of land as security, *see* 620–663 *infra*.
1081. An equitable charge is an appropriation of property to the contract of loan so that the creditor could attach same upon debtor's default. *See* generally, Idigbe JSC in *Ogundiani v. Araba supra* n. 1066.
1082. The old classification of mortgages in English law into living and dead pledge has since fallen into disuse.
1083. Although the main consideration behind this form of security is that the creditor shall take possession of the land and put it to use pending the debtor's liquidation of the debt, the former loses any improvements on the land once the pledge is redeemed by paying off the loan.
1084. A customary pledge is perpetually redeemable and the land cannot be sold to recover the loan.
1085. Whatever is attached to land belongs to the land: *See Francis v. Ibitoye* (1976) 12 SC 99; *NEPA v. Amusa* (1976) 12 SC 99 at 114–115.
1086. Cap L5 LFN 2010.
1087. *Ibid.*, s. 15.

advised, as compensation is payable mainly on the unexhausted improvements in the event of revocation of a right of occupancy.[1088]

610. Apart from the statutory charge expressed to be by way of legal mortgage,[1089] a charge is essentially equitable. An equitable charge by way of security is a devise by which land is specifically appropriated to the contract of loan and 'crystallises' only upon default by the charger (borrower) to repay the loan.

611. In addition to consensual security by way of a mortgage, charge or customary pledge, security over land may arise by operation of law. This arises in circumstances where it would be inequitable or unconscionable for a party to a land transaction to take benefit of the transaction and either refuse to furnish full consideration as in the case of the vendor's lien; or where a party fails or refuses to assign the subject matter of transaction (the land) to the other party after furnishing consideration, as in the case of the purchaser's lien. In either case, a lien arises by operation of law and attaches to the land as an encumbrance which may be enforced against transferees, except a bona fide purchaser of the legal estate without the claimant's equity.

§2. Mortgage of Land

612. A mortgage of land has been defined as 'a legal or equitable conveyance of title as a security for the payment of debt or the discharge of some other obligations for which it is given, subject to a condition that the title shall be reconveyed if the mortgage debt is liquidated'.[1090]

613. To create a valid and enforceable mortgage in law, lenders should take note of the following prerequisites:

(i) Property must be alienable[1091] and the conditions precedent for alienation where applicable must be met.[1092]
(ii) A valuation of the property to know how much it is worth is very important. The responsibility in this regard is that of a professional valuer. Where the holder is an actual grantee of a right of occupancy,[1093] it may be necessary to ascertain the ground rent and whether it has been paid up to date, as well as the remainder of the term granted. The state of repair of the property and the general character of the neighbourhood may affect the valuation.

1088. *Ibid.*, s. 29.
1089. *See*, e.g., Mortgage and Property Law No. 6 of Lagos State 2010, ss 15(1) and 16(1); Property and Conveyancing Law Cap 100 LWN 1959, ss 108(1), 109(1).
1090. *Santley v. Wilde* (1899) 2 Ch. 474; *Adetona & Anor v. First Bank* (2012) 3 BFLR 208 at 220.
1091. For example, s. 36(5) of the Land Use Act, 1978 Cap L5 2010 has placed a total bar on alienation of land in the non-urban area so that a mortgage cannot be created thereon.
1092. An example is the requirement of governor's consent. *See* s. 22 of the Land Use Act, *supra.*
1093. An actual grantee is the holder of a right of occupancy expressly granted by the Governor: *See* s. 5 of the Land Use Act, *supra.*

(iii) The borrower should be a holder of a valid legal or equitable title. This shall involve a thorough investigation of title from the document of title such as the old Deed of Conveyance or certificate of occupancy, to the actual root of title in the case of deemed grants.[1094] A rigorous search at the lands registry or the Companies Registry (in the case of corporate bodies) might reveal existing encumbrances. Third-party rights on the property must be ascertained and verified.

(iv) Compliance with the requisite Town Planning Laws and Regulations should be ascertained to ensure that all buildings on the land, extensions thereto, and any ongoing user of the land are all covered by planning permission.[1095]

(v) The decision to take a legal or an equitable mortgage would depend on the rules laid down by the bank, the nature of available title, consideration relating to enforcement of the security, and priority rules in law.

I. Creation of Mortgages

614. The mode of creating mortgages in Nigeria varies according to the applicable law and the nature of interest which forms the subject of the mortgage.

615. A legal mortgage may be created where the title of the borrower (mortgagor) is legal. Where the property is situated in States other than those covered by property legislation,[1096] the old common law mode of creation applies, and a legal mortgage is created by an assignment of the totality of the term over which a right of occupancy is held by the mortgagor, subject to cesser on redemption. A mortgage of a leasehold interest is created by an assignment of the residue of the term of lease to the mortgagee subject to cesser on redemption.

616. In States where the property legislation applies,[1097] a legal mortgage of a right of occupancy may be created by a demise for a term of years absolute[1098] subject to cesser on redemption. Where the title of the mortgagor is leasehold, a mortgage is created by a sub-demise for a term of years less one day at least than the

1094. *See* generally, Smith, I.O. *supra* n. 1053 at 26–28.

1095. *See*, for example, the Nigerian Urban and Regional Planning Act, Cap N138 LFN 2010, and corresponding legislation in the States.

1096. Very few of such States, if any, exists today.

1097. There is the Property and Conveyancing Law (PCL) Cap 100 Laws of Western Nigeria, 1959 applicable also in the old western and mid-western Region of Nigeria adopted by the States created there from. Many other States have property legislation in existence, e.g., Cap 110 Laws of Abia State of Nigeria 2005, Cap 100 Laws of Akwa Ibom State of Nigeria 2000, Cap P10 Laws of Kwara State of Nigeria 2007, Cap 122 Laws of Bauchi State of Nigeria 2006, Cap 114 Laws of Kebbi State of Nigeria 1996, Law No. 6 of Lagos State 2012 to mention but a few.

1098. Section 108(1)(a) Cap 100 Laws of Western Nigeria, 1959 as adopted in the various States created there from; s. 107(1)(a) Cap 110 Abia State of Nigeria 2005; s. 105(1)(a) Cap 100 Awa Ibom State of Nigeria 2000; Cap P10 Kwara State of Nigeria 2007, Cap 122 Bauchi State of Nigeria 2006; s. 107(3) Cap 114 Kebbi State 1996, Cap 114 Sokoto State 1996; s. 15(2) Law No. 6 of Lagos State 2012.

term vested in the mortgagor[1099] subject to cesser on redemption. A mortgagor with a right of occupancy or term of years may create a charge by deed expressed to be by way of legal mortgage,[1100] or a charge by deed expressed to be by way of statutory mortgage in the forms provided under the law.[1101] Where a legal mortgage is created by a charge or deed expressed to be by way of statutory mortgage, the mortgagee shall have the same protection, powers, and remedies of a legal mortgagee of a demise or sub-demise.[1102] Whether the mortgage is done by way of a demise or a sub-demise, the first mortgagee shall have the same right to the possession of documents as if 'his security included a right of occupancy' in the earlier case, or as if 'his security has been effected by assignment' in the latter case.[1103]

617. Any purported assignment of a right of occupancy or a term of years absolute by way of mortgage in any State with property legislation is not void, but shall operate in accordance with the tenor of the Law and, in the case of a purported assignment of a term of years, 'the term to be taken by a first or only mortgagee shall be ten days less than the term expressed to be assigned', and in the case of the second or subsequent mortgagee, 'shall be one day longer than the term vested in the first or other mortgagee whose security ranks immediately before that of the second or subsequent mortgagee, if the length of the last mentioned term permits, and in any other case, for a term less by one day at least than the term expressed to be assigned'.[1104]

618. The modes of creating equitable mortgages are uniform throughout the whole Federation. An equitable mortgage may be created in the following ways:

(1) Where the interest of the mortgagor is equitable, the mortgage created thereon must be equitable such as where the mortgagor at common law creates a second or subsequent mortgages over the same property in favour of subsequent mortgagee(s). This is possible, but would take effect as equitable mortgage only.[1105]

1099. Section 110 Cap 100 LWN 1959; s. 108(1) Cap 110 Abia 2005; s. 106(1) Cap 100 Akwa Ibom 2000, Cap P10 Kwara 2007, Cap 122 Bauchi 2006; s. 108(1) Cap 114 Kebbi 1996, Cap 114 Sokoto, 1996; s. 15(1) Law No. 6 Lagos State, 2010.
1100. *Ibid.,* subs. 1 thereto.
1101. Section 15(1) of Law No. 6 of Lagos State 2010.
1102. Section 110 Cap 100 LWN 1959; s. 109 Cap 110 Abia 2005; s. 107 Cap 100 Akwa Ibom 2000, Cap 123 Bauchi 2006, Cap P10 Kwara 2007; s. 109 Cap 114 Kebbi 1996, CAP 114 Sokoto 1996; s. 17(1) Law No. 6 of Lagos State 2010.
1103. Proviso to ss 15(1) and 16(1) of Law No. 6 Laws of Lagos State, 2010, and corresponding provisions in the Property Law of other States.
1104. Law No. 6 of Lagos State 2010, s. 16(2) and corresponding provisions in the Property Law of other States.
1105. Contrast to the position under the PCL, 1959 and the property legislation of the various States in Nigeria where such subsequent mortgagee holds a legal as opposed to equitable mortgage. But where the interest of the mortgagor is equitable, only equitable mortgage can be created: *See,* e.g., s. 18(1) of Law No. 6 of Lagos State 2010, and corresponding provisions in the property legislation of the various States of Nigeria.

(2) An agreement by the holder of a right of occupancy to create a legal mortgage in favour of a mortgagee who has advanced money to him is an equitable mortgage, and the execution of the legal mortgage may be enforced by the mortgagee suing in equity for specific performance.[1106]

(3) Delivery of title deed relating to the borrower's land with an intention to treat the land covered by such deed as security.[1107] Where such deposit is accompanied by a memorandum under seal, the equitable mortgagee is entitled to exercise the power of sale in law.[1108] In Lagos State, a mere deposit of title deed does not create an equitable mortgage except it is accompanied by an agreement to create a legal mortgage, or in case of mortgage of an equitable interest in a property, by an assignment of an equitable interest in favour of the mortgagee subject to cesser on redemption.[1109] In such cases, a mortgagee may, within thirty days, bring an application in court by an originating summons requiring the mortgagor to execute a legal mortgage in his favour, and thereafter, exercise the powers of legal mortgagee under the Law.[1110]

II. Documentation and Perfection of Security

619. An agreement for mortgage of land is a transaction within the ambit of section 4 of the Statute of Frauds, 1677 and corresponding provisions in the laws of other States,[1111] and must therefore be evidenced by a memorandum in writing signed by the party to be charged or his agent. The agreement shall normally contain particulars of parties; statement of the principal sum borrowed; interest payable; time and mode of repayment; proviso for redemption; and such other provisions as parties may agree upon. It is important to ensure that the agreement does not contain provisions which may constitute a clog on the mortgagor's equity of redemption. Among other provisions which may be contained in a mortgage agreement are the following:

(i) Covenant to insure: The risk of damage to or destruction of the mortgaged property by fire or other hazards may be taken care of by a covenant to insure in the mortgage agreement. The mortgagor may be required to insure the mortgaged property and prompt payment of premium by him may be ensured. However, the mortgagee may insure the property and add the premium and

1106. *Ogundiani v. Araba supra* n. 1066.
1107. *Russel v. Russel* ER vol. 28 1121; *Okuneye v. First Bank of Nigeria Plc* (1996) 6 NWLR (Pt. 475) 749.
1108. The statutory powers of sale under the Conveyancing Act, 1881, the Property and Conveyancing Law Cap 100 LWN 1959, and under the property legislation of the various States are applicable.
1109. Section 18(1) of Law No. 6 of Lagos State 2010.
1110. *Ibid.*, subs. 2 thereof.
1111. PCL Cap 100 LWN 1959, s. 67; Law Reform (Contract) Act 1961, s. 5(2) and corresponding provision in the Laws of the various States of Nigeria.

other incidental expenses to the interest to be agreed upon. This covenant may be implied by law unless otherwise expressly agreed.[1112]

(ii) Covenant to Repair or Keep in Repair: The covenant to repair or keep in repair by the mortgagor is a good option where the mortgagee does not intend to go into possession at any time considering the strict obligations imposed on the mortgagee in possession in equity. This covenant ensures that the mortgagor keeps the property in good state of repairs so long as the loan or any part of it remains unpaid. Where he defaults in that regard, the mortgagee may enter into possession to carry out the said repairs in which case the mortgagor would be obligated to indemnify the mortgagee for the cost of repairs, which shall be charged on the mortgaged property.

(iii) *Restriction on leasing powers:* Where parties intend to exclude statutory power to create or surrender leases, or restrict same under the ambit of the agreement, it is necessary that such exclusion or restriction be express otherwise, either of the parties in possession may create statutory leases.[1113]

(iv) Covenant to observe and perform lessee's covenant: Where the mortgage property is a leasehold property, the mortgagor may be required to covenant to observe and perform his covenants under the lease, whilst the mortgagee is given the benefit of all rights and remedies of the mortgagor in respect of any breach of covenant by the lessor.

(v) Consolidation of mortgages: Where it is intended by the mortgagee that two or more mortgages created shall be consolidated for purposes of redemption, it shall be so stated in the mortgage agreement otherwise the statutory restrictions on consolidation of mortgages for purposes of redemption[1114] would apply.

(vi) Entitlement to compensation in the event of acquisition of mortgaged property: In the event of revocation of the right of occupancy over the mortgage property, it is the mortgagor that is entitled to compensation as the 'holder' of a right of occupancy and the mortgagee is expressly excluded.[1115] To save the mortgagee from irreparable loss, it may be necessary to include in the agreement a declaration of trust in favour of the mortgagee in the event of payment of such compensation to the mortgagor pursuant to the provisions of the Land Use Act.

1112. *See,* for example, PCL Cap 100 LWN 1959, s. 123(1)(i) and corresponding provisions in the Property Law of other States.

1113. Conveyancing Act 1881, s. 18(1); PCL Cap 100 LWN 1959, s. 121(1); Law No. 6 of Lagos State 2010, s. 33; and corresponding provisions in the Property Law of other States.

1114. Conveyancing Act 1881, s. 17(2); PCL Cap 100 LWN 1959, s. 115(2) and corresponding provisions in the Property Law of other States.

1115. *See* the Land Use Act 1978 Cap L5 2010, s. 51 for the definition of a 'holder' which excludes the mortgagee; hence, the latter is not entitled to compensation since compensation is payable to the 'holder' i.e., the mortgagor.

620. The mortgagee must ensure that the mortgage is properly executed in law. Where the mortgagor is an illiterate, the relevant provisions of the Illiterates Protection Law[1116] must be complied with both as regards the illiterate jurat and execution before the Magistrate or Justice of the Peace.[1117] A Company registered under the CAMA may execute such agreement either by affixing its seal, or by authorising any of its Directors to execute same on its behalf.[1118] Trustees registered under Part C of CAMA may execute the mortgage agreement on behalf of the authorised body or organisation.

III. Stamping

621. A mortgage attracts ad valorem duty in law and must be duly stamped.[1119] An unstamped mortgage is inadmissible as evidence either of a loan agreement or of a security transaction.[1120] Such document may however be accepted for late stamping on payment of penalty or fine.[1121]

IV. Requirement of Consent under the Land Use Act

622. A legal or equitable mortgage requires Governor's consent under the Land Use Act.[1122] Failure to seek and obtain consent renders the mortgage transaction void and the content of the mortgage agreement with regards to the security ineffectual.[1123] This is so notwithstanding that the mortgagor as 'holder' of a right of occupancy owes the responsibility to seek and obtain Governor's consent.[1124] However, Governor's consent is not required with respect to a legal mortgage on a statutory right of occupancy over which an equitable mortgage had been created earlier with the consent of the Governor, or in the case of a reconveyance of the mortgaged property to the mortgagor upon liquidation of the loan.[1125] An agreement to create a mortgage without Governor's consent is not necessarily void, but remains inchoate until consent is obtained.[1126]

1116. *See,* for example, the Illiterates Protection Law Cap 13 Laws of Lagos State 2003 and other State Laws on Illiterates protection.
1117. *Ibid.,* s. 2.
1118. Cap C20 LFN 2010, ss 71 and 73.
1119. Stamp Duties Act Cap S8 LFN 2004, s. 22 and Schedule to the Act.
1120. *Ibid.,* s. 22(4). An equitable mortgagee under seal is treated as a legal mortgage for purposes of stamping.
1121. *Ibid.,* s. 80(3).
1122. Cap L5 LFN 2010, s. 22. Section 51 of the Act defines a mortgage to include an equitable mortgage: *See Jacobson Engineering Co. Ltd v. UBA Ltd* (1993) 3 NWLR (Pt. 283) 586.
1123. *Ibid.,* s. 26: *See Savannah bank Ltd v. Ajilo* (1989) NWLR (Pt. 97) 305; *Union Bank of Nigeria Plc v. Ayodare & Sons (Nig) Ltd* (2007) 13 NWLR (Pt. 1052) 567.
1124. *Union Bank of Nigeria Plc v. Ayodare supra* n. 1123.
1125. Proviso to s. 22 of the Land Use Act.
1126. *Awojugbagbe Light Industries Ltd v. Chinukwe* (1993) 1 NWLR (Pt. 270) 485.

V. Registration

623. A mortgage agreement is a registrable instrument[1127] and must be registered. However, the instrument shall not be accepted for registration where Governor's consent has not been obtained.[1128] All land instruments now relates to rights being subject of State grant,[1129] and it must therefore be registered within six months of the execution of such instrument otherwise, it is void.[1130] Failure to register the document makes it inadmissible in evidence to prove the existence of the security,[1131] but it may be evidence of payment and receipt of money.[1132] A registered mortgage instrument has priority over other competing mortgage instruments, and priority is reckoned from the date of registration as opposed to the date of execution of the document.[1133]

VI. Redemption of Mortgage

624. The law is: 'once a mortgage always a mortgage'.[1134] Consequently, the right of the mortgagor to redeem the mortgaged property upon payment of principal and interest exists both at law and in equity and may be exercised as appropriate. Payment of the principal and interest on the date fixed by the mortgage agreement entitles him to a release of the mortgaged property, or extinguishes the mortgage as it were. However, failure to repay the mortgage debt on the contract date extinguishes the mortgagor's right to redeem at law only; in equity, there is an implied condition giving the mortgagor a continuing right to redeem which he may exercise before it is destroyed by foreclosure, sale, release, or lapse of time.[1135] Any clause in a mortgage agreement which renders the right to redeem at law illusory, or which constitutes a clog on the equity of redemption is void.[1136]

1127. *See* Land Instrument Registration Act No. 36 1924, s. 2 and corresponding provisions in the Land Instrument Registration Law of the various States. *See also* the Lagos State Lands Registration Law No. 1 2015, s. 49.

1128. *Ibid.*, s. 15.

1129. All land rights emanates from the State either as an actual or deemed grant: *See* Land Use Act 1978 Cap L5 LFN 2010, ss 1, 5, 34, and 36.

1130. Land Registration Act No. 36 1924, s. 15 and corresponding provisions in the Land Instrument Registration Law of the States.

1131. *Oredola Okeya Trading Co. v. A.G Kwara State* (1992) 7 NWLR (Pt. 254) 412.

1132. *See Ogunbambi v. Abowaba supra* n. 356.

1133. *See* Registration Act No. 361924, s. 16 and corresponding provisions in the Land Instrument Registration Law of the States, and the case of *Amankra v. Zankley* (1963) 1 All NLR 304.

1134. This suggests that the mortgagor remains in equity, the real owner of the mortgaged property and that the mortgagee holds the mortgaged property mainly as security for the loan: *See Yaro v. Arewa Construction Ltd & 2 Ors* (2012) 1 BFLR 718 at 740. Thus, a mortgage transaction must not contain clauses that may render redemption of the mortgage illusory or operate as a clog on the equitable right to redeem: *See Fairclough v. Swan Brewery Co. Ltd supra* n. 341.

1135. *Majekodunmi & Anor v. African International Bank* (2012) 2 BFLR 232 at 244.

1136. *Fairclough v. Swan Brewery Co. Ltd supra* n. 341.

625. Where the mortgagor pays the principal and interest before his equity of redemption is destroyed,[1137] he is entitled to a reconveyance of the mortgaged property to him. In the States outside the old PCL States,[1138] a formal deed of release shall be executed reconveying the mortgage property to the mortgagor.[1139] However, in States that have adopted the PCL[1140] and in other States where property legislation exists,[1141] the requirement of a formal deed of release is not mandatory. A receipt endorsed on, written at the foot of, or annexed to the mortgage deed would be sufficient to extinguish the mortgage provided that it states the name of the person who pays the money and is executed by the person in whom the mortgage is vested.[1142] Such receipt shall operate, without any formal deed of release, as a surrender or release, and shall discharge the mortgaged property from all principal money and interest secured by, and from all claims under the mortgage, but without prejudice to any term or other interest of the mortgagee or other person in whom the mortgage property was vested.[1143] A receipt endorsed in the manner prescribed must be stamped as a reconveyance.[1144]

626. A mortgagor, who redeems the mortgage upon payment of principal and interest, is entitled to have the title deeds handed back to him.

VII. Enforcement of Mortgage Security

627. The essence of security is an assurance that the mortgagee would have something to fall back on in the event of the mortgagor's failure to pay back on the date fixed for repayment under the mortgage agreement. Thus, where the mortgagor defaults, the mortgagee reserves the right in law to enforce the mortgage security and thereby destroy the mortgagor's equity of redemption.

628. There are five methods of enforcement recognised by law depending on whether the mortgage is legal or equitable:

(i) Enforcement of Covenant to repay.
(ii) Taking possession.
(iii) Sale of mortgaged property.
(iv) Appointment of a receiver.
(v) Action for Foreclosure.

1137. The equity of redemption may be destroyed by sale or foreclosure.
1138. That is in the Eastern and Northern States without property legislation.
1139. *See,* e.g., Lagos State Lands Registration Law No. 1 2015, s. 55. Such reconveyance does not require Governor's consent: *See* proviso to s. 22 of the Act 1978 Cap L5 LFN 2010.
1140. That is in Oyo, Ogun, Ondo, Osun, Ekiti, Edo, and Delta States.
1141. See for example the Lagos State Mortgage and Property Law 2010.
1142. *See,* for example, the PCL Cap 100 LWN 1959, s. 135(1); Law No. 6 of Lagos State 2010, s. 47; Cap 110 Abia 2005, s. 134(1); Cap 100 Akwa Ibom 2000, s. 132(1), Cap 122 Bauchi 2006, Cap P10 Kwara 2007; Cap 114 Kebbi 1996, s. 134(1), Cap 114 Sokoto 1996.
1143. *Ibid.,* subs. (1) (a) and (b).
1144. *See* Law No. 6 of Lagos State 2010, s. 47(5) and corresponding provisions in the Property Laws of other States.

629. The various methods of enforcement are cumulative not exclusive, so that where one method did not satisfy the debt owing to the mortgagee, he could adopt another method accordingly, although where foreclosure proceedings are embarked upon, the mortgagee cannot afterwards fall back on any of the other remedies.[1145]

A. *Enforcement of Covenant to Repay*

630. A covenant to repay by the mortgagor is usually contained in a mortgage agreement but where it is inadvertently omitted, it is implied since in equity, receipt of money carries with it an implied obligation to repay.[1146] A mortgagee under a legal or equitable mortgage may enforce a personal covenant to repay in court where the mortgage property is still in existence and the mortgagee is in a position to reconvey.[1147] This personal action is statute barred twelve years after the right to recover the debt accrued,[1148] except where the mortgaged property comprises any future interest which has not matured.[1149]

B. *Taking Possession*

631. The right to take possession is the prerogative of the legal mortgagee mainly; an equitable mortgagee lacks the legal estate to entitle him to physical possession. Where physical possession by the mortgagee is not possible as a result of the existence of leases binding on him, he may enter into receipt of rent and profits by notifying the lessees in possession to pay to him as opposed to the mortgagor.[1150] Such rent should be applied by the mortgagee in satisfaction of his claim for principal and interest. Where the mortgagor is in physical occupation of the mortgaged property, the mortgagee takes possession by bringing an action in court to evict him. However, the mortgagee's right to take possession goes with attendant obligations such as a duty to keep the mortgaged property in good state of repairs[1151] which cost may be met from the rents and profits collected.

632. While in possession, the mortgagee may create leases[1152] and make reasonable improvements which enhance the value of the property.[1153] Where a mortgagee of land has been in possession of the mortgaged property for a period of sixteen

1145. *See Salako v. Federal Loans Board* (1967) NCLR 266 at 268.
1146. *See Sutton v. Sutton* (1882) 22 Ch. 511 at 516.
1147. *See Walker v. Jones* (1866) LR 1CP 50.
1148. *See* the Limitation Law Cap L67 Laws of Lagos State 2003, s. 28 with similar provision in the Limitation Law of other States.
1149. *Ibid.*, s. 28(2).
1150. *Horlock v. Smith* (1895) 1 Ch.D 516.
1151. *Sandon v. Hooper* 49 ER 820.
1152. Conveyancing Act 1881, s. 18; PCL Cap 100 LWN 1959, s. 12(1); Law No. 6 of Lagos State 2010, s. 33 and corresponding provisions in the Property Law of other States.
1153. *Shepherd v. Jones* (1882) 21 Ch. 469.

years from the date the right of action first accrued, the mortgagor's right to redeem is lost, and the property becomes vested in the mortgagee.[1154]

C. Sale of Mortgaged Property

633. The power of the legal mortgagee to sell the mortgaged property upon mortgagor's default without resort to court is statutory[1155] and need not be express. Recourse to sale of the property is dependent on two main conditions namely: whether the power of sale has arisen in the sense that the mortgage debt must have fallen due;[1156] and whether the power of sale has become exercisable. For the power of sale to become exercisable, at least one of the following must have happened:[1157]

(a) notice requiring payment of the mortgage money has been served on the mortgagor and default has been made in the payment of money for three months after such service; or
(b) some interest is in arrear and remains unpaid for two months after becoming due notwithstanding that the principal sum to be advanced in instalments under the mortgage deed has not been advanced in full; or
(c) there has been a breach of some provisions contained in the mortgage deed or in the statute which imposes an obligation upon the mortgagor.

634. The mortgagee may, upon fulfilling the above conditions, sell the mortgaged property at any time thereafter either by auction or by private treaty and at any price reasonably obtainable.

635. In exercising the power of sale, the law expects the mortgagee to act in good faith. As the court held in *Okonkwo v. Co-operative and Commerce Bank of Nigeria Plc*,[1158] 'if a mortgagee exercises his power of sale bona fide for the purpose of realising the debt and without collusion with the purchaser, the court will not interfere even though the sale is disadvantageous unless the price is so low as in itself to be evidence of fraud'.[1159] In *Eka-Ete v. Nigerian Development Society*

1154. *See*, for example, the Limitation Law of Lagos State 2003, ss 23, 27, and corresponding provision in the Limitation Law of other States.
1155. PCL Cap 100 LWN 1959, s. 123(3)(4); Law No. 6 of Lagos State 2010, ss 35(1), 36–40, and corresponding provisions in the Property Law of other States.
1156. This is the case where the contractual date for liquidation of the debt by the mortgagor has passed.
1157. Conveyancing Act 1882, s. 20; PCL Cap 100 LWN 1959, s. 125 with corresponding provisions in the various States with Property Legislation. *See also* Law No. 6 of Lagos State 2010, s. 37(1) for similar provision with slight modification.
1158. (1997) 6 NWLR (Pt. 507) 44.
1159. *Ibid.*, at 60.

Ltd & Anor,[1160] the finding of the lower court that the sale of the mortgagor's property by the mortgagee to the purchaser was at an undervalue, was held by the Supreme Court not to be sufficient reason to set aside the sale in the absence of bad faith or collusion on the part of the mortgagee and the purchaser.

636. The purchaser acquires an unimpeachable title on condition that the power of sale has arisen.[1161] Where the power of sale has not become exercisable, the remedy of the mortgagor lies in damages and not in an action to impeach the sale.[1162]

637. Upon a valid sale, a conveyance by way of an assignment subject to Governor's consent first had and obtained, shall operate to vest in the purchaser, a legal title in the property conveyed freed from all estates, interests and rights to which the mortgage has priority, but subject to all interests and rights which have priority to the mortgage.[1163] Such transfer to the purchaser destroys the mortgagor's equity of redemption and vests legal title in the purchaser absolutely.

638. The proceeds of sale of the mortgage property is meant to pay off the principal sum and accrued interest with the costs of sale of the property, while the remaining is paid to the mortgagor, as the mortgagee is not expected to take additional benefit beyond the principal, interest, and costs of sale.

639. An equitable mortgagee generally has no power in law to sell the mortgaged property by auction or private treaty.[1164] A judicial sale is normally the appropriate remedy.

D. Appointment of a Receiver

640. Appointment of a receiver by the legal mortgagee is necessitated by certain factors: the mortgagee may not be opportuned to go into physical possession as a result of the existence of binding leases, and where he has the opportunity, he may

---

1160. (1973) NSCC vol. 8 373. Also, in *ACB & Ors v. Ihekwoaba & Anor* (1998) 10 NWLR (Pt. 571) 590, the court held that the sale of a property at an undervalue price, by itself, would not vitiate the exercise of a mortgagee's power of sale, it must be shown that the sale was made fraudulently or at a gross undervalue.
1161. Conveyancing Act 1881, s. 21(1); PCL Cap 100 LWN 1959, s. 126(2) and corresponding provisions in the Property Law of other States: *See ACB & Ors v. Ihekwoaba & Anor supra* n. 431.
1162. *Ibid.*
1163. Law No. 6 of Lagos State 2010, s. 38(1) and corresponding provisions in the Property Law of other States.
1164. But where there is an agreement that the mortgagor shall give a legal mortgage if called upon to do so, the mortgagee may, upon default, sue in equity for specific performance, and if successful, he obtains a legal mortgage and can then pursue all the statutory remedies open to a legal mortgagee including sale of the mortgage property. *See* s. 18(2) of Law No. 6 of Lagos State 2012. *See also* the case of *Ogundiani v. Araba supra* n. 1066.

find the idea unattractive as a result of the attendant liabilities in law;[1165] the security may be in danger of being squandered by the mortgagor, or being in urgent need of capital, the mortgagee may be anxious to intercept the profits and apply same to the discharge of the mortgage debt. For the equitable mortgagee, appointment of a receiver is an appropriate remedy since the latter has no legal estate and therefore lacks the legal capacity to enter into possession. Thus, appointment of a receiver is a remedy in lieu of entering into physical possession for reasons mentioned.

641. The power of a legal mortgagee to appoint a receiver is statutory and need not be express.[1166] However, the power does not accrue to an equitable mortgagee automatically except where it is reserved in a mortgage agreement or where the mortgage is created by deed.

642. Although, it is usual for the mortgage agreement to provide for the appointment of a receiver, the court may also appoint a receiver in appropriate circumstances upon application made by a party whether the mortgage is legal or equitable.[1167]

643. The power to appoint a receiver becomes exercisable where:[1168]

(a) notice requiring payment of the mortgage money has been served on the mortgagor and default has been made in payment of the money for three months after such service; or
(b) some interest is in arrear and remains unpaid for two months after becoming due notwithstanding that the principal sum to be advanced in instalments under the mortgage deed has not been advanced in full; or
(c) there has been a breach of some provision contained in the mortgage deed or in the statute and which imposes an obligation upon the mortgagor.

644. The receiver is truly an agent upon appointment, but of whom? This question is pertinent in the event of liability arising from the fulfilment of receivership obligations in law. Where the appointment is made under a mortgage deed by the mortgagee, the receiver is presumed to be the agent of the mortgagor in law,[1169] but where the power to appoint a receiver is contained in a mortgage instrument not under seal, the receiver is the agent of the appointor-mortgagee.[1170] Where the appointment is made by the court, the mortgagor is an agent of the court. Where the

1165. Mortgagee in possession may be liable not only for rents and profits realised from the mortgage property but also for those he ought to have realised but for his negligence or wilful default.
1166. *See* generally, the Conveyancing Act, s. 19; PCL Cap 100 LWN 1959, s. 131; Law No. 6 of Lagos State 2010, s. 43 and corresponding provisions in the Property Law of the various States.
1167. The powers of the court to appoint a receiver are contained in the various High Court Rules: *See,* for example, Or 38 rr. 9–10 of the High Court of Lagos State (Civil Procedure) Rules 2012, and corresponding provisions in the High Court Rules of other States.
1168. *See* Conveyancing Act 1881, s. 19; PCL Cap 100 LWN 1959, s. 131 and corresponding provisions in the Property Law of the various States.
1169. *Ibid.,* subs. (2).
1170. *Intercontractors Nigeria Ltd v. UAC of Nigeria Ltd* (1988) 1 NSCC vol. 19 (Pt. 1) 737.

receiver is taken to be the agent of the mortgagor despite his appointment by the mortgagee, the mortgagor takes responsibility in law for mismanagement of the mortgaged property by the receiver without compensation from either the receiver or the appointor-mortgagee, for any loss suffered as a result of the risk thrust on him.[1171] The receiver shall be responsible for collection of rents, profits, and other moneys accruing from the mortgage property, and shall apply the money:[1172]

(a) in the discharge of all rents, taxes, rates, and outgoings whatever affecting the mortgaged property;
(b) in keeping down all annual sums or other payments and the interest on all principal sums having priority to the mortgage in right whereof he is receiver;
(c) in payment of his commission, and of the premiums of fire, life or other insurances if any, properly payable under the mortgage deed or under statute, and the cost of executing necessary or proper repairs directed in writing by the mortgagee;
(d) in payment of interest accruing or due in respect of any principal money due under the mortgage; and
(e) in or towards discharge of the principal money if so directed in writing by the mortgagee.

645. Normally, a receiver is expected by law to receive rents, profits, and other moneys accruing from the mortgaged property and apply moneys received in a manner prescribed by law, but where he is appointed also as a manager of the mortgaged property, he owes in addition, a duty to the mortgagor to act in good faith.[1173] While liability for breach of duty of care by the receiver-manager is not generally established by judicial authorities in Nigeria, statute has established this concept of duty of care in corporate law.[1174] A detailed discussion of the receiver's duty of care under the CAMA is beyond the scope of this chapter.

E. Action for Foreclosure

646. An action for foreclosure is open to a legal mortgagee who for some reasons,[1175] may not be disposed to sale of the mortgaged property. It is also a potent remedy for an equitable mortgagee created by deposit of title deed accompanied by an agreement by the borrower to give a legal mortgage if required to do so.[1176]

1171. *Ibid.*
1172. *See* the Conveyancing Act 1881, s. 28(4); the PCL Cap 100 LWN 1959, s. 131(8) and corresponding provisions in the Property Law of the various States.
1173. *Intercontractors Nigeria Ltd v. UAC of Nigeria Ltd supra* n. 1170.
1174. Companies and Allied Matters Act Cap C20 2010, s. 390(2)(a).
1175. The market price may not be favourable at the time; or there may be need to put the property in good shape before selling to enhance its value.
1176. *Ogundiani v. Araba supra* n. 1066.

647. An application to court for a foreclosure order shall be made by originating summons supported by an affidavit verifying the claim.[1177] The mortgagee-applicant shall make the mortgagor, any other person interested in the equity of redemption, and any subsequent mortgagees, parties to the action.[1178] But a foreclosure order will not be made until the contractual date has passed with the principal and/or interest remaining unpaid after a demand and a reasonable time allowed to lapse without compliance.[1179] The court may however make an order for the sale of the mortgaged property as opposed to foreclosure upon application by the mortgagor or any person entitled to the equity of redemption, where the justice of the case demands.[1180]

648. Where the court deems it fit to decree foreclosure, an interim order known as foreclosure nisi is first made giving the mortgagor and subsequent encumbrancers six months within which to repay the amount due to the first in time.[1181] Where there is default to pay at the expiration of the decree nisi, the foreclosure order is made absolute by the court. The effect of the foreclosure absolute is to enlarge the limited estate conveyed to the mortgagee[1182] or make title already vested in him absolute,[1183] and to consequently destroy the mortgagor's equity of redemption. In Lagos State[1184] and the old PCL States[1185] an order of foreclosure obtained by the mortgagee shall operate to enlarge the limited title hitherto conveyed to the mortgagee, and vest absolute title of the mortgagor in the mortgagee subject to Governor's consent being had and obtained. In the other States of the Federation where the whole estate had hitherto been assigned subject to cesser on redemption, the effect of the order of foreclosure shall only make absolute the title initially conveyed to the mortgagee, and Governor's consent is not required.[1186] In both cases however, the equity of redemption is destroyed and all mortgage terms extinguished. But the rights of prior mortgages are not foreclosed so that the mortgagee granted a foreclosure order takes subject to their interests.[1187]

649. Foreclosure may be reopened and equity of redemption revived in some circumstances such as where the mortgagee proceeds to sue on the personal covenant

1177. That affidavit should contain all relevant facts relating to the mortgage and breach of covenant to repay.
1178. For the court rules relating to third-party procedure, *see*, e.g., Or 13 rr 19–22, High Court of Lagos State(Civil Procedure) Rules 2012 and Or. 16 r. 1 of the English Rules.
1179. *Fitzgerald's Trustee v. Mellersh* (1892) 1 Ch. 385.
1180. *See* the Conveyancing Act 1881, s. 25(2); PCL Cap 100 LWN 1959, s. 114(2) and corresponding provisions in the Property Law of the various States.
1181. The court may decree in the order nisi that each encumbrancer repay the amount due to the first in time.
1182. This is the position in the PCL States and the States with property legislation: *See* PCL Cap 100 LWN 1959, s. 111(2); Law No. 6 of Lagos State 2010, ss 19(2) and 20(2) and corresponding provisions in the Property Law of other States.
1183. The order absolute merely removes the condition attached to the initial vesting of title so that the mortgagor's equity of redemption merges in the estate.
1184. *See* Law No. 6 of Lagos State 2010, s. 19(2).
1185. *See supra* n. 1182.
1186. There is no transfer as contemplated under s. 22 of the Land Use Act 1978 Cap L5 LFN 1990.
1187. The rule is 'redeem up, foreclose down'.

after obtaining an order absolute,[1188] or where a third party purchases the property from the mortgagee after foreclosure.[1189] In addition, the court may exercise discretion to reopen a foreclosure if such relief appears in the special circumstances of the case to be due to the mortgagor.[1190]

650. An action for foreclosure being an action to recover land, must be brought within twelve years from the date upon which the right of recovery accrues, i.e., the date fixed for payment of the principal, otherwise, it becomes statute barred.[1191] However, there is a fresh accrual and the limitation period starts to run again from any payment of principal and interest by the mortgagor, or from his written acknowledgement of the mortgagee's title.[1192]

§3. Charge of Land

I. Equitable Charge at Common Law

651. An equitable charge of land is a devise in equity by which land is appropriated as security for loan without conveying proprietary or possessory interest to the creditor.[1193] The chargee (creditor) takes no estate whatsoever in the land, but has merely a right of payment out of the property upon default by the chargor (debtor).

II. Advantages of Equitable Charge over a Mortgage

652. The evolvement of an equitable charge on land as security for loan has some advantages over a mortgage. The chargee unlike the mortgagee has no inherent right to enter into possession of the land and cannot therefore overstretch the powers accruing to him in law as a creditor; his primary entitlement being to the principal sum and interest. Where the charge is registered,[1194] it vests in the chargee the rights, powers, and remedies conferred by the charge subject to encumbrances but free from any unregistered interest in the land.[1195] Because a charge transfers neither proprietary nor a possessory interest in land, its valid creation does not require Governor's consent under the Land Use Act.[1196]

1188. *See Perry v. Barker* (1806) ER vol. 32 459.
1189. *See Campbell v. Holyland* (1877) Ch. 166.
1190. *Ibid.*, at 172–173.
1191. *See,* for example, the Limitation Law of Lagos State Cap L67 Laws of Lagos State 2003, s. 12 and corresponding provisions in the Limitation Law of the various States.
1192. *Ibid.*, s. 38.
1193. *Tancred v. Delagoa Bay* (1889) 28 QB 239 at 242; *Ogundiani v. Araba supra* n. 1066.
1194. *See,* e.g., Lagos State Lands Registration Law No. 1 2015, s. 53.
1195. *Ibid.*, s. 54.
1196. The consent provisions in the Land Use Act apply to transfer of interest in land only.

III. Creation of Equitable Charge by Agreement

653. An equitable charge of land may be created by a simple agreement appropriating specific property of the borrower with clear details to the loan granted, with a clear express of intention that the property be made available and applied for the liquidation of the said loan in the event of default by the borrower. It is not required that title documents be deposited with the lender unless the intention is to charge such documents as opposed to the land.[1197] An equitable charge does not require consent under the Land Use Act[1198] and is not a registrable instrument[1199] although where it is registered, it constitutes notice of encumbrance on the land.[1200]

IV. Evolvement of Equitable Charge by Operation of Law

654. An equitable charge may evolve by operation of law in favour of a third party in circumstances where a mortgagor's financial obligation to the mortgagee is met by a third party who then takes custody of the title deeds.[1201] But although the third party steps into the shoes of the former creditor, he is only a chargee as opposed to a mortgagee since the delivery of title deeds to him does not vest title in the property whether legal or equitable in him.

V. Effect of Creation or Evolvement of Equitable Charge

655. Upon creation or evolvement of an equitable charge, the chargee becomes a secured creditor for the purposes of bankruptcy or insolvency.[1202]

VI. Enforcement of Equitable Charge

656. The equitable chargee unlike a legal mortgagee, cannot enter into possession since there is no legal title to sustain possession in law, and cannot foreclose the title of the chargor because the chargee acquires no title under the charge and

1197. Also, deposit of title deeds may be construed as an act of part performance pursuant to an oral agreement to create a legal mortgage so that equitable mortgage may evolve: *Russel v. Russel supra* n. 1107.
1198. *See* n. 1196.
1199. While the content of a charge may be registered under s. 53 of the Lagos State Lands Registration Law No. 1 2015, the document creating a charge is not an instrument which confers, transfers, limits, charges or extinguishes in favour of another party any right or title to or interest in land … : *See,* e.g., Land Registration Act No. 36 1924, s. 2 and corresponding provisions in the Land Instrument Registration Law of other States.
1200. *See* Lagos State Lands Registration Law No. 1 2015, s. 54.
1201. *Khoury v. Azar* (1952) 12 WACA 268.
1202. *Mathews v. Goodday* (1961) 31 LJ Ch. 282.

therefore has nothing to be made absolute. A chargee can however apply to court for a judicial sale of the property or to appoint a receiver of the rents and profits in the event of the chargor's default.[1203]

§4. Agricultural Charge

I. Nature of Agricultural Charge

657. A farmer in Nigeria may create agricultural charge in favour of a lender for credit facility granted. This may be necessary in order to acquire major equipment and diversify farming activities. The Central Bank of Nigeria may guarantee such credit facility under the Agricultural Credit Guarantee Scheme Fund set up by the Federal Government of Nigeria under the Agricultural Credit Guarantee Scheme Fund Act 1977.[1204]

II. Definition of Agricultural Charge

658. There is no definition of an agricultural charge under the existing legislation in Nigeria, and case law authorities are not helpful. However, the Agricultural Credit Guarantee Scheme Fund Act, has defined agricultural holdings required for security as 'a charge on land on which the borrower holds a legal interest or a right to farm or a charge on the crops on such land'.[1205]

A. Charge on Land in Which the Borrower Holds a Legal Interest

659. Since all rights on land have been converted to rights of occupancy, a holder of either a statutory or customary right of occupancy under the Land Use Act qualifies as a holder of a legal interest. This is so for both cases of actual grant by the Governor or the local government or deemed grants conferred over existing rights on land. A holder of a right of occupancy is defined as:

> a person entitled to a right of occupancy and includes any person to whom a right of occupancy has been validly assigned or validly passed on the death of a holder but does not include any person to whom a right of occupancy has been sold or transferred without a valid assignment nor a mortgagee, sub-lessee or sub-underlessee.

1203. *Ogundiani v. Araba supra* n. 1066.
1204. Decree No. 20 1977 which is deemed to be an Act of the National Assembly pursuant to s. 315 of the Constitution of the Federal Republic of Nigeria 1999.
1205. *Ibid.,* s. 10.

660. The purport of the above provision is to limit the holders of a legal interest in land to persons who applied for and were granted a right of occupancy over land, and all those who before the advent of the Land Use Act, had land vested in them. The same goes for assignees of such rights with the requisite consent. Others like the sub-lessee or sub-underlessee, mortgagees, and assignees of invalid assignments are obviously excluded.

B. A Charge on Land in Which the Borrower Holds a Right to Farm

661. This has taken into cognisance the incidence of the customary land tenure system. Thus, a customary pledgee or customary tenant in occupation does not qualify as a holder but as an occupier under the Land Use Act. An occupier is defined under the Act as:

> any person lawfully occupying land under customary law and a person using or occupying land in accordance with customary law and includes the underlessee of a holder.

662. This definition is wide enough to cover not only cases of a customary pledge or a member of the family using and occupying land in accordance with customary law, but also that of a tenant who can conveniently be regarded as the 'sub-underlessee of a holder'.

C. Charges on Crops on Such Land

663. Although the Agricultural Credit Guarantee Scheme Fund Act restricts forms of real security to 'a charge on crops on such land', by virtue of the powers conferred on the Central Bank as the Managing agent for the purposes of the fund, it has, under its guidelines, made pursuant to the powers, extended the real security to cover not only assets on the land including fixed assets but also crops and livestock.[1206]

III. Security of Tenure

664. The Land Use Act certainly ensures security of agricultural land holding for, section 36(2) of the Act provides that:

> Any occupier or holder of such land whether under customary rights or otherwise howsoever shall, if the land was on the commencement of this [Act] being used for agricultural purposes continue to be so entitled to possession of

1206. *See* Guidelines on the Agricultural Credit Guarantee Scheme issued by the Central Bank in the Central Bank Gazette February 1986.

the land for use for agricultural purposes as if a customary right of occupancy has been granted by the appropriate local government.

665. Such security is made more attractive to creditors by ensuring that creditors rely on a viable record of title traceable to an identifiable individual in possession of such land whether under customary right or otherwise who can show that the land is being used for agricultural purposes. Thus section 36(3) of the Land Use Act provides:

> On the production to the Local Government by occupier of such land at his discretion, of a sketch or diagram or other sufficient description of the land in question and on application therefore in the prescribed form the Local Government shall if satisfied that the occupier or holder was entitled to the possession of such land whether under customary rights or otherwise however, and that the land is being used for agricultural purposes at the commencement of this [Act] register the holder or occupier as one to whom a customary right of occupancy had been issued in respect of the land in question.

666. It is no longer possible following a long line of judicial decisions,[1207] for the Governor to make an inconsistent grant thereby divesting the holder of such agricultural holding of his interest otherwise known as a customary right of occupancy. And although section 36(5) places a total bar on alienation of land situate in non-urban areas, this provision does not, in any way, hamper the effective creation of an agricultural charge. The traditional method of creating a charge does not involve any transfer of interest in land. It is at best an assurance that the creditor will have something to fall back on upon default by the debtor and can easily appropriate same in satisfaction of the debt owed. It follows also, that consent under the Land Use Act is not required.

IV. Enforcement of Agricultural Charge

667. While section 12(1) of the ACGSF Act gives the creditor the power 'to dispose of any security obtained in respect of the loan',[1208] section 15(1) of the Act provides that 'all legal proceedings of a civil nature arising from the failure of any borrower to repay a loan granted by a bank and guaranteed under this [Act] or given pursuant to this [Act] shall be instituted and conducted by or against the Board'. Also, the amendment Act empowers the board inter alia, to pursue defaulters through judicial action. Reading the two provisions together would suggest that enforcement of an agricultural charge like the common law charge, is by way of

1207. *Dzungwe v. Gbishe* (1985) 2 NWLR (Pt. 8) 528; *Kyari v. Alkali* (2001) 11 NWLR (Pt. 274) 412; *Dantsoho v. Mohammed* (2003) 6 NWLR (Pt. 817) 457; *Ibrahim v. Mohammed* (2003) 6 NWLR (Pt. 817) 615 to mention but a few.

1208. This provision gives the impression that chargor could sell without application to court.

judicial sale of the property and/or things on, or attached to it. It is doubtful if the bank can appoint a receiver since this remedy is not provided for under the ACGSF Act, and foreclosure is obviously not a remedy as there is no title conditionally vested in it to enlarge.

A. *Enforcement Through Judicial Sale*

668. One of the challenges confronting the lender is the enforcement of security through judicial sale. The order of court directing sale of the charged real property cannot vest title in a third party, and no transfer is effectual without requisite consent first had and obtained by the creditor. The time and prohibitive cost involved are constraints making the remedy unattractive. Another is the slim possibility of realising the security in crops or livestock as these may have been moved or sold by the debtor when enforcement is anticipated. Where the land is sold to a bona fide purchaser of the legal estate without notice of the charge, the interest of the creditor is destroyed as the purchaser takes free of it. In most cases, banks would have to rely on the Guarantee of the Central Bank[1209] or on extrajudicial steps by the Agricultural Loans Board within the parameters of the law.[1210] While these may be a way of mitigating the creditor's loses, it has in no way provided an effective instrument of enforcement against the unwilling debtor.

§5. Conveyancing Liens

I. Nature of Conveyancing Lien

669. A vendor of land who has conveyed the land to the purchaser has in equity, a lien upon the property for the unpaid purchase money,[1211] while a corresponding lien will arise in favour of a purchaser who has made a full or part payment of the purchase price but who has not obtained a conveyance of the property.[1212] Being a specie of equitable lien, a conveyancing lien differs from the common law lien (otherwise known as a possessory lien) in the sense that unlike the latter, it does not depend on possession of either the land sold or the title deed.[1213] Without being in possession of the property in respect of which the debt is due, the creditor may be

1209. The Central Bank Guidelines to the principal legislation assures the bank of 75% of the debt which percentage of loan shall be made available by the Central Bank of Nigeria in the event of the farmer's inability to pay back the loan: For Central Bank Guidelines as contained in the gazette of February 1986.

1210. Such steps include publishing the names of defaulters in national newspapers or soliciting the assistance of government loan machineries: s. 3(i)(h) of the Act.

1211. *Re Birmingham* (1959) Ch. 523; *Barclays Bank Plc v. Estates & Commercial Ltd* (1997) 1 WLR 415.

1212. Kindersley V-C in *Wythes v. Lee* 61 ER 954 at 957–958.

1213. *Goode v. Burton* (1847) 1 Exch. 189.

entitled in equity to have the property applied to the satisfaction of his debt. Its enforcement depends on its establishment by a judicial decree, and it is by way of sale pursuant to a court order.

670. A conveyancing lien gives security to a creditor who otherwise would have had no remedy in law on some technical ground e.g., where the conveyance attest to purchase money having been paid when in fact, none was paid.[1214] But where any form of security has been taken to cover the shortfall, this precludes a lien arising in favour of such creditor.[1215] The lien may arise in favour of the vendor or the purchaser.

II. Vendor's Lien

A. Nature of Lien

671. The vendor is entitled to a lien for the unpaid purchase money by the purchaser. This lien secures the price, so long as the price is money whether it is payable in a lump sum or periodically.[1216]

B. When Vendor's Lien Arises

672. While there appears to be divergent views as to when the lien arises,[1217] a better view and one in line with juristic basis for the evolvement of the security in equity is that the lien arises in equity upon completion. Before completion, the vendor's remedy lies in legal lien on the land which entitles him to retain possession of both the land and the title deeds. It is only after conveyance of the legal estate and delivery of possession that a conveyancing lien arises on the conveyed land for the unpaid purchase money in equity.[1218] It is said that 'to the extent that conveyancing lien is of no moment and its enforcement impossible until after the date fixed for completion and upon failure of the purchaser to pay the purchase price in full, there is no doubt that it arises when the purchase money becomes due upon completion'.[1219]

1214. *See Rice v. Rice* (1854) 61 ER 646.
1215. *See Capital Finance Co. Ltd v. Stokes* (1969) 1 Ch. 261.
1216. *Re Mead* (1880) 15 CR. D 651.
1217. One school of thought is that the lien arises upon exchange of contract: *See* Kindersley V-C in *Wythes v. Lee supra* n. 1212; *Barclays Bank Plc v. Estates & Commercial Ltd supra* n. 1211. The other school of thought is that it arises after completion, or the purchaser is allowed into possession prior to completion without payment in full of the purchase price: *See* Lindley LJ in *Kettlewell v. Watson* (1884) 26 Ch. 501; *Davies v. Little John* (1923) 34 CLR 174 at 181.
1218. *See* Barnsley, *Conveyancing Liens* 61 Conv. 336 (Sweet & Maxwell 1997).
1219. Smith, I.O. *supra* n. 1053 at 137.

C. Exclusion or Destruction of the Lien

673. The vendor's lien may be excluded by the parties in their contract of sale, or where there is something in the transaction itself from which it may be inferred that parties must be taken to have excluded it.[1220] It may be destroyed by sale to a bona fide purchaser of the legal estate for value without notice of the lien,[1221] or postponed to a subsequent equitable mortgagee having no notice of the lien.[1222]

D. Notice to Subsequent Purchaser or Mortgagee

674. The precarious nature of this lien has made it imperative that the unpaid vendor affect any subsequent purchaser or mortgagee with notice of his security. A number of ways has been suggested[1223] as follows:

(a) Endorsement of the conveyance to show that part of the purchase price remains unpaid. Such an endorsement at the lands registry of any State in Nigeria is notice to a third party of the encumbrance.
(b) Lodgement of a caveat with the Registrar of title under the Registration of Titles Law.[1224]
(c) Registration of the written agreement to pay the balance within thirty days.
(d) Keeping the title deed as collateral security for the unpaid balance.

675. A lender of the purchase money or part of it to the purchaser may be subrogated to the vendor's lien[1225] provided the transaction with the lender is enforceable.[1226]

E. Enforcement of Vendor's Lien

676. The unpaid vendor's lien is enforceable not only against the purchaser and his successors in title upon his death, but also against all persons taking as volunteers under him, as well as his trustees in bankruptcy.[1227] Where the purchaser creates a mortgage of land or subsequently sells the land to a third party, enforceability

1220. *See Parrott v. Sweetland* 40 ER 250; *Capital Finance Co. Ltd v. Stokes supra* n. 1192.
1221. *Ayorinde v. Scott* CCHCJ/2/72 (Unreported) 149.
1222. *Rice v. Rice supra* n. 1214.
1223. Per Odesanya J. in *Ayorinde v. Scott supra* n. 1221.
1224. The Registration Law of Lagos State entitles the vendor to register this type of interest. Any title registered by the purchaser or a third party subsequently becomes subject to the encumbrance.
1225. *Boodle & Hatfield & Co. v. British Films Ltd* (1986) PCC 176.
1226. *Nottingham Permanent Benefits Building Society v. Thurston* (1903) AC 6; *Orakpo v. Mason Investments Ltd* (1971) Ch. 81.
1227. *Ex parte Hanson* 33 ER 131.

depends on whether the lien has been duly protected against the purchaser's successors in title by taking any of the precautions listed earlier.[1228] Subject to such precautions being taken, a vendor's lien may be enforced against the purchaser's successors in title (i.e., a subsequent purchaser or mortgagee) unless he obtained a legal estate for value without actual or constructive notice of the lien,[1229] or unless though his interest is equitable, he has a better equity than the vendor.[1230]

677. The lien is enforced by commencing proceedings in court for a declaration that the vendor is entitled to a lien and seeking reliefs such as a court order to sell the property, take possession or appoint a receiver.

F. Waiver or Loss of Lien

678. The vendor may waive his lien by taking a security such as a mortgage for the purchase money or abandon his right to it, and this may be express or may be implied from the circumstances of the case. Also, the vendor may lose his lien and his claim barred by the Statute of Limitation after twelve years.[1231]

III. Purchaser's Lien

A. When Purchaser's Lien Arises

679. Purchaser's lien arises in respect of the property in possession of the vendor for any deposit or instalment of the purchase money which the purchaser has paid to the vendor as opposed to a stakeholder, without obtaining a conveyance.[1232] Its existence depends on there being a valid contract between the parties. Thus, where the vendor's title is defective or where the purchaser has been deprived specific performance by the court due to his own delay in completing the contract, the lien does not arise. The lien arises even where time for completion has not arisen and this is the case where the contract goes off for want of title, or where he rescinds the contract under a condition enabling him to do so,[1233] or the vendor repudiates the contract.[1234]

1228. *See.* Para. 674.
1229. *Ayorinde v. Scott supra* n. 1221.
1230. *Rice v. Rice supra* n. 1214.
1231. *See,* e.g., Limitation Law of Lagos State Cap L67 Laws of Lagos State 2003.
1232. *Snell's Equity* 529 at 532 (30th ed. Sweet & Maxwell).
1233. *Whitbread & Co. Ltd v. Watt* (1901) 1 Ch. 911 at 915.
1234. *Lee-Parker v. Izzt* (1971) 1 WLR 1688.

B. Coverage of Lien

680. In the absence of default under the contract or abandonment of the contract by the purchaser, the purchaser has a lien to secure return of the deposit paid to the vendor[1235] as opposed to a stakeholder; return of any other part paid of the price to the vendor;[1236]reimbursement for the cost of investigating title;[1237] reimbursement for cost of an unsuccessful action for specific performance where the vendor fails because he has not adduced a good title;[1238] and expenditure on improvements incurred under a contractual term.

C. Enforcement of Lien

681. Where a lien inures in favour of the purchaser, the latter becomes a secured creditor, the security being the lien over the land contracted to be purchased.[1239] This security may be enforced by sale of the property pursuant to a court order by bringing an action for a declaration that he is entitled to the lien.[1240] The purchaser may sue in the same action for specific performance or may sue for a lien and sale of the property.[1241]

682. The lien binds the vendor's successors in title[1242] and may be enforced against them provided it is protected.[1243] However, a donee from the vendor or his testamentary beneficiary will be bound in any event.[1244]

§6. Customary Pledge

I. Nature of Customary Pledge

683. A pledge of land is a form of security known exclusively to Customary or Islamic law in Nigeria. It is created where the owner/occupier of land known as the pledgor, in order to secure an advance of money or money's worth, gives possession, and use of the land to the creditor known as the pledge until the debt is fully discharged.[1245] The usual understanding under customary pledge transaction is that the pledge shall enter upon the pledgor's land and enjoy rents and profits from the land until the pledgor settles the debt owed. It is essential that possession be given

1235. *Whitbread & Co. v. Watt supra* n. 1233.
1236. *Rose v. Watson* (1864) 10 HLC 672.
1237. *Kitton v. Hewett* (1904) WN 21.
1238. *Turner v. Marriott* (1867) LR 3 Eq. 744.
1239. Barnsley *supra* n. 1218.
1240. *Ibid.*
1241. Fry on Specific Performance 6th ed. (1921) 677.
1242. Barnsley *supra* n. 1218 at 355.
1243. *Ibid.*
1244. *Ibid.*
1245. Elias, *Nigerian Land Law* 153–154 (4th ed. Sweet & Maxwell 1971).

at the time of the transaction, because 'it is out of the possession granted the pledgee under the agreement that the pledgee's right spring'.[1246]

II. Creation of Customary Pledge

684. In its original form, customary pledge could be created orally in which case, witnesses were generally required to evidence the transaction, but the recognition of the use of writing under customary law in modern times has made documentation of the transaction a popular phenomenon.[1247]

685. Where the land is subject of family ownership, consent of the head of the family and the principal members must be sought and obtained and in the case of the community, consent of the head of the community must be sought and obtained. The reason is that family or communal land is the subject to joint ownership with the individual having only a right of user.[1248]

686. Where the land is situate in an urban area but undeveloped, the borrower (pledgor) cannot pledge more than half hectare since that is the maximum quantum that the Land Use Act allows.[1249] Where the land is situate in the Federal Capital Territory Abuja, customary pledge can only be created over land the subject of a statutory right of occupancy mainly, for a customary right of occupancy does not exist there.[1250] Creation of customary pledge is susceptible to the application of the consent provisions of the Land Use Act; thus consent of the local government is required with regards to customary right of occupancy and Governor's consent with regards to statutory right of occupancy since transfer requiring consent is expressly made to cover 'transfer of possession'.[1251] A holder of a customary right of occupancy granted by the local government is not entitled to more than 500 hectares in the case of agricultural land and 5,000 hectares in the case of land meant for grazing. Such a holder cannot ipso facto create a pledge over land which exceeds the maximum quantum prescribed by law.[1252]

III. Pledgee in Possession

687. Since the main security held by the pledge lies in being in possession of the land, he must not only assume possession at the time of creating the pledge, but

1246. Per Mitchelin J. in *Adjei v. Dabanka* (1930) 1 WACA 63 at 66–67.
1247. It is advisable that all pledge transactions be recorded in writing to foreclose any claim that the land was sold to the person in possession.
1248. *See Amodu Tijani v. Secretary, Southern Nigeria* (1921) AC 399.
1249. Land Use Act Cap L5 LFN 2010, s. 34(5).
1250. *Ona & Anor v. Atenda* (2000) 5 NWLR (Pt. 656) 244.
1251. Land Use Act Cap L5 LFN 2010, s. 22(1).
1252. *Ibid.*, s. 6(2).

must continue in uninterrupted possession during the continuance of the pledge otherwise, he loses his right to the pledge.[1253]

688. The pledgee has exclusive possession and may therefore sue any intruder for trespass and thereby protect the property.[1254] The pledgee's right in the security is however limited to that of retention until the pledge is redeemed by the pledgor; the pledgee has no power to sell the pledged land to discharge the pledgor's obligation to him, neither can he foreclose.[1255]

689. While in possession, he may cultivate the land and plant trees and crops for his benefit during the period the pledge lasts. The pledgee is however advised not to plant cash crops as he is not entitled to compensation for such improvements when the pledgor redeems the pledge. The law is that the pledgee should quit the land and hand possession back to the pledgor when the latter repays the loan.[1256]

690. As a general rule, the pledgee is not entitled to charge interest on the loan under customary law; the enjoyment and/or cultivation of the land is construed as sufficient interest accruing to the pledgee from the land.[1257] It is advisable therefore that a pledge desirous of charging interest on the loan should ensure that same is expressly provided for in the pledge instrument.

IV. Pledgee's Duty of Accountability

691. The pledgee is liable to account for any unjustifiable benefit derived from the land. For example, the pledgee is accountable for rents collected while in possession[1258] and where palm trees or other economic trees are pledged, the pledgee shall be liable to account for the difference between the value of the yield and the amount of customary tribute paid so that the capital borrowed may be reduced by the difference.[1259]

V. Rights of the Pledgor

Pledgor's Right of Disposition of Pledged Property

692. A pledgor who pledges a property of which he is the owner may, by virtue of his legal title, sell the said property although any purchaser of the property buys subject to the pledge. But the pledgor cannot repledge the property subject matter

1253. *Otubu v. Omotayo* (1995) 6 NWLR (Pt. 400) 24 at 252.
1254. The owner of land who is not in physical possession is not competent to maintain an action from trespass: *See Ayinde v. Salawu* (1989) 3 NWLR (Pt. 109) 297.
1255. This prohibitions hinge on the rule that a pledge under customary law is perpetually redeemable.
1256. *Okoiko & Anor v. Esedalue & Anor* (9174) 1 All NLR (Pt. 1) 425 at 465.
1257. *Ibid.,* at 464.
1258. *Amao v. Adigun* (1957) WRNLR 55.
1259. *Kuahen v. Avose* (1889) LE Colonial at 16; *Amao v. Adigun supra* n. 1258.

of the pledge for, possession once given to one person cannot be given to another during the subsistence of the earlier transaction.

Pledgor's Right of Redemption

693. The pledgor has the right to redeem the property at any time[1260] and where a date is stipulated for redemption, he may redeem before or after the date.[1261] The maxim 'once a pledge always a pledge' is an age old maxim under customary law which signifies two basic principles:

(1) That a thing which is pledged is never lost. So long as it is possible to identify the land, the parties and the original purpose and understanding behind the transaction, the right to redeem subsists notwithstanding that many years have elapsed from the date of the transaction.
(2) That notwithstanding any stipulation in the agreement for the postponement of the redemption date, the pledgor would be allowed to redeem his property at any time notwithstanding that the pledgee has expended money on the improvement or that he has invested money and labour in growing crops yet to be harvested.

694. It follows from these customary law principles that the right of the pledgor to redeem cannot be defeated by lapse of time,[1262] and the right may be exercised by the pledgor's successor in title.[1263] The right is absolute and cannot be fettered by agreement.

695. The customary right of the pledgor to redeem the land together with all the improvements on it upon settlement of the debt owing to the pledgee has not been altered by the Land Use Act. The right to occupy and use the land by the pledge automatically terminates upon repayment of the loan notwithstanding that he has been registered as one to whom a customary right of occupancy had been issued in respect of the land in question.[1264]

Determination of Customary Pledge and Governor's Consent

696. Upon the determination of the customary pledge, it is doubtful whether Governor's consent is required for a valid transfer of possession back to the pledgor. What happens may be likened to a reconveyance of land upon the mortgagor's liquidation of the debt owing to the mortgagee and since such act does not require Governor's consent under the Act, it is very unlikely that a separate consideration is conceived by the Act as regards customary pledge of land.

1260. *Okoiko & Anor v. Esedalue & Anor supra* n. 1256.
1261. *Dapaah v. Poku* Unreported WACA decision of 13/6/50.
1262. *Iwuchukwu v. Anyawu* (1993) 8 NWLR (Pt. 311) 307.
1263. *Kofi v. Kofi* (1933) 1 WACA 284.
1264. That principle of customary law as laid down in *Okoiko & Anor v. Esedalue & Anor supra* n. 1256 has not been altered by the Land Use Act.

Chapter 2. Security in Movable Property

Nature of Security over Movables

697. Commercial goods of different kinds, fixtures, and growing crops when separately assigned or charged, trade machinery and other corporeal movables may be subject matter of security. Movable properties unlike immovables, generally have no title deeds which may be appropriated by the creditor to forestall further dealings in the chattels by the debtor. The debtor's possession of them enables him to represent that he is the owner and thus, able to sell them or fraudulently use them to obtain credit from others. The hazards posed by these shortcomings may be overcome by the creditor only where he takes possession of the chattels or registers same; the former ensures physical control over the movables and the latter gives notice to prospective purchasers or creditors. The law recognises in these regards, a pledge of the movables or the creation of a registered mortgage bill of sale as security respectively.

698. Sometimes, the continuance of business may require not only that the debtor remain in possession of the movables, but also that he should be able to deal with the movables free from the creditor's security so as to make profit and pay off his debts. Security in the form of a floating charge given over stock in trade is a typical example. Also where it is difficult or impracticable to give possession of the movables to the creditor, a charge known as hypothecation may be created over such movables in the debtor's possession or in the custody of a third party with the debtor's authority.

Creation and Evolvement of Security over Movables

699. Security over movables may be created by agreement or may evolve by operation of law such as where a lien arises in favour of bailee of chattels or persons authorised to sell same on commission or at a fee. These and various other statutory liens constitute the major mechanism for creditors' protection in commercial transactions.

§1. Mortgage of Personal Chattels

I. Nature of Mortgage of Personal Chattels

700. Proprietary security in the form of mortgage may be created over personal chattels by the mortgagor (the borrower) assigning title legal or equitable over the chattels to the mortgagee (the lender) as security for advances, subject to cesser on redemption. In such cases, transfer of possession is not contemplated and the mortgagor remains in possession.

701. While the intention of the parties transformed into writing may be of paramount importance as in the case of mortgage of land, the parties' freedom of contract is circumscribed by law. Where an instrument in writing purports to transfer proprietary interest in personal chattels by one party to another and possession is not intended to be given, a bill of sale is contemplated by statute and the document of transfer must comply with the provisions of the Bills of Sale Law as regards form and registration.

II. The Applicable Law

702. In Nigeria, the Bills of Sale Act 1923[1265] as Federal Law re-enacted the English Bills of Sale Acts of 1878 and 1882 as amended by the English Bills of Sale Acts of 1890 and 1891, with a proviso that where any provision of the English Acts is inconsistent with that of the local legislation, the latter shall prevail.[1266] Although the old western and mid-western Nigeria repealed the incorporated English Acts and replaced same with the Bills of Sale Law,[1267] the provisions of the State Law remains substantially the same as in the English Acts. The Constitution of the Federal Republic of Nigeria 1999 (as amended) has placed bills of sale transactions under the concurrent list[1268] enabling both the Federal and the States to legislate thereon.

703. The Bills of Sale Law Cap B2 Laws of Lagos State 2003 is adopted for discussion in this Chapter, but the provisions of the Bills of Sale Law of other States are the same.

III. Nature of Bills of Sale

704. A transaction constitutes a bill of sale when the subject matter of the transaction involves personal chattels, and title to the security is derived from a document.

705. The Bills of Sale Law defines personal chattels as 'goods, furniture and other articles capable of complete transfer by delivery and (when separately assigned or charged) fixtures and growing crops … '.[1269] It however excludes:[1270]

1265. This law is omitted from both the 1990 and 2004 versions of the Laws of the Federation of Nigeria.
1266. *Ibid.*, s. 1.
1267. Cap 11 LWN 1959.
1268. *See* item No. 18 on the Concurrent Legislative List, Second Schedule, Part II.
1269. *See,* for example, s. 3(1) of the Bills of Sale Law Cap B2 Laws of Lagos State 2003 and corresponding provision in the Bills of Sale Law of other States.
1270. *Ibid.*

(i) chattels real (i.e., leasehold interests on land);
(ii) fixtures [except trade machinery[1271]] when assigned together with a freehold or leasehold interest in any land or building to which they are affixed;
(iii) growing crops when assigned with land in which they grow;
(iv) stocks and shares;
(v) choses in action;
(vi) stock or produce upon land which either by contract or custom of the country ought not to be removed at the time of making or giving of such bill of sale.

706. Title to the security must be derived from the instrument; it does not matter that it is accompanied with possession by the mortgagee. The question is whether the security is created by virtue of a document as opposed to the fact of possession outside the document accompanying the transaction.[1272] Following this analogy, the Bills of Sale Law enumerates the categories of transactions covered by the Law to include: 'bill of sale [in its true form]; assignment, transfers or declaration of trust; inventories of goods with receipts thereto attached, or receipts for purchase moneys of goods; other assurances; Power of Attorney; or authorities or licences to take possession … '.[1273] In all these cases, title to the security is derived from documents as opposed to the fact of possession. However, the following categories of transaction are specifically excluded from the ambit of the Bills of Sale Law:[1274]

(a) assignments for the benefit of creditors;
(b) marriage settlements;
(c) transfer of any ship or vessel or any share thereof;
(d) transfer of goods in the ordinary course of business or any trade or calling; goods abroad or imported; and
(e) debenture of incorporated companies.

IV. Form and Content of Bill of Sale

707. Where a document qualifies as a bill of sale, it must comply with the statutory form as contained in the schedule thereto.[1275] The following particulars are prescribed by statute.[1276]

1271. 'Trade machinery' means the machinery used in or attached to any factory or workshop but excluding … the motive powers and the fixed appurtenances thereof which transmit the action of the motive powers to other machinery, fixed and loose, and the pipes for steam, gas or water and the wiring and other fixed fittings for transmitting electrical current, in the factory or workshop: *See* s. 3(1) of Cap B2 Laws of Lagos State 2003, and corresponding provision in the Bills of Sale Law of other States.
1272. *Ex Parte Hubbard* (1886) 17 QBD 690.
1273. *See* s. 3(1) of the Bills of Sale Law Cap B2 Laws of Lagos State 2003, and corresponding provisions in the Bills of Sale Law of other States.
1274. *Ibid.*
1275. *Ibid.*, s. 8.
1276. *Ibid.*, Form A of the Schedule.

Parties

708. An inaccurate description of parties to the transaction, their addresses or other particulars relating to them avoids the bill notwithstanding the existence of extrinsic information.

Consideration

709. A statement of consideration is required otherwise the bill is void for non-compliance. Such consideration must not be less than sixty Naira,[1277] must be an amount actually received by the grantor[1278] and must be a pre-existing debt not arising from the contract of loan.[1279]

Specific Assignment

710. Chattels to be assigned of which the grantor is required to be the true owner[1280] must be specifically described in the form of an inventory in the schedule to the bill,[1281] and not in the body of the bill.[1282] Thus, all forms of after acquired chattels are outside the purview of the Act and where meant as security, the instrument is void.[1283] Where such after acquired chattels are contained in the body of the bill, it is absolutely void,[1284] but where the personal chattels of which the grantor is not the true owner are contained in the schedule, the bill is void only in respect of the after acquired chattels and as against the grantor mainly.[1285]

The Amount Secured with Interest

711. The amount secured with interest must be clearly stated otherwise, the bill is void for non-compliance with the statutory form.

Covenant to Repay

712. Covenant to repay entails statement of the amount payable with interest, the time of repayment, and the manner of repayment. Covenant to repay cannot be implied, and failure to state same avoids the bill of sale and discharges the debtor from any liability to repay.

Maintenance and Defeasance of Security

713. While parties are permitted to insert 'terms as to insurance, payment of rent, or otherwise which the parties may agree to for maintenance or defeasance of

1277. *Ibid.,* s. 15.
1278. It follows therefore that a bill of sale is not the appropriate method of creating security over an overdraft to be drawn from time to time.
1279. An example is where the consideration relates to expenses charged in addition to the loan.
1280. *Ibid.,* s. 10.
1281. *Ibid.,* s. 9.
1282. *See Thomas v. Kelly* (1888) 13 AC 506.
1283. *Ibid.,* s. 10.
1284. *Supra* n. 1283 above..
1285. *See* s. 10 of Cap B2 Laws of Lagos State 2003.

security', any other term outside these shall be void for non-compliance with the statutory form. For the maintenance of the security, clauses as to repairs, replacement of damaged or worn out chattels are permitted, while defeasance clause is however limited by the proviso in the statutory form precluding seizure for any cause outside those specified in the law.[1286]

Restriction on Seizure, Power of Sale and Redemption

714. The concluding paragraph of the Form incorporates by reference, the provisions of the law[1287] restricting seizure of the chattels to specific instances such as where there has been a default in the payment of the loan or performance of any agreement or covenant necessary for maintaining the security; or if the grantor becomes bankrupt or suffers the goods or any of them to be distrained for rent, rates or taxes; or if the grantor fraudulently removes or suffers the said goods or any of them to be removed from the premises; or if the grantor fails, upon request by the grantee to produce his last receipts for rent, rates, and taxes; or if execution is levied against the goods of the grantee under any judgment.[1288] Any covenant in the bill giving the creditor power of seizure in any circumstances outside those prescribed by the Bills of Sale Law is not only void as to those circumstance but also absolutely void for non-compliance with the statutory form.

715. The grantee's power of seizure is subject to the provision of the law[1289] which prohibits the removal or sale of the chattels until five clear days from the day they were so seized or taken possession of.

Testimonium

716. The form requires the incorporation of a testimonium[1290] as a link between the parties and the content of the document, and a bill of sale without testimonium is not in accordance with the statutory form and shall be void for all purposes.

The Schedule

717. A bill of sale must have a Schedule annexed to it containing an inventory of all personal chattels given as security,[1291] and failure to provide for it makes the bill void for all purposes for non-compliance with the statutory form. Where some personal chattels are not specifically described in the schedule, the bill of sale is void with respect to such personal chattels against all third parties including an assignee in bankruptcy,[1292] but it is not void as between the grantor and grantee of the bill.[1293]

1286. *Ibid.*, s. 12.
1287. *Ibid.*
1288. *Ibid.*
1289. *Ibid.*, s. 13.
1290. *Ibid.*, Form A of the Schedule.
1291. *Ibid.*, s. 9.
1292. *Ibid.*
1293. It follows that a grantee could sue for the debt as an independent transaction.

Execution and Attestation

718. A bill of sale must not only be signed by the parties thereto, but must be attested by one or more credible witnesses not being party thereto.[1294] The attestation shall include details of the witnesses such as the name, address, and description of the witness. As these details are part of the statutory form, any omission renders the bill void in respect of the personal chattels.[1295]

Registration

719. A bill of sale shall be registered within seven days after the execution thereof, or if executed out of the State, then within seven days after the time at which it would, in the ordinary course of post, arrive at the principal registry if posted immediately after the execution thereof.[1296] But the bill will not be late for registration if the lateness was due to the fault of the registry in making necessary entries in the register after the submission of the required documents within seven days.[1297] A bill of sale not registered within seven days is void in respect of the personal chattels comprised in it,[1298] but not void as to the personal covenant for repayment.

720. The procedure for registration is contained in the law.[1299] The law requires that the following documents be delivered to the Registrar:

(a) the bill of sale together with every schedule or inventory annexed or referred to in the bill;
(b) a true copy of the bill of sale, every schedule or inventory annexed and every attestation of the execution of the bill;
(c) an affidavit proving the time of making the bill and of its due execution and attestation. It must also contain a description of the residence and occupation of the grantor (or where the bill of sale is made or given by any person under or in execution of any process, then a description of the residence and occupation of the person against whom such process is issued) and of every attesting witness to the bill.

721. Any collateral agreement of defeasance, condition or declaration of trust to which the bill of sale is subject but not contained therein is deemed to be part of the bill and must be written on the same document as the bill of sale before registration otherwise, the registration shall be void.[1300]

1294. *Ibid.*, s. 14.
1295. *See Adetoyin v. Bank of the North Ltd* (1976) 3 OYSHC 217.
1296. *See* s. 14 of Cap B2 Laws of Lagos State 2003.
1297. *Ibid.*
1298. *Ibid.*
1299. *Ibid.*, s. 18(1)(a).
1300. *Ibid.*, s. 18(1)(b).

722. Upon filing the required documents, the Registrar shall enter the particulars of the bill in the register as prescribed in the form contained in the schedule to the law.[1301] Registration does not only give notice, priority as between two or more security bills of sale is determined according to the date of registration.[1302]

723. Where in the affidavit accompanying a bill of sale when presented for registration describes the residence of the person making or giving the same, or of the person against whom process is to be issued, or the chattels enumerated in the schedule to the bill, to be in some place or places within the Magisterial district outside the one within which the principal registry is situate, the Registrar shall, within three clear days after registration in the principal registry, transmit a copy of such bill of sale and of every schedule or inventory annexed, to the Magistrate exercising jurisdiction in such place or places.[1303] Any copy so transmitted shall be filed by the Magistrate and is open to inspection by the public.[1304]

Renewal of Registration

724. Registration is valid for five years and shall thereafter become void unless renewed by filing an affidavit of renewal with the Registrar stating the date of the bill of sale and of the last registration thereof; the names, residences, and occupations of the parties thereto; and that the bill of sale is still an existing security.[1305]

Failure to Register or Renew Registration

725. Where there is failure to register or renew registration within the period prescribed by law due to inadvertence, the High Court may, upon application by a party, extend the time upon terms and conditions as to security, notice by advertisement or otherwise or as any other matter as the court thinks fit to direct.[1306] An order may also be made for rectification of the register on application by a party, upon accidental or inadvertent omission or misstatement of the name, residence, or occupation of any person on the register.[1307] However, the power of rectification by the court does not extend to correcting errors in the bill of sale and its attendant documents.

V. Enforcement of Security

726. A potent method of enforcement of security under a bill of sale is by selling the chattels. The power of sale is derived exclusively from the provisions of the

1301. *Ibid.*, Form C thereto.
1302. *Ibid.*, s. 18(2).
1303. *Ibid.*, s. 19(1).
1304. *Ibid.*, s. 19(2).
1305. *Ibid.*, s. 20.
1306. *Ibid.*, s. 22.
1307. *Ibid.*

Bills of Sale Law,[1308] which provisions negative the power of sale by the Conveyancing Act 1881,[1309] the Property and Conveyancing Law 1959,[1310] or the Property Law of the various States in Nigeria.[1311] In exercising this power, the grantee of the bill (i.e., the mortgagee) shall comply with the provisions of the law on seizure, and the conditions under which the chattels may be removed or sold.[1312]

VI. Discharge of Obligation and Right to Redeem by the Mortgagor

727. The debtor/mortgagor discharges his obligation under the bill of sale by paying off the loan to the mortgagee/creditor, or where the latter waives that obligation upon prescribed evidence being given that the debt for which the bill was given has been satisfied or discharged, the Chief Registrar of the High Court may order a memorandum of satisfaction to be endorsed upon any registered copy of a bill of sale in accordance with the rules made under the law.[1313]

728. Apart from the right of the grantor of the bill of sale (i.e., the mortgagor) to redeem after the seizure of the chattels by the grantee (i.e., the mortgagee), the grantor may, within five days after the seizure on account of the circumstances prescribed by law,[1314] apply to the High Court to restrain the grantee from removing or selling the chattels, and if the court is satisfied that by payment of money or otherwise, the said cause of seizure no longer exists, may grant the order as prayed or make such other order or orders as may seem just.[1315]

§2. PLEDGE OF PERSONAL CHATTELS

I. Nature of Pledge of Chattels

729. Pledge as a security may be a better option than a mortgage where personal chattels are involved, and the reasons are not far-fetched: a pledge gives the creditor control over the chattels through the exercise of a right to possession and obviates the possibility of the debtor removing the chattels in the event of default, or dealing with it as an ostensible owner in possession as in the case of a mortgage bill of sale.[1316] Apart from the dangers posed by the requirements of the Bills of Sale Law in creating and enforcing the mortgage bill of sale[1317] which requirements do

1308. *Ibid.,* ss 12 and 13.
1309. Applicable in the Eastern and Northern States of Nigeria. *See* ss 19 and 20.
1310. Cap 100 LWN 1959 applicable in the old western and mid-western Nigeria.
1311. *See ss. 12 and 13 of the Bills of Sale Law..*
1312. Ibid. .
1313. Section 23 of the Law.
1314. Sections 12 and 13 thereof.
1315. Proviso to s. 12.
1316. The nature of chattels as movables and the fact that the mortgagee more often than not retains the documents of title, make it easy for sale to be effected in the absence of the mortgagee.
1317. *See* ss. 8, 10, 12 and 13 of the Law.

not apply to a pledge, a third party who obtained title from the mortgagor in the ordinary course of the mortgagor's business takes free of a prior legal registered bill of sale.[1318] A pledge of chattels is a simple act of delivery of possession cheaper to create, easier to realise and, unlike a mortgage bill of sale, requires no registration, and the pledgee is not bound to check the register of bills of sale before taking the pledge. While personal chattels contained in a mortgage bill of sale may be attached consequent upon a successful claim by the landlord for arrears of rent or in the event of liability for taxes or preferential rates, such chattels in the possession of a pledgee cannot be so attached.[1319]

II. Creation of Pledge of Chattels

730. A pledge of personal chattels is created by the pledgor-debtor delivering actual or constructive possession of the chattels to the pledgee-creditor as security for advance of money. Possession is actual where the pledgor hands over the chattels directly to the pledgee; it is constructive where:

(i) the pledgor delivers the keys to the place where the chattels are kept,[1320] or gives instruction to the person in charge of the place to allow the pledge remove the chattels;[1321]or
(ii) the pledgor delivers documents to goods to the pledgee;[1322] or
(iii) the pledgor gives instruction to the carrier of goods to deliver same to the pledgee or by delivery to the pledgee, an endorsed bill of lading.[1323]

731. An actual or constructive possession, to properly constitute a valid pledge, must be, unequivocal and continuous; a return of the goods to the pledgor except for a purpose endorsed by law,[1324] nullifies the pledge.

732. A pledge need not be created in writing; the fact of possession by the pledgee is sufficient. However, it may be necessary to reduce the intention of the parties as to their rights and obligations into writing and this would be legitimate in law. Where parties decide to reduce the transaction into writing, care should be taken to ensure that the document merely evidences the fact of possession already taken by the pledgee as opposed to giving possession by it, otherwise, the document amounts to a bill of sale, and unless it is in the statutory form, it is absolutely void.[1325]

1318. *National Mercantile Bank v. Hampson* (1880) 5 QB 177.
1319. *Tomlinson v. Consolidated Credit Corporation* (1889) 24 QB 135.
1320. *Hilton v. Tucker* (1888) 39 Ch.D 669.
1321. *Wrightson v. Mc Arthur Hutchisons Ltd* (1921) 2 KB 807.
1322. Such delivery is, by virtue of s. 3 of the Factor Act 1889, deemed to be a pledge of the goods.
1323. *Sewell v. Bardick* (1884) 10 AC 74 at 78.
1324. *Official Assignee of Madras v. Mercantile Bank of India* (1935) AC 53.
1325. *Dublin distillery v. Doherty* (1914) AC 832.

III. Obligations of Pledgee in Possession

733. Maintenance and protection of the chattels are the main obligations of the pledgee while in possession, although all expenses incurred as a result are recoverable from the pledgor upon redemption or enforcement of the security.[1326] The pledgee cannot, while the security subsists, transfer title in any manner[1327] and cannot consume the chattels[1328] otherwise, he forfeits the security and becomes liable in the tort of conversion for dealing in the chattels in a manner inconsistent with the right of the owner.

IV. Rights of the Pledgee in Possession

734. A pledgee in possession has special property in the subject matter of security by virtue of which he is entitled to protect his possession by excluding every other person including the pledgor from it, and enabling him to enforce the security in the event of the pledgor's default.[1329] He may sue a third party to recover possession of the chattels pledged without joining the pledgor.[1330]

V. Enforcement of Security

735. In the event of default by the pledgor to pay on the due date under the contract of loan, the pledgee may enforce the covenant to repay in the agreement,[1331] or exercise an implied power[1332] of sale upon giving the pledgor reasonable notice of pledgee's intention to sell.[1333]Where parties did not agree on any date for repayment and the pledgee gives no notice or gives inadequate notice to the pledgor before selling the chattels, the sale is void and the pledgee is liable in conversion.

736. There is a duty imposed on the pledgee in law to sell in good faith and obtain the best price reasonably obtainable in the market,[1334] and the pledgee must not sell more than is reasonably sufficient to pay off the debt. A pledgee who sells the pledgor's chattels upon default 'does so by virtue and to the extent of the pledgor's ownership and not with a new title of his own'.[1335] Thus, since the pledgee would be exercising the power of sale as agent of the pledgor, it is implied that he shall be able to convey the pledgor's title as it were, to the third-party purchaser.

1326. *Ahmed El-Hag v. Amachree* (1962) LLR 10.
1327. *Johnson v. Stear* (1863) 15 CBNS 330.
1328. *Cooke v. Haddon* (1862) 3 F & F 229.
1329. *Donald v. Suckling* (1886) LR 1 QB 585.
1330. *Saville v. Tankred* (1747–1756) 2 Ch. 27–28.
1331. This is usual in all contracts of loan.
1332. This implied power arises from the special property vested in the pledgee when the pledge was created.
1333. *Carter v. Wake* (1877) 4 Ch.D 605; *Re Morritt* (1886) 18 QBD 222.
1334. *The Odessa* (1916) 1 AC 145.
1335. Per Coker J. in *Ahmed El-Hag v. GKJ Amachree supra* n. 1303.

737. Upon sale, the pledgee shall appropriate the proceeds of sale to the payment of the pledgor's debt and in paying off incidental expenses, while he pays any surplus to the pledgor.[1336]

VI. Hypothecation of Personal Chattels

A. Nature of Hypothecation

738. Hypothecation as a security is basically a charge created over chattels under circumstances that make transfer of proprietary interest inconceivable,[1337] less appealing or risky;[1338] or where it is difficult[1339] or impracticable[1340] for the lender to have possession of the chattels or goods.

B. Creation of Hypothecation

739. In this form of security, goods remain in the borrower's or a third party's possession, while security over them is granted by means of a letter of hypothecation instructing the banker to hypothecate the chattels to the borrower's indebtedness. In order for the letter of hypothecation to avoid the application of the Bills of Sale Law in terms of content and registration,[1341] it must be couched in a way as to constitute a document 'used in the ordinary course of business as proof of possession or control of the goods',[1342] as opposed to where lender's title to the security is derived from the document itself. It is important that the chattels or goods hypothecated should be in existence and ascertained at the time of transaction; unascertained or future goods are ineffectual since no such chattels can be appropriated upon debtor's default.

C. Enforcement of Security

740. In the event of failure to repay the loan, the creditor appropriates the charged assets and ipso facto, the ownership rights of the borrower through judicial sale or by appointing a receiver. The creditor cannot foreclose as there is no title in

---

1336. *The Odessa supra* n. 1334.
1337. A legal mortgage may have been created over the personal chattels.
1338. The requirements of the Bills of Sale Law as it affects mortgage of chattels is seen as a trap for the unwary and sometimes weak against competing security.
1339. For example, where goods are contained in the borrower's warehouse which cannot be sealed off to enable the lender become pledgee of them.
1340. Goods may be temporarily in the custody of a third party, e.g., a carrier or bailee of goods for specific purposes, or where goods are abroad or at sea.
1341. For the various requirements of the Bills of Sale Law, *see* 704–722 ante.
1342. *See,* for example, *Re Hamilton Young & Co.* (1905) 2 KB 772.

whatever form to make absolute.[1343] However, the enforcement right of the creditor is subject to the right of the bona fide purchaser of the legal interest for value without notice of the encumbrance.[1344]

D. Right of Redemption

741. Where the borrower liquidates the loan, the encumbrance hanging on the assets automatically disappears without any conscious effort at reconveying same since there was no conveyance of the proprietary interest in the chattels originally.

VII. Lien over Personal Chattels

A. Nature of Lien of Personal Chattels

742. A lien is a right exercisable over the property of another person (the owner) which constitutes that property a security for any claim arising from the unfulfilled obligations of the obligor-owner.[1345] In relation to chattels, a lien could arise in a variety of circumstances either under an agreement[1346] or by operation of law. A lien arises by operation of law where it arises at common law or created by statute. While the existence of statutory lien depends on the construction of provisions in different statutes, common law lien may arise in at least three circumstances namely:

(1) Where the creditor in possession of debtor's property refuses to hand it over to the debtor until the latter pays the debt. A good example is the repairer's possession of personal chattels consequent upon refusal of the owner to pay for work or repairs done by the repairer on the chattels.
(2) Where the right of retention is coupled with the right to sell the chattels and proceeds of sale applied towards the liquidation of the indebtedness. The popular example is the innkeeper's lien for charges over the client's luggage.
(3) When the creditor intercepts chattels en route the debtor and either retains or sells them.

743. A right of lien may be exercised in any of the foregoing circumstances and may be by the creditor against the debtor in the event of failure of the latter to discharge the debt either separately or in conjunction with other remedies in law[1347] to which the creditor may be entitled.

1343. This is the position with any form of equitable charge.
1344. All equitable interests are subject to this frailty.
1345. *Co-operative Bank of Eastern Nigeria v. Eke* (1979) NCLR 491 at 501; *Afrotec Technical Services (Nig) Ltd v. MIA & Sons Ltd* (2000) 15 NWLR (Pt. 692) 730 at 756.
1346. *Afrotec Technical Services (Nig) Ltd v. MIA & Sons Ltd supra* n. 1345 at 788.
1347. For example, set off and damages for breach of contract.

B. Types of Lien over Personal Chattels

744. A lien may be special or general. A special lien arises from the particular transaction connected with the property subject of lien, e.g., repairer's lien on chattel for the cost of repairs; a general lien is that arising not only from the particular transaction, but also from the general dealing between the parties in respect of other transactions of a similar character, e.g., factor's lien for goods in his possession for commission and other entitlements arising from his employment.

VIII. Common Law Possessory Lien

A. Classification of Common Law Possessory Lien

745. Common law lien may be classified as Agency lien e.g., factor's and auctioneer's lien; Mercantile lien e.g., vendor's and purchaser's lien on goods sold or purchased; innkeeper's lien arising from bailment; and Maritime lien. All but Maritime lien are discussed in this chapter. Discussion on Maritime liens is beyond the scope of this monograph and may be sought elsewhere.[1348]

B. Agency Lien

746. A lien may arise in favour of an agent appointed to act for the principal in the ordinary course of business. Every agent has a general or particular possessory lien on the goods and chattels of his principal in respect of all lawful claim either for remuneration earned or advances made, or losses and liabilities incurred, in the course of the agency or otherwise arising in the course of the agency provided that:

(a) the possession of the goods or chattels was lawfully obtained by him in the course of the agency, and in the same capacity as that in which he claims the lien;
(b) there is no agreement inconsistent with the right of lien; and
(c) the goods and chattels were not delivered to him with express directions, or for a special purpose, inconsistent with the right of lien.[1349]

747. The possessory lien of an agent is a particular or special lien mainly except where he has a general lien by agreement, express or implied, with his principal.[1350] Where a lien arises by the contract between parties, the court shall construe the provisions of such contract and give effect to it accordingly.[1351] Examples of Agency lien can be found in factor's and auctioneer's lien.

1348. Smith, I.O. *supra* n. 1053 at 244–255.
1349. *Witt & Busch Ltd v. Alraine (Nig) Ltd* (1968) NCLR 301 at 306–307.
1350. *Bock v. Gorrisen* (1861) 30 LJ Ch. 39.
1351. *Witt & Busch v. Alraine (Nig) Ltd supra* n. 1349.

Factor's Lien

748. A factor is a person to whom goods are assigned for sale by a merchant who entrusts him with the actual possession of the goods or the documents of title thereto and gives him authority to sell in his own name.[1352]

749. Every factor has a general lien over goods in his possession as factor for any balance owed to him as a factor.[1353] For the lien to arise, the factor's possession of the goods must have arisen out of his activity as factor,[1354] and the goods must have come into his possession and so remain throughout his transaction with regard to the goods.[1355]

The factor's right is mainly that of retention until he is paid; he has no right of sale.[1356] However, if a sale took place in the ordinary course of business, the purchaser gets a good title under the Factors Act, 1889.[1357]

750. A factor who has a lien over goods given to him by his principal for sale can in general, sell them pursuant to his authority and reimburse himself out of the proceeds before remitting the balance to his principal.[1358] But he cannot exercise a right of lien where the principal had revoked his authority to sell for, such sale would be wrongful as against the principal although the buyer would a good title if the sale came within the Factors Act 1889.

Auctioneer's Lien

751. An auctioneer has a lien over the proceeds of sale to the extent of his charges in conducting the sale.[1359] Thus as against the highest bidder, the auctioneer has a lien over the goods for the purchase price so that if the purchaser fails to take delivery, he can sue for the price enough to pay off his commission and other expenses incurred in the transaction.[1360]

752. The auctioneer has a lien over the goods sent to him for sale in respect of the general balance arising out of advances made to the principal against future proceeds of sale.[1361] For the lien to arise in this regard, the rights against goods or proceeds of sale must have arisen mainly in connection with the auction,[1362] otherwise, the auctioneer's right is that of equitable set-off.

1352. *Baring v. Gorrie* 106 ER 317.
1353. *Kruger v. Wilcox* 27 ER 168.
1354. *Burns v. Bruce* (1799) Hume 29.
1355. *Kruger v. Wilcox supra* n. 1353.
1356. This is typical of possessory liens generally although statute has come to protect the purchaser in the event of a wrongful sale: *See,* e.g., Factors Act 1889.
1357. *Ibid.,* s. 2.
1358. *Gardiner v. Alexander Milner & Co.* (1858) 208 565.
1359. *Webb v. Smith* (1885) 30 Ch.D 192.
1360. *Chelmsford Auctions Ltd v. Poole* (1973) QB 542.
1361. *Neillay's Trustee v. Hutchison* (1881) 8 R 489.
1362. *Brown v. Smith* (1893) 13 LT 158.

C. Innkeeper's Lien

753. An innkeeper has a lien over personal chattels brought into a hotel by a guest for the amount of the bill incurred[1363] and this is so, notwithstanding that the subject matter of lien does not belong to him.[1364] To the extent that each item of the guest's belonging is security for the whole bill, it is a general lien,[1365] but to the extent that the lien is limited to charges for lodging and storage of goods mainly to the exclusion of debts arising from loans made to the guest or disbursements made on his behalf, the lien is special.[1366]

754. The innkeeper's lien subsists notwithstanding that the bill has exceeded what was agreed on by the parties.[1367] But the lien is restricted to the guest's belongings deposited with the innkeeper; it does not extend to his person or the clothes he is wearing.

755. The innkeeper loses his lien when he parts with the property of the guest, and he cannot exercise his lien over the goods in respect of that particular debt if the guest happens to return to the hotel at a subsequent date. Also, a lien does not arise where the guest gives an alternative security for payment of the bill, and there is an intention to rely on that other security to the exclusion of the lien.

756. Although the right of the innkeeper over the goods of a guest who has incurred unpaid bills is that of retention at common law and no right of sale exists in favour of the innkeeper, section 6 of the Innkeepers Law applicable in many parts of Nigeria[1368] gives the innkeeper the right to sell such property. But the power of sale afforded the innkeeper by this law is subject to the proviso that the debt for the payment of which a sale is made shall not be any other or greater debt than the debt for which the goods or chattels could have been retained by the innkeeper under his lien. The power of sale is not exercisable until after six weeks of the property being in the custody of the innkeeper without having been paid[1369] and only after advertisement of the auction sale by the innkeeper in one newspaper at least one month before any such sale.[1370] Such advertisement shall contain notice of such intended sale and give a short description of the goods or chattels intended to be sold together with the name of the owner or person who deposited or left same where known.[1371] The proceeds of sale shall be applied to the payment of any such debt together with

1363. This does not extend to a charge for damage caused by the guest: *Ferguson v. Peterkin* (1953) SLT 91.
1364. The owner of such property may recover the same but not without settling the guest bills, and may sue the guest thereafter to recover money paid. However, no lien attaches to the goods brought to the guest after his arrival. And which ownership the innkeeper knows is that of a third party: *See Broadwood v. Granada* (1854) 10 Exch. 417.
1365. *Mulliner v. Florence* (1878) 3 QBD 484.
1366. *Chesham Automobile Supply Ltd v. Beresford Hotel (Birchington) Ltd* (1913) 29 TLR 584.
1367. *M'Kichen v. Muir* (1849) Shaw j 223.
1368. *See,* e.g., Cap 50 LWN 1959.
1369. *Ibid.,* s. 6(2).
1370. *Ibid.,* s. 6(4).
1371. *Ibid.*

the costs and expenses of such sale and the surplus if any, shall on demand, be paid to the person leaving any such goods or chattels.[1372]

D. Lien Arising from Bailment for Reward

757. A bailment has been defined as a delivery of personal chattels on trust on the understanding that the trust shall be duly executed and the chattels redelivered in either their original or altered form as soon as the time for, or condition on which they are bailed, shall have elapsed or been performed.[1373]

758. Where goods are delivered to a person under a contract or an arrangement of bailment so that conditions be fulfilled with respect thereto for a charge, a lien may arise in favour of the bailee with respect to certain costs or expenses incurred in discharging the obligation undertaken by him in respect of the goods. Such lien may arise with regards to storage of goods, improvement of goods, packaging of goods, and carriage of goods.

Storage of Goods

759. A warehouseman or other depository has a special lien on property for safe-keeping until the deposit charges are paid.[1374] The right of the custodian of such property is mainly that of retention and the latter has no right to sell the property.[1375] Where the depositor of the property is not the owner, the lien prevails against the owner if the depositor acted with authority, express or implied.[1376]

Lien for Improving Goods

760. A person who has done some work on goods delivered to him for improvement, repairs or change of form has a lien on such goods for the cost of improvement, repairs or change of form. However, mere improvement on goods is not enough; there must be facts from which the law will imply a contract to repay or give a lien in the sense that the lienee must have acted at the request express or implied of the lienor, and upon an undertaking, express or implied, on the part of the lienor to reimburse the lienee.[1377]

761. To acquire a right of lien, the person improving the goods must be in possession of them continuously; where goods are taken and returned at will by the owner, the right of lien is lost. Also, the lien exists over goods the subject of the contract only. A lien existing over improved goods being a special lien, it secures

---

1372. *Ibid.*, s. 6(3).
1373. *Re S Davies & Co. Ltd* (1945) Ch. 402.
1374. *Laurie v. Denny's Trustee* (1853) 15 D 404.
1375. Where the custodian sells the chattel without express or implied permission of the bailor, he becomes liable in conversion: *See Sacks v. Miklos* (1948) 1 All ER 67 at 68 CA; *Munro v. Wilmot* (1949) KB 295.
1376. *Singer Manufacturing Co. v. London and Southwestern Railway Co.* (1894) QB 833.
1377. *Midaf Industrial Holding v. Western Nigeria Development Corporation* (1971) NCLR 236.

charges for work done on the goods retained only; it does not cover debts for work or improvement done on other goods delivered in the past to the owner's possession in the absence of special agreement or trade custom.[1378]

762. Where goods subject of bailment for improvement are delivered to a bailee for repairs or other improvements by a hirer of the chattels under a hire purchase agreement, and the hirer defaults on his hire purchase agreement resulting in the exercise of the owner's power of seizure, the question whether the bailee has a lien on the goods as against the owner of the goods for the cost of repairs or improvements depends on whether the hirer had an obligation to carry out the repairs or improvement and whether he had express or implied authority to carry out the repairs or improvement. The following rules have been laid down by judicial authorities:

(1) Where there is express obligation on the part of the hirer to carry out repairs on the hired goods and he is not expressly prohibited from creating a repairer's lien, the lien binds the owner.[1379]
(2) Where the hire purchase agreement prohibits the hirer from creating repairer's lien over the goods but the bailee is not aware of such prohibition, lien arises in favour of the latter as against the owner for the cost of repairs provided that there is an obligation on the part of the hirer to keep the goods in repair.[1380]
(3) In the absence of an obligation on the part of the hirer to repair, the hirer nonetheless has implied authority to create a repairer's lien if it is reasonable to do so and it is not prohibited by the hire purchase contract. Alien created in such situation also binds the owner who shall be responsible for the cost of repairs.[1381]

763. Where the original bailee of goods for repairs sub contracts same to another bailee for the same purpose without the knowledge or authority of the owner of the goods, no lien arises in favour of the subcontractor in the absence of a trade custom.[1382]

Lien for Packaging of Goods

764. The bailee has a general lien on the goods delivered to him for packaging for the cost of packaging and may refuse to deliver them to the customer until he is paid what is due to him generally for packaging those goods or other goods of the same customer.

1378. *Green v. Farmer* 98 ER 154.
1379. *Green v. All Motors Ltd* (1917) 1KB 625.
1380. *Albemarie Supply Co. Ltd v. Hind & Co.* (1928) 1 KB 307.
1381. *Tappenden v. Artus* (1964) 2 QB 185.
1382. *Pennington v. Reliance Motor works Ltd* (1925) 1 KB 127.

Lien for Carriage of Goods

765. A carrier of goods has a special lien on each item of the goods subject of the contract of carriage for payment of his freight and may retain such goods until he is paid for the services.[1383] It is immaterial that the bailor of such goods is not the owner of them for the lien attaches to the goods as against the actual owner and the latter is liable to pay before collection.[1384] It is also immaterial that the goods are delivered to the carrier against the Will of the owner since the carrier is obliged to carry all goods delivered to him for carriage.[1385]

766. Since the carrier's lien is a special lien, it does not extend to the general balance of account due in respect of other good although a general lien may be created on the latter by contract.

767. A carrier cannot exercise a right of lien where there is an agreement to give credit for the carriage,[1386] and its right of lien does not arise until the transit is complete. Where the carrier is obliged to preserve the goods at the end of the transit, he may recover the charges incurred, but he has no right of lien for such charges in the absence of an agreement to the contrary.[1387]

768. The right of lien exists so long as the carrier retains the goods, but where the consignee carries away the goods against the Will of the carrier, the lien is lost and can only be revived when the carrier retakes the goods.[1388]

E. Lien Arising from Bailment Without Reward

769. A bailee of goods without reward either by agreement or by virtue of certain special circumstances has a lien on the goods and the right to detain same until paid all the expenses incurred by him in full.[1389] But being a bailment without reward, the bailor must have acknowledged that such expenses would be settled by him or by a person so authorised by him.[1390]

IX. Power of Sale of the Possessory Lienee

770. As could be observed from the various types of possessory lien discussed, a possessory lienee at common law has a right to possess and retain the goods subject of the lien until the debtor's financial obligation is met by him; he has no right

1383. *George Baker Transport Ltd v. Eynon* (1973) 1 WLR 1461.
1384. This may be justified on the ground of ostensible authority.
1385. Halsbury's Laws of England 4th ed. vol v 447.
1386. *Raitt v. Mitchell* (1815) 4 Camp 146.
1387. *Great Northern Railway Co. v. Swaffield* (1874) LR 9 Exch. 132.
1388. Halsbury's Laws of England *supra* n. 1385.
1389. *Balonwu v. Odunuko* (1971) 2 NCLR 388.
1390. *Ibid.*

to sell and unless such power is conferred by statute, a sale by him amounts to the tort of conversion as against the debtor. This is so notwithstanding that the debtor is not forthcoming or unable to pay. This position at common law is fraught with difficulties especially where perishable goods are involved, or where the retention of the goods involves costs or expenses borne by the lienee and the security may not be worthwhile afterwards. It has been held that in such cases, an application may be made to court for an order to sell the property.[1391]

X. Statutory Lien over Goods

771. In Nigeria, a number of statutes exist regulating the creation and enforcement of lien apart from the common law. These are discussed under different heads.

A. Lien and Other Rights of Retention under the Sale of Goods Act

772. Section 39 of the Sale of Goods Act ('the Act') gives an unpaid seller certain rights exercisable over goods either in possession of the seller or in transit in the form of lien or other rights of retention enforceable by resale.

Unpaid Seller's Lien

773. Section 41 of the Act creates a lien in favour of an unpaid seller of goods[1392] who is in possession of them notwithstanding that property in the goods has passed to the buyer,[1393] and regardless of the fact that the seller is in possession as agent, bailee, or custodier for the buyer.[1394] Such unpaid seller is entitled to retain possession of the goods until payment or tender of the price where the goods have been sold without any stipulation as to credit,[1395] or where the goods have been sold on credit but the term of credit has expired,[1396] or where the buyer becomes insolvent.[1397]

774. Where part delivery of the goods has been made by the seller, he may exercise his right of lien or retention on the remainder unless such part delivery has been made under such circumstances as to show an agreement to waive the lien or right

1391. *Larner v. Fawcett* (1950) 2 All ER 727.
1392. The seller of goods is said to be an 'unpaid seller' 'when either the whole price has not been paid or tendered, or a bill of exchange or other negotiable instrument has been received as conditional payment and the condition on which it was received has not been fulfilled by reason of the dishonour of the instrument or otherwise': *See* s. 38(1) of the Act.
1393. For rules relating to passing of property in the goods, *see* Sale of Goods Act 1893, s. 18.
1394. *Ibid.*, s. 41(2).
1395. *Ibid.*, s. 41(1)(a).
1396. *Ibid.*, s. 41(1)(b).
1397. *Ibid.*, s. 41(1)(c).

of retention.[1398] But where the contract is severable, the unpaid seller cannot exercise a lien over subsequent instalments after default if the buyer is prepared to pay for a subsequent instalment.

775. Subject to any express agreement between the parties,[1399] a right of lien is lost by the unpaid seller of goods in accordance with section 43(1) of the Act when he delivers the goods to a carrier or other bailee for the purpose of transmission to the buyer without reserving the right of disposal of the goods, or when the buyer or his agent lawfully obtains possession of the goods, or by waiver thereof. The lien is not lost by the unpaid seller obtaining judgment or decree for the price of the goods,[1400] and the sellers right to be paid the contract price is independent of the existence of the lien; a lien being an additional security given to the unpaid seller.[1401]

776. Where an unpaid seller exercises a right of lien, he resells the goods as provided by section 48(3) of the Act.

Stoppage in Transit

777. Section 44 of the Sale of Goods Act gives the unpaid seller, in the event of the buyer becoming insolvent, the right to resume possession of goods in the course of transit to such buyer, and retains possession of them until payment of the price. An exercise of this right by the unpaid seller put the carrier in transit under an obligation to redeliver possession of the goods to the seller. If the buyer or his agent obtains delivery of the goods before their arrival at the appointed destination, the transit is at end.[1402] If after the arrival of the goods at the appointed destination, the carrier or bailee acknowledges to the buyer or his agent that he holds the goods on his behalf and continues in possession of them as such, the transit is at end notwithstanding that a further destination for the goods may have been indicated by the buyer.[1403] If the goods are rejected by the buyer and the carrier, or bailee continues in possession of them, the transit is not deemed to be at end, even if the seller has refused to receive them back.[1404] Where goods are delivered to a ship chartered by the buyer, it is a question of fact whether they are in the possession of the master as a carrier or as agent to the buyer.[1405] If the carrier or other bailee wrongfully refuses to deliver the goods to the buyer or his agent, the transit is said to be at end.[1406] When the carrier has delivered some of the goods, the seller may stop the remainder in transit, unless the partial delivery was made under such circumstances as to show an agreement to give up possession of the whole of the goods.[1407]

1398. *Ibid.*, s. 42.
1399. *Afrotec Technical Services (Nig) Ltd v. MIA & Sons Ltd supra* n. 1345 at 730.
1400. Sale of Goods Act 1893, s. 43(2).
1401. *Afrotec Technical Services (Nig) Ltd v. MIA & Sons Ltd supra* n. 1345.
1402. Sale of Goods Act 1893, s. 45(2).
1403. *Ibid.*, s. 45(2).
1404. *Ibid.*, s. 45(4).
1405. *Ibid.*, s. 45(5).
1406. *Ibid.*, s. 45(6).
1407. *Ibid.*

778. Section 46 of the Act provides for method of stoppage. By virtue of that provision, the unpaid seller may stop the goods by taking actual possession of them or by giving notice of stoppage to the carrier or bailee in whose possession the goods are.[1408] The notice may be given either to the person in actual possession of the goods or to his principal and in the latter case, the notice to be effectual, must be given at such time and under such circumstances that the principal, by the exercise of reasonable diligence, may communicate it to his servant or agent in time to prevent a delivery to the buyer.[1409] On receiving notice of stoppage, the carrier or bailee must redeliver the goods to the seller or according to the directions of the seller at the latter's expense.[1410]

B. Unpaid Seller's Right and Disposition by Buyer

779. The seller's lien or his right of stoppage in transit are not affected by any sale or other disposition of the goods without the seller assenting thereto, except where documents of title have been given to the buyer and have been transferred on sale to a person taking the documents in good faith and for valuable consideration. Where the person taking the document from the buyer does so not on sale but by way of pledge or other disposition for value, the unpaid seller's right of lien or stoppage in transit can only be exercised subject to the rights of the transferee.[1411]

C. Unpaid Seller's Right to Resell

780. An unpaid seller may find a potent remedy in resale, and a contract of sale is not rescinded by the mere exercise by an unpaid seller of his right of lien or stoppage in transit.[1412]

781. Where the goods are of perishable nature,[1413] or where the unpaid seller gives notice to the buyer of his intention to resell, and the buyer does not, within a reasonable time, pay or tender the price, the unpaid seller may resell the goods and recover from the original buyer damages for any loss occasioned by his breach of

1408. *Ibid.,* s. 46(1).
1409. *Ibid.*
1410. *Ibid.,* s. 46(2).
1411. *Ibid.,* s. 47.
1412. *Ibid.,* s. 48(1). This is however subject to the provisions of the section particularly, s. 48(4) of the Act where the seller reserves the right of resale in case the buyer defaults and the seller resells the goods upon the buyer's default.
1413. Goods are of 'perishable nature' when they are likely to deteriorate physically as time elapses so as to become unmerchantable: *See Sharp v. Christmas* (1892) 8TLR 687 at 688; *Asfer v. Blundell* (1896) 1 QB 123 at 126.

contract.[1414] Where the seller expressly reserves the right of resale in case of buyer's default, and upon the buyer's default resells the goods, the original contract of sale is rescinded but without prejudice to any claim the seller may have for damages.[1415]

782. Since there is no specific mode of resale stipulated by statute, the sale may be by public auction or by private treaty to anyone at any price provided the seller acts reasonably.[1416] The unpaid seller who, in exercising a right of lien or right of stoppage in transit sells the goods, passes good title to the buyer as against the original buyer.[1417]

XI. Lien Arising under the Factors Act 1889

783. Section 7 of the Factors Act provides that where the owner of goods gives possession of them to another person for the purpose of consignment or sale, or ship goods in the name of another person, and the consignee has no notice that the person in possession of the goods is not the owner of them, the consignee has the same lien on the goods in respect of advances made to or for the use of the person in possession of the goods as if the latter were the owner of them.

XII. Lien Arising under the Nigerian Railway Act

784. Where a person fails to pay on demand made by or on behalf of the Nigerian Railway Corporation any rate, charge, or debt due from him to the corporation, the latter may detain any goods delivered by him or delivered to the corporation for conveyance to him until the debt is paid.[1418] This creates a special lien in favour of the corporation over each item of the goods to the extent equal to the amount of indebtedness. But a general lien may arise over any other goods of the debtor then being in or thereafter coming into possession of the corporation, if the particular goods delivered by the debtor have been removed from the railway.[1419]

785. The corporation has the power to sell the goods or any part of them by public auction after calling for tenders for the purchase thereof.[1420] In the case of perishable goods, the corporation may sell at any time otherwise in the case of other goods, no sale shall take place until two months after the date of the demand made by the corporation for the payment of any rate, other charge, or debt due to it.[1421]

1414. Sale of Goods Act 1893; s. 48(3).
1415. *Ibid.*, s. 48(4).
1416. Chitty on Contract vol II para. 4610.
1417. Sale of Goods Act 1893, s. 48(2).
1418. Nigerian Railway Corporation Act Cap N129 LFN 2010, s. 61(1).
1419. *Ibid.*
1420. *Ibid.*, s. 61(2).
1421. *Ibid.*, s. 61(2).

786. From the proceeds of sale, the corporation may retain the rate, charge, or debt due including all expenses of detention[1422] and sale and render any surplus and any such goods as remain unsold to the person entitled thereto.[1423] Where any goods remain after sale by the corporation, the latter may, by notice oral or written, require the debtor to remove the goods from the railway within fifteen days from the date of the notice.[1424] Failure to comply with such notice by the owner may result in the corporation selling the goods and applying the proceeds towards satisfaction of the debt owed and other expenses incurred by the corporation, while the balance goes to the owner of such goods.[1425]

XIII. Lien Arising under the Customs and Excise Management Act

787. The Customs and Excise Management Act requires report to be made of every ship, vehicle, or aircraft and all goods carried therein and of every vehicle entering Nigeria by land and all goods carried therein.[1426] If at the expiration of twenty-one days from the date of making the report, or where no report was made on the date it should properly have been made or such longer period as the customs and excise management allow and any goods are still on board the ship, aircraft, or vehicle, the board may authorise the detention of that ship, aircraft, or vehicle until any expenses properly incurred in watching and guarding the goods beyond the said period have been repaid to the board.[1427] Where the goods are removed from the ship, aircraft, or vehicle to a government warehouse, the board may retain the goods until the expenses of removal are paid.[1428] Where it is necessary to station any officer in charge of any ship, aircraft, or vehicle for the protection of revenue, such officer may detain the ship, aircraft, or vehicle until any expenses incurred have been paid to the board.[1429]

XIV. Retention Right

788. *See* paragraphs 593–595.

XV. Compensation

789. Compensatory remedy exists in equity where there is a breach of trust or other fiduciary duties owed to the defendant by the plaintiff. Since its decision in

1422. In the case of animals, the expenses of detention shall include the cost of feeding, watering, and tendering them: *See* s. 61(3) of the Act.
1423. *Ibid.*, s. 61(3).
1424. *Ibid.*, s. 61(4).
1425. *Ibid.*
1426. Customs and Excise Management Act Cap C45 2010, s. 26(1).
1427. *Ibid.*, s. 35(1)(a).
1428. *Ibid.*, s. 35(10(b).
1429. *Ibid.*, s. 35(2).

Norton v. Lord Ashburton,[1430] the House of Lords has extended the remedy for a breach of fiduciary duty beyond the duty to account for loss of trust assets by the trustees, to liability for the loss suffered by the beneficiary. Thus, the general equitable compensatory remedy is applicable, or considered potentially applicable in actions against trustees for the loss caused by the latter's breach of trust;[1431] in action against fiduciaries for the loss caused by to the plaintiffs by breach of a fiduciary duty;[1432] in action against defendants who though not fiduciaries in respect of the breach in question, have acted in breach of an equitable obligation;[1433] or in action for breach of confidence resulting in loss to the plaintiff;[1434] and in an action for loss flowing from a breach of contract founded on estoppels.[1435]

790. The essence of compensation in equity is to restore persons who have suffered loss to the position in which they would have been if there had been no breach of the equitable obligation.

791. The measure of equitable compensation is determined by equitable principles as to what is fair and just taking the totality of circumstances into consideration and without being constrained by the measure of damages for breach of contract or for tort.

§3. Delegation and Direct Claim

792. At law, by a device of a Power of Attorney donated by the creditor (assignor) to an assignee, an assignee of a debt could sue a debtor using the assignor's (creditor's) name to press the claim. This device is however fraught with dangers for, not only could the creditor (assignor) terminate the power thereby jeopardising the interest of the assignee who may equally be the assignor's creditor, such power is automatically terminated upon the death of the assignor (creditor) and if death occurs before an assignee makes or collects his claim, the power would be of no help to him. But by the ingenious devise in equity, such a debt or any other chose in action may be assigned to a third party directly in law or in equity. (*See* paragraphs 437–442 for detailed discussion of Assignment of choses in action in law or equity.)

1430. (1914) AC 932.
1431. *Patridge v. Equity Trustees Executors & Agency Company Ltd* (1947) 75 CLR 149.
1432. *Mckenzie v. Mc Donald*(1927) VLR 134.
1433. *Mahoney v. Purnell*(1996) 3 All ER.
1434. *Green v. Folgham* 57 ER 159.
1435. *Glumelli v. Glumelli* (1999) 196 CLR 101.

Chapter 3. Company Charges

793. The power to borrow money and create debentures secured by a charge is vested in companies by the CAMA 2020.[1436] Section 191 of CAMA gives a registered company the power to 'borrow money for the purpose of its business or objects and may mortgage or charge its undertaking, property and uncalled capital, or any part thereof [and] to issue debentures, debenture stock and other securities whether outright or as security for any debt, liability or obligation of the company or of any third party'.

794. Although a debenture is generally an acknowledgement of the company's indebtedness, it is unlikely that creditors would create naked debentures and more often than not, the company is required to charge its assets as security. A secured debenture is that which is secured either by a fixed charge on the specific or ascertainable company properties or by a floating charge over the whole or a specified part of the company's undertaking and assets or both.

§1. Fixed Charge or Mortgage Debenture

795. There is no statutory definition or detailed description of a fixed charge in Nigeria; consequently, the common law concept of fixed charge applies subject to some statutory modifications.

796. At common law, a fixed charge is a charge over specific property of a company which fastens on the property when the charge is created.[1437] It is not necessary that the property should exist when the charge is created or that the company should own them at the time; it suffices if the property or the class of assets to which it belongs is sufficiently defined in the instrument creating the charge so well that there can be no doubt as to whether the property is caught by the charge when it comes into existence or when the company acquires it.[1438] When a charge is fixed, the assets are appropriated to the satisfaction of the debt immediately or upon the debtor acquiring an interest in it, in the case of future or after acquired property.[1439]

797. A debenture secured by a fixed charge takes the form of a mortgage legal or equitable with the attendant rights and obligations of the parties as in the case of the ordinary mortgage involving the individual.[1440] The fixed charge prevents the chargee from disposing of the property subject to charge without the consent of the chargee.[1441] Sections 232 and 233 of CAMA set out the events under which a fixed charge may be realised as well as the remedies available to the fixed chargee.

1436. This repealed and replaced CAMA Cap C20 LFN 2010.
1437. *Illingworth v. Houldsworth* (1904) AC 355.
1438. *Tailby v. Official Receiver* (1888) 13 AC 523 at 533.
1439. *Ibid.*
1440. Section 222(13) of CAMA 2020 defines a mortgage to include a charge.
1441. It is this fettered freedom that qualifies it a fixed charge.

798. The advantage of the fixed charge from the point of view of the chargee lies in the availability of a particular asset or group of assets to satisfy the creditor upon default by the debtor company and in the priority of the charge over any floating charge created prior or subsequent to the fixed charge,[1442] unless the earlier floating charge contained a negative pledge clause. The major disadvantage of a fixed charge is that the chargee, having chosen and ascertained the charged assets, is confined to those and cannot have recourse to other assets in the event of enforcement even where the assets charged are depreciating in value and/or insufficient to meet the company's debts.

799. The fixed charge belongs to the regime of general mortgages as opposed to an equitable charge. Where the assets include land, it requires perfection such as consent under the Land Use Act,[1443] stamping,[1444] and registration under the relevant Land Registration Law[1445] as in the case of mortgage of land, and the rights and obligations of the mortgagor and mortgagees follow as in the case of mortgage of land earlier discussed. Where the assets consists of personal chattels, the debenture is not a bill of sale for purposes of the application of the Bills of Sale Law of the State[1446]and consequently, the provisions of the Bills of Sale Law as to form and registration of the mortgage instrument do not apply.

§2. Floating Charge

800. A floating charge is an equitable charge on all or any of the company's property or assets, the constituent items of which are constantly changing. It is an invention of equity[1447] dictated by the business exigencies of the times[1448] and its course has been influenced by the ingenuity of draftsmen[1449] and statutory provisions.[1450] The nature of a floating charge is such that it creates an immediate security over all company's assets or undertaking or a particular category of them but without attaching to any until crystallisation.[1451] Section 178(1) of CAMA defines a floating charge as:

1442. CAMA Cap C20 LFN 2010, s. 204.
1443. Cap L5 LFN 2010.
1444. Stamp Duties Act Cap S8 LFN 2010.
1445. Land Registration Act 1924, s. 2 and corresponding provisions in the Registration Laws of the States.
1446. Bills of Sale Act 1882. s. 17.
1447. *Pennington Company Law* 555 at 561 (9th ed.).
1448. The huge demand for funds by companies could only be met by a fixed charge which restricts the company's power to deal with the charged assets in the ordinary course of business and consequently, reducing the company's prospect of repayment of loan through profitable business operations. The floating charge enables the company to raise money without removing any of its property from the business.
1449. An example of draftsmen innovation is the negative pledge clause meant to protect the floating chargee against priority of a fixed charge created subsequently.
1450. *See* CAMA 2020, ss 203, 222–234.
1451. *Evans v. Rival Granite Quarries Ltd* (1916) 2 KB 979 at 999.

an equitable charge over the whole or a specified part of the company's undertakings and assets including cash and uncalled capital of the company both present and future, so that the charge shall not preclude the company from dealing with such assets until –

(a) the security becomes enforceable and the holder thereof, pursuant to a power in that behalf in the debenture or the deed securing the same, appoints a receiver or manager or enters into possession of such assets; or
(b) the court appoints a receiver or manager of such assets on the application of the holders; or
(c) the company goes into liquidation.

801. The foregoing provision of CAMA on the definition of a floating charge is an amplification of the common law position on the nature and consequences of a floating charge created over all assets of the company. The nature of floating charge is characterised by three main features:[1452]

(1) it is a charge on a class of assets both present and future;
(2) the class of assets is one which in the ordinary course of business of the company would be changing from time to time; and
(3) it is contemplated that, until the charge attaches to assets by crystallisation, the company may dispose of or deal with the assets in the ordinary course of business. The expression 'ordinary course of business' is construed widely to cover a sale of the whole undertaking[1453] including payment of its unsecured creditors and the power to grant mortgages on the same property unless it is otherwise provided in the charge instrument.

802. The difference between a fixed and a floating charge is not necessarily situated in the nature of assets as to being fixed or shifting for a fixed charge, like a floating charge, may be secured over book debts[1454] as well as future and after acquired property; the distinction actually lies in the freedom or restriction of the chargee to manage the assets in the ordinary course of business. Thus, while a floating chargee has the power to deal with the assets of the company in the ordinary course of business, a fixed chargee cannot deal with the assets subject matter of the charge.

803. A floating charge is essentially an equitable charge and creates neither proprietary nor possessory security in favour of the creditor but represents an appropriation of the property to the satisfaction of an obligation without any transfer.[1455]

1452. *Re Yorkshire Woolcombers Association Ltd* (1903) Ch. 284 at 295.
1453. *Re Boras Co.* (1901) 1 Ch. 326; *Harmer v. London City and Midland Bank Ltd* (1918) 87 LJ KB 973.
1454. *Siebe Gorman & Co. Ltd v. Barclays Bank Ltd* (1972) 2 Lloyds Report 12.
1455. *Intercontractors Nigeria Ltd v. UAC* (1988) 2 NWLR (Pt. 76) 303.

It is advantageous in various ways: it enables the company operating as a going concern to create security over its assets while preserving the company's power to deal with them in the ordinary course of business. For a company with limited fixed assets but with large and valuable stock in trade, the floating charge is the most convenient way of creating security over the company's assets. The floating charge affords protection against an unsecured creditor upon crystallisation, and the fact that the company can deal with its assets in the ordinary course of business makes it possible to create a later fixed legal or equitable charge over the floating charge unless the latter provides otherwise.

I. Creation of a Floating Charge

804. To create a floating charge, no particular form is necessary; it suffices that there is the intention to impose a charge on the assets present and future and to allow the company to continue to deal with those assets in the ordinary course of business.

805. Where land is the subject matter of a charge and the creation of the charge involves alienation of legal or equitable interest in land as in the case of a fixed charge, Governor's consent is required for a valid creation. This is not the case with a floating charge which merely appropriates the land to the satisfaction of the debt without any transfer.

§3. Perfection of Company Charges

806. The law requires all charge instruments to be stamped as a prerequisite for admissibility in court,[1456] and the CAMA requires all companies not only to keep a copy of any charge instrument,[1457] a register of charges,[1458] a register of debenture holders,[1459] and to register debenture transfers[1460] for purposes of inspection by the public,[1461] but also, to register a charge created by a company[1462] with the CAC.[1463]

Registration at the CAC

807. Registration with the CAC has to be done within ninety days of creation of the charge otherwise, it is void against the liquidator and any creditor of the

1456. Stamp Duty Act Cap S8 LFN 2010, s. 22(4).
1457. *Ibid.,* s. 215.
1458. *Ibid.,* s. 216.
1459. *Ibid.,* s. 218.
1460. *Ibid.,* s. 220.
1461. This is the publicity rule which enjoins companies to make corporate information available to the public. In this respect, CAMA prescribes penalty for non-compliance: *See* CAMA, s. 219 (4)(5)
1462. CAMA, Cap C20 LFN 2010, s. 222(1).
1463. *Ibid.,* s. 222(2)(f)

company,[1464] and when the charge becomes void for non-registration, the money secured shall immediately become payable.[1465] But the court may, upon application to it by the chargor, extend the time for registration or make an order to rectify omission or misstatement of any particular on terms and conditions as the court may deem just where the delay in registration or the omission or misstatement in the register was accidental, or due to inadvertence or to other sufficient cause, or is not of a nature to prejudice the position of creditors or shareholders of the company, or that it is just and equitable to grant the relief.[1466]

808. A chargor shall deliver to CAC the instrument by which the charge is created and the prescribed particulars of the charge. The particulars required in the case of a charge to the benefit of which the holder of a series of debentures are entitled are: the total amount secured by the whole series and where amount uncertain, the maximum sum secured; the date of the resolution authorising the issues of the series and the date of the recovering deed if any, by which the security is created or defined; description of the property charged; and the names of the trustees if any, for the debenture holders.[1467] In the case of other charges, the required particulars are: the date of creation of the charge;[1468] the amount secured by the charge; short particulars of the property; and the person entitled to the charge. A debenture which entitles the holder to a charge on land shall not, for the purpose of section 197 of CAMA be deemed to be an interest in land.[1469] A certificate issued by the Commission shall be prima facie evidence of compliance with the requirements of registration.[1470] But registration of a charge does not cure any defect in the charge as the charge may be impugned on other grounds.

809. Where a charge affects property situate in Nigeria but registration elsewhere in Nigeria is required to make the charge valid, a Certified True Copy of the original instrument may be delivered to CAC.[1471] In the case of a charge created out of Nigeria with respect to property situate outside Nigeria, the delivery to and receipt by the Commission of a copy of the instrument verified in the prescribed manner is sufficient compliance with section 197(1) provided it is delivered within ninety days after the date on which the instrument or its copy could, in due course by post, and if dispatched with diligence, have been received in Nigeria.[1472] Where a charge is created in Nigeria but affects or relates to property outside Nigeria, the

1464. *Ibid.,* s. 222(1). However, an unregistered charge is valid against the chargor on the strength of s. 224 of CAMA which makes it a primary duty of the chargor to register the charge; and unregistered charge is valid against an unsecured creditor before liquidation: *See Re Kris Cruisers Ltd* (1949) Ch. 138 at 140–141.

1465. The contract or obligation to repay the debt secured is not discharge as the chargee may enforce the covenant to repay.

1466. CAMA 2020, s. 230.

1467. *Ibid.,* ss 222 (9); 223 (1)(a).

1468. *Ibid.,* s. 223(1)(b).

1469. *Ibid.,* s. 222 (8).

1470. *Ibid.,* s. 223(2).

1471. *Ibid.,* s. 222(3).

1472. *Ibid.,*. s. 222(5).

instrument may be sent for registration notwithstanding that further proceedings may be necessary to make the charge valid or effectual under the law of the country in which the property is situate.[1473]

810. Where particulars of a charge are registered pursuant to sections 222(9) and 223(1) of CAMA, third parties are deemed to have constructive notice of them.[1474] It is therefore necessary for a prospective creditor of the company to conduct a search not only at the company's registered office, but also at the CAC.

Registration at the Lands Registry

811. A floating charge on land unlike a fixed charge, requires no registration of the land under the land registration laws in Nigeria; not only is a charge not a transfer of proprietary or possessory interest requiring registration, the ambulatory nature of a floating charge does not make it possible to deliver its particulars for registration.[1475]

§4. Priority of Company Charges

812. The rules of priority in relation to Company charges are as follows:

(1) By virtue of section 179 of CAMA, a floating charge will be postponed to a later fixed charge whether legal or equitable, even if the later fixed chargee had notice of the existence of an earlier floating charge. To forestall a situation where a fixed charge created after a floating charge will have priority over an earlier floating charge, the practice is to insert a negative pledge clause in the debenture prohibiting the creation of any later charge subsequently having priority over the floating charge. However, for the negative pledge clause to have effect, section 179 of CAMA requires not only that the fixed chargee be aware of the existence of a prior floating charge, but must also have actual notice of the prohibition contained in the negative pledge clause at the time the charge was granted to him. The registration of the charge under section 197 of CAMA does not constitute notice of the content of the charge, save the particulars in the register of particulars of charges which particulars does not include particulars of prohibitions, conditions or restrictions including any negative pledge clause in the charge.[1476]

(2) As between two floating charges created, the first in time has priority, and the company cannot create a subsequent floating charge on the same assets that will rank in priority to or pari passu with the original floating charge.[1477]

1473. *Ibid.*, s. 222(6).
1474. *Ibid.*, s. 92.
1475. *JIA Enterprises et al v. British Commonwealth Insurance Co* (1962) All NLR 363.
1476. That is the implication of s. 92 of CAMA.
1477. *Re Automatic Bottle Makers Ltd* (1926) Ch. 412.

(3) An unsecured creditor has priority over a floating chargee prior to crystallisation and if such creditor has levied and actually completed execution, the floating chargee cannot compel him to restore the money, nor can he be restrained from levying execution.[1478]
(4) The interest of the floating chargee is postponed to any lien or set-off accruing prior to crystallisation.[1479]
(5) The interest of the floating chargee is subject to any claim by title paramount. Thus, the landlord can enter and distrain on chattels in the leasehold premises if rent is unpaid notwithstanding that the chattels are comprised in a charge which has crystallised.[1480]

I. Statutory Limitations

813. There are provisions of CAMA restricting the creation of a floating charge and retaining the protection it affords creditors in the interest of the company, its employees, and the general public. The various statutory limitations are discussed below:

(a) *Preferential creditors:* Section 494(1) of CAMA provides that in winding up a company, claim in respect of employees such as wages, salaries, accrued holiday remunerations, and social security contributions under the National Provident Fund are given preference over claims of other creditors including those of crystallised floating charges. For the purpose of application of this provision, any person who advanced money to pay such wages or salaries is subrogated to the rights of employees so paid.[1481] Also, a duty is created by the section incumbent on the company to pay, in preference to all other creditors, all rates and taxes due from the company within twelve months.[1482] Where a floating chargee or his receiver collects funds out of which preferred debts could have been paid, he will be personally liable to the extent of these funds if the preferred debts are not paid.[1483] However, the statutory duty does not arise until the preferential claim is proved and becomes payable,[1484]and fixed charges are not postponed to the claims of preferential creditors. These statutory limitations do not apply to fixed charges.
(b) *Defective floating charges:* Section 498 of CAMA provides that a floating charge created within three months of the commencement of winding up of the company shall be invalid unless it is proved that the company immediately after the creation of the charge was solvent otherwise, the charge is valid only to the extent of cash paid to the company at the time of, or subsequently to the creation of, and in consideration for the charge, together with interest on that

1478. *Evans v. Rival Granite Quarries Ltd supra* n. 1451.
1479. *Rother Iron works Ltd v. Canterbury Precision Engineers Ltd* (1974) QB 1.
1480. *Re Roundwood Colliery Co.* (1897) 1 Ch. 373.
1481. CAMA 2020, s. 657 (3)
1482. *Ibid.*, s. 657 (1)(a).
1483. *IRC v. Goldblatt* (1972) Ch. 458.
1484. *Ibid.*

amount at the current bank rate. The effect of this provision is to make it impossible for Directors to 'retrospectively convert themselves into secured creditors in respect of moneys which they have previously advanced without demanding security'.[1485]It does not also avail directors to advance further money on a floating charge on the understanding that it is to be used to repay their existing loans.[1486] This restriction on the creation of a floating charge close to winding up is inapplicable to fixed charges, and a fixed charge is not invalid on the ground that it was granted by an insolvent company immediately before liquidation, although it may be attacked on the ground of fraud or as a fraudulent preference under section 495 of CAMA.

(c) *Cost of liquidation*: Section 647 of CAMA provides that the expenses of the company's liquidation are payable out of the assets of the company in priority to other claims.

II. Crystallisation of Floating Charge

814. Crystallisation is the attachment of specific assets of the company hitherto constituting a floating charge, upon the happening of certain event recognised or prescribed by law. By crystallisation, the floating charge is converted into a fixed charge[1487] fastening on all charged assets in which the company then has or subsequently acquires an interest. It ends the authority conferred on the floating chargee to manage the assets comprised in the security and attaches specific assets available at the time.[1488]

815. The events which crystallises a floating charge are listed in section 203(1) of CAMA. The events are:

(a) where the security becomes enforceable and the chargee appoints a receiver pursuant to a power so to do in the debenture or the deed securing same, or enters into possession of such assets; or
(b) where the court appoints a receiver or manager of such assets on the application of the holder; or
(c) where the company goes into liquidation.[1489]

1485. *Gower's Principles of Modern Company Law* 471 at 478 (4th ed. Stevens).
1486. *Re Destone Fabric Ltd* (1914) Ch. 319.
1487. *Re Crompton & Co. Ltd* (1914) 1 Ch. 963 at 964.
1488. *Robbie & Co. Ltd v. Witney Warehouse Ltd* (1963) All ER 613.
1489. The provision of s. 203(1) of CAMA has limited the instances of crystallisation to the foregoing events mainly thus making inapplicable other events at common law like cessation of business, or sale of substantial assets other than in the ordinary course of business. Also, the provision has neither rendered inoperative the concept of automatic crystallisation upon the occurrence of a particular event of default prescribed by the charge instrument, or semi-automatic crystallisation in the sense of a mere requirement of notice being given to the chargor by the chargee to terminate the company's licence to carry on business; nor does the breach of terms of the charge per se permit crystallisation. In any such event, the chargee may bring about crystallisation only by taking possession or by appointing a receiver or manager of the assets.

816. When the floating charge becomes fixed, it constitutes a charge on all the assets of the company and has priority over any subsequent equitable charge and over unsecured creditors.[1490] The evolving fixed charge after crystallisation does not require re-registration at the companies registry as no new security interest is created.[1491]

817. Crystallisation may be reverted to cause the charge to float again over the assets. This may be necessitated by a new arrangement agreed upon between the parties to the charge which gives the debtor company an extension of time within which to pay upon certain considerations.

818. Section 203(2) makes decrystallisation possible in Nigeria provided that the charge has not been fully discharged. To decrystallise, the receiver or manager is either withdrawn with the consent of the chargee or the chargee withdraws from possession before the charge is fully discharged.

III. Remedies Available to a Debenture Holder

819. The remedies available to a debenture holder secured by a fixed or floating charge are as follows:

(1) *Recovery of principal and interest based on the implied covenant on the part of the debtor to pay back the loan*

(2) *Petition for winding up on the ground of the latter's inability to pay its debt.*[1492]

To rely successfully on this ground for winding up, the petitioner must show that the company is indebted in the sum exceeding =N=2000; that the Petitioner has issued a demand in writing requiring the company to pay the sum due; and that the company has for three weeks thereafter, neglected to pay the sum or to secure or compound for it to the reasonable satisfaction of the petitioner.[1493]

(3) *Sale*

A power of sale may be exercised by a debenture holder or a trustee where such power is contained in the debenture or trust deed or pursuant to a court order following a debenture holders' action.

(4) *Foreclosure*

A debenture holder or a trustee in the case of a trust deed may realise his security by bringing a foreclosure action.[1494] An action for foreclosure and the effect of a foreclosure order are the same as for any mortgagee. But an order of foreclosure will not be made unless all the debenture holder of every class

---

1490. *Mandilas and Karaberis Ltd v. Anglo Canadian Cement Company Ltd* (1967) NCLR 42.
1491. *Fasakin v. Fasakin* (1994) 4 NWLR (Pt. 340) 597.
1492. CAMA, 2020, s. 571(d).
1493. *Ibid.,* s. 572.
1494. *Ibid.,* s. 233 (2)(b)(i).

are parties to the action so that all interests in the company's assets may be represented.[1495] The court may, where it considers it just to do so, make an order for sale of the property instead of making an order for foreclosure.

(5) *Appointment of a Receiver*

The power to appoint a receiver may be statutory, contractual or a combination of both. It may be made out of court where there is a power in the debenture for such appointment to be made,[1496] or may be made by the court pursuant to an application by the debenture holder or a trustee.[1497] The general ground on which the court will appoint a receiver is the preservation or protection of the property for the benefit of persons who have an interest in it.[1498] A receiver appointed by the court shall cause a notice of such appointment to be advertised in the official gazette and two daily newspapers.[1499] In the case of a receiver/manager appointed by the debenture holder out of court, Notice of appointment of any receiver or manager must be given to the CAC within fourteen days.[1500] An order for the appointment of a receiver or manager pursuant to any powers contained in any instrument must within seven days of such order, give notice to the Commission, and the latter shall enter same in the register of charges.[1501] Upon receipt of any Notice, the company shall, within fourteen days submit to the receiver, statement of affairs of the company in the prescribed form.[1502] Within two months of receipt of the statement, the receiver must send: to the court a copy of the statement and his comment thereon if any; to the Commission a copy of the statement, his comment on it if any; to the company, a copy of his comment thereon if any, and if he does not comment, a note to that effect; and to any trustees of the debenture and every debenture holder whose address is known, a copy of the summary of the statement of affairs. It is also required that every invoice, order for goods, or business letter issued by or on behalf of the company shall contain a statement that a receiver or manager has been appointed. Failure to do so by the company attracts a fine under CAMA.[1503]

820. A receiver simpliciter has the power to stop the business, collect debts, and realise the assets of the company.[1504] Pursuant to these general powers, and subject to any order made by the court, the receiver is statutorily empowered to take possession of the assets subject to the mortgage, charge or other security, protect the company's property, receive rents, and profits, discharge outgoings, and realise the

1495. *Re Continental Oxygen Co.* (1871) 1 Ch. 311.
1496. *Intercontractors Nigeria Ltd v. National Provident Fund Management Board* (1988) 2 NWLR (Pt. 76) 280.
1497. *Okoya & Ors v. Santili & Ors* (1990) NWLR (Pt. 1310) 172.
1498. *Ibid.*
1499. CAMA 2020, s. 206.
1500. *Ibid.*, s. 555 (1).
1501. *Ibid.*, s. 231.
1502. *Ibid.*, s. 559 (1) (a) (b).
1503. *Ibid.*, s. 555(2).
1504. *Uwakwe Ors v. Odogwu & Ors* (1989) 5 NWLR (Pt. 123) 562.

security for the benefit of those on whose behalf he is appointed. However, he shall not have power to carry out any of the company's business or undertaking unless he is appointed a manager.[1505]

821. All moneys realised from sale of assets, rents and/or general debts shall be distributed by the receiver in accordance with his instrument of appointment in the case of appointment out of court. Where the receiver is appointed by the court, an application shall be brought for an order setting out the manner of distribution among various claimants.[1506] Except otherwise expressly provided or ordered by the court, the moneys in the hand of the receiver may be applied in the settlement of the cost of realising the security; other expenses of the receiver including remuneration and costs; costs, exchanges, other outgoings, and expenses of trustees under a debenture trust deed if any, including their remuneration; cost of debenture holders action (if any); preferential debts out of the property subject to a floating charge in priority to the claims of the debenture holder;[1507] and the debenture debt with interest accruing thereon up to the date of payment.

1505. CAMA 2020, s. 556(1).
1506. *Omojasola v. Plison Fisko Nig Ltd* (1990) 5 NWLR (Pt. 151) 434.
1507. CAMA 2020, s. 207.

Chapter 4. Security Transactions In Movable Assets Act 2017

§1. Main Objective

822. Recent efforts by the Federal Government of Nigeria in quest for rapid economic development include the drive to encourage the development of the micro, small, and medium enterprises (MSMEs) and enhance their access to expanded credit using movable properties at their disposal as security for lending. Towards this end, the Security Transactions In Movable Assets Act ('STIMA' or 'Act') was enacted in 2017[1508] codifying (with few modifications) the provisions of the Central Bank of Nigeria Regulations on registration of security interests in movable property by banks and other financial institutions in Nigeria.[1509]

§2. Framework

823. Basically, STIMA provides a framework for the creation of security interests in movable assets; the mandatory terms to be provided in parties' agreement; the rights and obligations of parties to registered security agreements; the creation of a national collateral registry and mechanism for perfection of security interests in movable assets; as well as the determination of priority of competing interests therein among others.

§3. STIMA and the Pre-existing Legal Landscape

824. Before the enactment of STIMA, the main legislation regulating the creation, perfection, maintenance, and enforcement of security interests in movables in the form of personal chattels not being the subject matter of a secured debenture, was the Bills of Sale Law applicable in the various states of the federation.[1510] That Law exists side by side with STIMA which is a federal legislation. The Bills of Sale Law like STIMA creates a principal registry and establishes the procedure for the registration, renewal, and security of bills of sale. But while the provisions of the Bills of Sale Law do not apply to security interests in the form of companies charges registered as a debenture under the CAMA,[1511] section 2(3) of STIMA provides that nothing in the Act shall prevent the creation of such security interests.

1508. Act No. 3 2017.
1509. *See* the Central Bank of Nigeria Collateral Registry Regulation issued in September 2014 accessed online at www.cbn.gov.ng/out/2014/dfd/collateralregistryregulations2014.pdf.
1510. *See,* for example, the Bills of Sale Law, Cap B2 Laws of Lagos State 2015.
1511. Cap C20 Laws of the Federation of Nigeria, 2010.

§4. Scope of Application

825. While STIMA applies to all security interests in movable assets created by an agreement to secure repayment of loans or performance of some other obligations, it does not apply to any right of set-off; the creation or transfer of an interest in land other than account receivables; and any interest created by a transfer, assignment or mortgage in movable property governed by a law for which a registry has been established with regards to ships and aircrafts.[1512]

826. The Act generally applies to secured transactions in movable assets. Section 63 of the Act defines 'movable property' broadly as 'tangible or intangible property other than real property'. This goes beyond the narrow limit covered by the Bills of Sale Law in the form of 'personal chattels' covering mainly 'goods, furniture, other articles capable of transfer by delivery', including 'fixtures and growing crops when separately assigned or charged'.[1513] Thus, any form of asset capable of being moved or transferred by delivery falls within the ambit of assets to which the Act applies.

827. The implication of the disparity in the definition of assets covered by STIMA and the Bills of Sale Law is that where assets are potentially covered by both statutes such as where both personal chattels and other movables are the subject matter of security, it is not clear whether to assume that the Act creates a parallel regime in which case, the personal chattels would still have to comply with the mandatory requirements of the Bills of Sale Law regarding creation, registration and enforcement,[1514] or whether the Act should be regarded as covering the field sufficiently thereby superseding the state law[1515] in which case, the Act applies exclusively to the secured transaction. Since there is no judicial authority on this matter, it is advisable that a separate instrument creating security in personal chattels contained in the assets subject matter of security be made to conform with the provisions of the Bills of Sale Law as well. However, where the assets do not qualify as personal assets under the Bills of Sale Law but falls within the scope of the Act, its provisions apparently apply.

§5. Creation of Security Interests

828. Section 3(1) of the Act provides that a security interest is created in movable assets by a security agreement between a grantor (the borrower) and the creditor. Where such agreement provides that the security interest extends to the grantor's present and future assets, any future asset acquired by the grantor which

1512. *Ibid.*, s. 2(2).
1513. Cap B3 Laws of Lagos State 2015, s. 3.
1514. *Ibid.*, 5, 7, 8, 9, 10, and 13.
1515. *See* the Constitution of the Federal Republic of Nigeria 1999, s. 4(5).

falls under the collateral description in the security agreement shall take effect as security under the agreement without further consent or any other act of the grantor.[1516]

829. The Act provides that a security shall be created only to the extent of the rights enjoyed by the grantor in the assets.[1517] Consequently, no valid security interests shall be created over assets in which the grantor has no title. However, the provision of section 4(3) of the Act makes it possible for security interest to be created over movable assets notwithstanding any agreement limiting the grantor's right to create such security interest. This provision has the effect of weakening the efficacy of negative pledge clauses in floating charges and would render other limitations to the creation of further security usually included in security documentation valueless. The lesson in this is that lenders advancing credit secured by movable assets have the obligation to conduct proper due diligence to discover the existence of any negative pledges or other pre-existing security.

§6. Content of Security Agreement

830. Section 5 of the Act contains mandatory terms required to be included in the Security Agreement. It requires that the agreement reflects the intention of the grantor and creditor to create security interest; identifies the grantor and creditor; describes the secured obligation including the maximum amount for which the security interest is enforceable; describes the collateral adequately; indicates the tenor of the obligation secured; and confirms the agreement by parties to submit to arbitration, as first recourse in a situation that any civil dispute arises. A collateral is adequately described if it is accompanied with '(a) item, kind, type or category, year of manufacture or any other description that can identify the collateral; or (b) a statement that a security interest is taken in all the present and future assets of the grantor; and (c) for the purpose of (a) and (b), a description of the insurance cover on the collateral'.

831. The effect of non-compliance is not stated in the provision above and would ultimately depend on judicial pronouncement. Pending such judicial pronouncement however, it would appear, following the mandatory effect of the use of the word 'shall' in that provision, that failure to include any of the mandatory terms may result in failure of the security interest.

§7. Preservation of Security Interests

832. An existing security interest created under the Act shall extend to the identifiable or traceable proceeds of a collateral, whether or not the security agreement

1516. Act No. 3 2017, s. 3(2).
1517. *Ibid.*, s. 4(1).

contains a description of the proceeds.[1518] Also, an interest in tangible property which is subsequently co-mingled with other property of the same class or nature shall continue notwithstanding that it now forms part of a mass.[1519] These provisions protect the interest of the creditor and preserves the res in any case for purposes of enforcement of the security interest in the assets.

§8. Perfection of Security Interest in the Collateral or in the Proceeds

833. A collateral Registry has been established for purposes of receiving, registering, and storing information about security interests, or for providing access to persons who may seek information on security interests from the Registry.[1520]

834. Security interests in movables may be perfected by registering a financing statement in respect thereof.[1521] It is worthy of note that the completion and registration of such financing statement generally requires the consent of the grantor in writing to be effective.[1522] Registration of an amendment financing statement is ineffective without the consent of the grantor in writing where the amendment financing statement adds a description of new collateral, or adds a new grantor, unless the new grantor is a transferee of the collateral already described in the registration. Proceeds of collateral which are specifically described in the financing statement or, are in the form of money, accounts receivables, negotiable instruments, or bank accounts, are automatically perfected.[1523]

835. Although a financing statement may be registered by or on behalf of a creditor at any time under the Act, where the assets are personal chattels under the Bills of Sale Law, or a company charge under a debenture deed, the period of registration is seven days[1524] after making the relevant Bill of sale or within ninety days of creating the charge respectively.[1525] The effect is that neither of the security interests created under these parallel regimes shall be valid unless the period stipulated for registration is complied with.[1526]

1518. *Ibid.*, s. 7(1).
1519. *Ibid.*, s. 7(2).
1520. *Ibid.*, s. 11.
1521. *Ibid.*, s. 12.
1522. *Ibid.*, s. 13.
1523. *Ibid.*, s. 9(1). If the proceeds are not of the kind covered in the preceding subsection, the security interest will remain perfected if the creditor registers an amendment adding a description of the asset that is proceeds within fifteen days after they arose: *See* s. 9(2) thereof.
1524. *See* the Bills of Sale Law Cap B2 Laws of Lagos State 2015.
1525. *See* the Companies and Allied Matters Act 2020, s. 222.
1526. Under both regimes, the effect of non-registration is that the transaction is void: *See,* for example, ss 8 and 14 of the Bills of Sale Law Cap B2 Laws of Lagos State 2015. *See also* CAMA 2020, s. 222.

836. The registered financing agreement shall be valid until the expiration of the term specified in it,[1527]or its cancellation, whichever comes first.[1528] Duration of a registered financing statement may be renewed or extended by an amendment of the financing statement before its expiration.[1529] No information shall be deleted from the Registry, whether or not an amendment financing statement cancelling the registered financing statement has been registered.

837. While security interest requires registration under the Act at least for purposes of the application of the priority rule, stamping of the security agreement is not required.[1530] However, the potency of this provision in relation to company charges is in doubt, as it is unlikely that the CAC will accept an unstamped security document for the purpose of registration of a charge in accordance with CAMA.

§9. Contents of a Financing Statement

838. It is mandatory for a creditor to provide in the financing statement information as to the grantor type description (whether individual, micro, small, or large business); in the case of a company, co-operative or registered business name, the unique identification number which shall be the CAC registration number or other registration number issued by the appropriate authority for registering these types of debtors; in the case of an individual, the unique identification number derived from approved biometric based identification,[1531] gender, name, address including telephone and date of birth; the name and address of the creditor or its representative; a description of the collateral;[1532] the maximum amount for which the secured obligation may be enforced; the period of time for which the registration is to be effective; a confirmation of parties' agreement to submit themselves to mediation or arbitration mechanism as first recourse in the event of any civil dispute;[1533]and such other information as the Registrar may consider necessary.[1534] If there is more than one grantor or creditor, then the required information must be entered in the designated field separately for each grantor or creditor.[1535]

1527. An expired registered financing statement shall be maintained in the Registry and searchable by the public for six months following its expiration after which it shall be kept in the archive: *See* s. 18(4) of the Act.
1528. *See* s. 18(1) of the Act.
1529. *See* s. 18(2) of the Act.
1530. *See* s. 54 of the Act.
1531. If the grantor is an individual who is neither a citizen nor a resident of Nigeria, the secured creditor shall enter the debtor's name and unique identification number appear on the grantor's passport issued by a foreign government or any other document as the Central Bank of Nigeria may prescribe: *See* s. 14(4) of the Act.
1532. A description of collateral is sufficient if the collateral is described by item, kind, type or category; or a statement that a security interest is taken in all the grantor's present and after acquired property; or any other description that reasonably identifies the collateral: *See* s. 15(2).
1533. *Ibid.,* s. 14(5).
1534. *Ibid.,* s. 14(1).
1535. *Ibid.,* s. 14(3).

839. Circumstances under which a financing statement shall be ineffective and as against whom are stated in section 16 of the Act. It shall be ineffective where there is error in the unique identification number of the grantor or the serial number of the collateral that causes the registration not to be retrieved in a search.[1536] Where a registered financing statement contains information on multiple grantors or collaterals, an error in the unique identification number of the grantor shall render the registration ineffective only with respect to that grantor; and an error in the serial number of a collateral shall render the registered financing statement ineffective only with respect to the collateral identified by such serial number.[1537]

840. However, an error in the name or address of the grantor; the maximum amount for which the security interest may be enforced; or the name or address of the creditor does not render the registered financing statement ineffective.[1538] An error in the collateral description other than in the serial number may render the registered financing statement ineffective with respect to that collateral if the error seriously misleads the searcher.[1539] An incorrect description of some collateral shall not render the registered financing statement ineffective with respect to other collateral sufficiently described.[1540] An error in other information does not render the registered financing statement ineffective.[1541]

§10. Priority of Registered Security Interests

841. Priority of perfected security interests in the same collateral is determined by the order of registration,[1542] so that a security interest which is earlier in time may be defeated by a later registered security interest. A security interest is to have the same priority in respect of all secured obligations and advances, whether existing or future,[1543] and a prior interest shall attach to both the collateral itself and any proceeds of disposal thereof. A security interest that is transferred shall have the same priority as it had at the time of the transfer.[1544] Transfer of a security interest perfected by registration is valid without registering an amendment financing statement in the Registry.[1545]

842. A creditor may enter into an agreement to sub-ordinate its priority in favour of any other claimant, and such sub-ordination is effective without registering and amendment financing statement in the Registry.[1546]

1536. *Ibid.*, s. 16(1).
1537. *Ibid.*, s. 16(2).
1538. *Ibid.*, s. 17(1).
1539. *Ibid.*, s. 17(2).
1540. *Ibid.*, s. 17(3).
1541. *Ibid.*, s. 17(4).
1542. *Ibid.*, s. 23.
1543. *Ibid.*, s. 24(2).
1544. *Ibid.*, s. 25(2).
1545. *Ibid.*, s. 25(3).
1546. *Ibid.*, s. 26(1)(2).

843. A purchase money security interest in a collateral or its proceeds shall have priority over a non-purchase money security interest in the same collateral created by the same grantor if the purchase money security interest in the collateral or its proceeds is perfected when the grantor obtained possession of the collateral.[1547]

844. A perfected security interest in goods that subsequently become part of a product or mass shall continue as a perfected security interest in the product or mass if the goods are so manufactured, processed, assembled, or co-mingled that their identity is lost in the product or mass.[1548] If more than one security interest is perfected in the goods before they become part of a product or mass, the security interests rank equally in proportion to the value of the goods at the time they became part of the product or mass.[1549]

845. A financial institution's right of set-off shall have priority over a perfected security interest that extends to a deposit account.[1550] A transferee of funds from a deposit account or cash other than from a deposit account takes the funds or cash free of a security interest unless the transferee acts in collusion with the grantor or the borrower in violating the rights of the creditor.[1551] A transferee of cash for this purpose does not include a bailee.[1552]

846. A lien arising out of materials or services provided in the ordinary course of business in respect of goods that are subject to a security interest shall have priority over that security interest.[1553]

847. A holder of a negotiable instrument or title document shall have priority over a perfected security interest in the negotiable instrument or the title document where the holder gave value; acquired the negotiable instrument or the title document without knowledge that the transaction is in breach of the security agreement to which the security interest relates; and took possession of the negotiable instrument or the title document.[1554]

848. The provisions of the Sheriff and Civil Process Act notwithstanding, a perfected security interest has priority over the rights of an unsecured creditor that has obtained a judgment or an order of attachment, unless the judgment creditor, before the security interest is perfected, registers a financing statement; seizes the collateral; or serves a notice of its claim on the third party holding property for the debtor.[1555] The priority of the credit interest extends to credit disbursed by the creditor before the expiry of thirty days after the judgment creditor notified the creditor

---

1547. *Ibid.*, s. 27.
1548. *Ibid.*, s. 28(1).
1549. *Ibid.*, s. 28(2).
1550. *Ibid.*, s. 29(1).
1551. *Ibid.*, s. 29(2).
1552. *Ibid.*, s. 29(3).
1553. *Ibid.*, s. 30.
1554. *Ibid.*, s. 31.
1555. *Ibid.*, s. 34(1).

that it had taken the steps highlighted above or pursuant to an irrevocable commitment in a fixed amount without any limitation if the commitment was made before the judgment creditor notified the creditor.[1556]

849. One significant challenge pertaining to the application of the priority rules under the Act relates to lack of uniformity in the priority rules of other laws such as the Bills of Sale Law and the provisions of CAMA. Where a security requiring mandatory registration under either of these laws is not so registered, the security is void notwithstanding registration under the Act, and the rule of priority which should ordinarily flow from the registration under the Act would be inconsequential in relation to such security.

§11. Validity of Assignment

850. Section 25(1) of the Act enables a secured creditor to transfer its rights without the consent of the grantor or borrower and/or in breach of the relevant agreement. Upon assignment, a security interest shall have the same priority as it had at the time of transfer.[1557]

§12. Rights and Duties of a Grantor, Borrower, and Creditor

851. All rights and duties that arise under the Act shall be exercised and discharged in good faith and in accordance with reasonable commercial standards.[1558] But a person does not act in bad faith merely because he acts with knowledge of the security interest of some other person, unless he knows that his actions would violate rights of the other person.[1559] A person in possession of an encumbered asset shall preserve the asset from damage, impairment and loss, excluding fair wear and tear having regard to the nature of the asset.[1560]

§13. Enforcement of Security Interests

852. In the event of default, a creditor may exercise his rights under the Act and in the security agreement or resort to any appropriate judicial remedy.[1561] Such remedies are in addition to any other remedy provided in CAMA.[1562] Prior to the

1556. *Ibid.*, s. 34(2).
1557. *Ibid.*, s. 25(2).
1558. *Ibid.*, s. 35(1).
1559. *Ibid.*, s. 35(2).
1560. *Ibid.*, s. 35(3).
1561. *Ibid.*, s. 29(1).
1562. *Ibid.*, s. 29(5).

enforcement of security, the creditor shall serve a notice of default and wait for ten days before exercising his right to take possession of the collateral or render same inoperative.[1563]

853. A creditor may repossess a collateral under the Act pursuant to judicial process; or without judicial process if the grantor consented to relinquishing possession without a court order in the security agreement.[1564] In the case of repossession without judicial process, a creditor may request for assistance from the Nigerian Police having authority within the location of the collateral, and the Nigerian Police shall provide assistance for the peaceable possession of the collateral, upon presentation by the creditor of a copy of the relevant security agreement and duly certified confirmation statement.[1565]

1563. *Ibid.*, s. 40(3).
1564. *Ibid.*, s. 40(4).
1565. *Ibid.*, s. 40(6).

Selected Bibliography

Books

Adigun, O. *Cases and Texts on Equity, Trusts and Administration of Estate.* Mabrochi International Books, 2003.
Baker, P.V. *Megarry's Manual of the Law of Real Property,* 5th ed. Stevens & Sons Ltd., 1975.
Banire, M. *The Nigerian Law of Trusts.* Excel Publications, 2002.
Barnsley, G. *Conveyancing Law and Practice.* Butterworths, 1973.
Beale, H. *Chitty on Contract,* Vol. II.
Bentham J. *The Theory of Legislation* (69 Oceania Publications Inc 1975) (1690).
Bridge, M. et al. *The Law of Personal Property.* Sweet & Maxwell, 2013.
Chorley, R. *Law of Banking,* 6th ed. Sweet & Maxwell.
Coker, G.B.A. *Family Property Among the Yorubas* 2nd ed. African Universities Press & Sweet & Maxwell, 1966.
Douglas A., Phillips. *Nigeria.* Chelsea House Publisher, 2004.
Elias, T.O. *Nigerian Land Law,* 4th ed. Sweet & Maxwell, 1971.
Elias, T.O. *British Colonial Law.* London: Sweet & Maxwell, 1962.
Emiri, F. *Equity and Trust in Nigeria.* Malthouse Publishers, 2012.
Fabunmi J.O., *Equity and Trust in Nigeria.* University of Ife Press Ltd., 1986.
Falola, Toyin. *The History of Nigeria.* Greenwood Histories of the Modern Nations (Greenwood Publishing Group), 1999.
Fekumo, J.F. *Principles of Nigerian Customary Law.* Port Harcourt-Nigeria: F&F Publishers (Nig) Ltd., 2002.
Fry, E. *Specific Performance,* 6th ed. 1921.
Gower L.C.B. *Principles of Modern Company Law,* 4th ed. Stevens, 1979.
Halsbury's Laws of England, vol. 16. 4th ed. Lexis Nexis, 2006.
Holden, J.M. *Laws and Practice of Banking* 5th ed., Universal Law Publishing, 1991.
James, R.W. *Modern Land Law in Nigeria.* University of Ife Press 1973.
Jegede, M.I. *Principles of Equity.* Ethiope Publishing Corporation Benin City, 1981.
Jegede, M.I. *Law of Trusts, Bankruptcy and Administration of Estate.* MIJ Publishers, 1999.
Kasumu, A.B. & James, R.W. *Alienation of Family Property in Southern Nigeria.* Ibadan University Press, 1966.
Keeton, G.W. *Law of Trusts.* 9th ed. Professional Books Ltd, 1974.

Selected Bibliography

Keeton, G.W & Sheridan, L.A. *The Law of Trusts*. 12th ed. Barry Rose Law Publishers Ltd, 1993.

Kodilinye, G. *An Introduction to Equity in Nigeria*. Sweet & Maxwell, 1975.

Locke, J. *Two Treaties of Government*. 358 3rd ed. John Churchill at the Black-Swan 1698 .

Luckham, R. *The Nigerian Military: A Sociological Analysis of Authority and Revolt 1960–67*. Cambridge University Press, 1971

Maitland. *Equity*. Brunyante ed. 1936. Cambridge University Press, 2011.

Mbaku, J.M. & Takogang. *Decolonisation, Reunification in the Leadership Challenge in a Federation in Cameroon: Cameroon under Pal Biya*. Trenton & Asmara: African World Press, 2004.

McGhee, J Snell's. *Equity*. 30th ed. Sweet & Maxwell, 2015

Megarry, R.& Wade, W. *The Law of Real Property*. London: Sweet & Maxwell, 2012.

Moffat, G. *Trusts Law (Text and Materials),* 2nd ed. Butterworths, 1994.

Nasir, J. *The Islamic Law of Personal Status*. Graham & Totnam, 1986.

Nwechue R. *Reflection on the Nigerian Civil War: Facing the Future*. New York Africana Pub. Corp, 1971.

Olawoye, C.O. *Title to Land in Nigeria*. University of Lagos/Evans Brothers, 1974.

Oluyede, P.A.O. *Legal Development in Nigeria since 1960: The Land Use Act 1978*. Unilag Publication, 1992.

Oluyede, P.A.O. *Modern Nigerian Land Law,* Evans Ibadan, 1989.

Omotola, J.A. *Essays on the Land Use Act,* Lagos University Press, 1980.

Orojo, O. *Nigerian Commercial Law and Practice*. Sweet & Maxwell, 1983.

Paton, G.W. *Jurisprudence,* 3rd ed. Oxford University Press, 1972.

Pennington, R. *Company Law,* 8th ed. Butterworths, 2001.

Pollock, F. *Jurisprudence and Legal Essays*. MacMillan & Co. Ltd, 1961.

Quadri, A.A. *Islamic Jurisprudence in the Modern World*. Taj Publishers, 1999.

Sagay, I. *Nigerian Law of Succession*. Malthouse, 2006.

Salmond. *Jurisprudence*. 12th ed. Sweet & Maxwell, 1966.

Schacht J. *An Introduction to Islamic Law*. Clarendon Press, 1964

Smith, I.O. *Nigerian Law of Secured Credit*. Lagos-Nigeria: Ecowatch Publications (Nig) Ltd., 2001.

Smith, I.O. *Practical Approach to Law of Real Property in Nigeria,* Revised edition. Ecowatch Publications (Nig) Ltd., 2013

Smith, I.O. (ed.). *The Land Use Act: Twenty Five Years After*. Department of Private and Property Law, University of Lagos, 2003.

Smith, I.O. (ed.). *Secured Credit in a Global Economy*. Department of Private and Property Law, University of Lagos, Nigeria 2005.

Smith, I.O. (ed.). *Law and Land Rights*. Department of Private and Property Law, University of Lagos, 2006.

Stock, R. '*Nigeria',* Microsoft Encarter 2006 [CD]. Microsoft Corporation, 2005.

Articles in Learned Journals

Akanle, O. 'Post-Colonial Nation Building, Global Governance, Globalization, and Development in Nigeria and Africa'. *Africa Insight* 41(3) (2011): 1–15.

Selected Bibliography

Akanle, O. & Olutayo, A.O. 'Globalization and Development Nexus: Nigeria Entangled'. *Mambayya House Journal of Democratic Studies* 2 (2010): 18–39.

Asante, S. 'Judicial Principles in Anglo-American Law and the Customary Law of Ghana: A Comparative Study'. *CLQ* 1 (1965): 1144.

Barnsley, G. 'Conveyancing Liens'. *Conv.* 61. Sweet & Maxwell, 1997, 336.

Battersby, G. 'A Consideration of Property and Title in the Sale of Goods Act'. *JBL* 1 (2001).

Egwemi, V. 'The Interrelationship Between Culture and National Development in Nigeria'. *Continental Journal of Social Sciences* 2 (2009): 12–20.

Ekpo A.H.& Umoh O.J. *An Overview of the Nigerian Economic Growth and Development.* Available at www.onlinenigeria.com/economics/.

Goodhart W. & Jones, G., 'The Infiltration of Equitable Doctrine into English Commercial Law'. *MLR* 42 (1980): 489 at 496–498.

Jegede, M.I. 'The Position of the Head of Family in Relation of Family Property'. *NBJ* 21 (1966).

Olawoye, C.O. 'Meaning of Family Property'. *NJCL* 1(2) (1970): 300.

Pedrazzini F & Simpson W: 'The Legal Framework for Secured Credit: A Suitable Case for Treatment' *BLI* 1 (1999): 127.

Selected Bibliography

Index

The numbers here refer to paragraph numbers.

www.ingramcontent.com/pod-product-compliance
Ingram Content Group UK Ltd.
Pitfield, Milton Keynes, MK11 3LW, UK
UKHW020136290926
15471UKWH00003B/519

9 789403 547244